tana's
habitat

because life doesn't come with a manual

tana's

the ultimate guide to

finding,
affording,
and styling

your first place

tana march
with **scott acord**

habitat

because life doesn't come with a manual

a perigee book

A PERIGEE BOOK
Published by the Penguin Group
Penguin Group (USA) Inc.
375 Hudson Street, New York New York 10014, USA
Penguin Group (Canada), 90 Eglinton Avenue East, Suite 700, Toronto, Ontario M4P 2Y3, Canada
(a division of Pearson Penguin Canada Inc.)
Penguin Books Ltd., 80 Strand, London WC2R 0RL, England
Penguin Group Ireland, 25 St. Stephen's Green, Dublin 2, Ireland (a division of Penguin Books Ltd.)
Penguin Group (Australia), 250 Camberwell, Victoria 3124, Australia
(a division of Pearson Australia Group Pty. Ltd.)
Penguin Books Pvt. Ltd., 11 Community Centre, Panchsheel Park, New Delhi—110 017, India
Penguin Group (NZ), Cnr. Airborne and Rosedale Roads, Albany, Auckland 1310, New Zealand
(a division of Pearson New Zealand Ltd.)
Penguin Books (South Africa)(Pty.) Ltd., 24 Sturdee Avenue, Rosebank, Johannesburg 2196, South Africa

Penguin Books Ltd., Registered Offices: 80 Strand, London WC2R 0RL, England

While the authors have made every effort to provide accurate telephone numbers and Internet addresses at the time of publication, neither the publisher nor the authors assume any reponsibility for errors, or for changes that occur after publication. Further, the publisher does not have any control over and does not assume any responsibility for author or third-party websites or their content.

First edition: August 2006

Library of Congress Cataloging-in-Publication Data

March, Tana.
    tana's habitat : the ultmate guide to finding, affording, and styling you first place
    by Tana March with Scott Acord.
        p. cm.
    Includes bibliographical references and index.
    ISBN 0-399-53292-7 (alk. paper)
    1. Moving, Household.   2. Housekeeping.   3. Interior decoration.
  I. Acord, Scott.   II. Title.
    TX305.M37 2006
    643'.1—dc22

                                                            2006014531

PRINTED IN THE UNITED STATES OF AMERICA

10 9 8 7 6 5 4 3 2 1

Most Perigee Books are available at special quantity discounts for bulk purchases for sales promotions, pre-
miums, fund-raising, or educational use. Special books, or book excerpts, can also be created to fit specific
needs. For details, write: Special Markets, The Berkley Publishing Group, 375 Hudson Street, New York,
New York 10014.

acknowledgments

i owe an enormous amount of gratitude to a million people without whom this book or my life as I know it would not be possible. Thank you from the bottom of my heart for your excitement and encouragement, your generous and selfless support, your countless hours of dedication, and your open ears. I am ever thankful.

Mom, Dad, Barrie, Gram, Joe, Nancy, Scott Acord, Laurie Liss, Christel Winkler, Jeanette Shaw, Ian Rogers, Michi Broman, Mike Petty, Laura Blanchard and Put on the Dog, Tommi Lewis-Tilden, Kevin Stein, Stefanie B. Stark, Jane Fort, Ernie Gates and the *Daily Press*, Robyn Heller, Myrna Valdez, Cathy Bahn, Scott Kozinchick, Nancy Anderson, Josephine Lowry, Helen Lowe, Robert Lyons, Michael Matisse, Lauren McCormack, Lora Hart, Doug McMahon, Phil Mondello, Norma Loehr, Apryl Lundsten, Darick Chamberlin, Kyle Pollock, Ellen Olson-Brown, Victoria Herd, Lahly Poore, Kristin and Matthew, Shannon and Captain Pat, Clif y Sara, Jennifer Chandler, Katie Rodda, Keri and Raymond, Dr. Gavin, Beau Des Hotel, Andrew Apfelberg, Michael Cioffoletti, Chris Gernon, Leah Miller, Perigee Books, Jay Shanker, Sydney Shipps, Vic Spicer, Erin Zimring, Amy Cook, Ashlea Tate, Barbara Card Atkinson, Brandon Oropallo, Candice Fink-Benson, Carra Gamberdella, Kay Daly, Lee Arcuri, Rebecca Giantonio, Stephanie Mantello, Tamar Love-Grande, Ian Fergusson, Jill Murry, Bonnie McIntosh, Mike Bisch, Jake Bailey, Howard Levitan, Felicia Lansbury, Wendy Weatherford, Jim Connor, David Shipps, Dean Testerman, Audrey Fine, Michael Dare, T. J. Campbell, and Darin, who inadvertantly taught me that art is in the everyday.

—tana march

v

many people over the years have given me guidance and encouragement to help mold me into the man and artist I am today, and I thank all of you.

I want to give special thanks to Tana, for letting me partner with her and giving me an outlet to express my many creative visions that have helped me attain many of my artistic goals. Stephen Gavin, you've given me much love and support over the years; you're like a brother to me. Tom Gentile, you always make me want to be a better man and strive for more. Beau Des Hotel, you've been a great friend and I've learned so much from you artistically over the last twenty years. Vanessa Reyes, you've been a great friend for many years and have stood by me through all the craziness. A big special thanks to Laurie Liss, for believing in us and the book and helping us get it published.

To my parents, Jim and Glenda Hall, and the rest of my family: Keith; Angie; Lindsey; Jordan; Brenda; Obie; Michael; Claudine; my dad, Gene, and his wife, Elaine; Yvonne; Crystal; and my grandmother Wilma Acord—I think the world of you.

I'd also like to thank all of my friends who continue to give me much love and encouragement and never tell me I'm crazy—even when I'm sure you want to: Chris Gernon; Marti, Julia and Robbie Browning; Renée, John, Dylan, Carly, and Chloe Litt; Wendy Weatherford; John Barrentine and David Fikse; the Foote family: Michelle, Brad, Kimberly, Evan, and Lauren; Jeff Powell, Greg Hall, Elaine Gavin, Tom Rollerson, Sarah Beatty-Buller, Naomi Bulochnikov, Chris Delhommer, Tracy McGraw, Toni Herron, Lori Hornik, Maura Wozniak, Michelle Clark, Luis Defrank, Laura Nelson, Surayyah McCarthy, Brett Henne, Lynne Davis, Lisa Chader, Cindy McLean, Nicole Pope, Amanda Murphy, and Natasha Powell.

—scott acord

acknowledgments

contents

introduction

from the day we're born to the moment we leave home, we're being schooled to live on our own. Every species does it. For most animals it's instinctive, but for us humans, survival of the fittest is a little more complicated. So, while you've probably acquired some life skills along the way, chances are there's a lot about living on your own you simply haven't been taught. ***tana's habitat: the ultimate guide to finding, affording, and styling your first place*** is here to help fill in the blanks. This do-it-(all)-yourself manual makes moving out an easy transition for every first timer.

Each section of the book is designed to help you save money, plan for your future, and still have a life:

Making the Break is filled with simple, practical advice to prepare you financially for moving out and keep you fiscally independent once you get there. Chock-full of questionnaires and helpful hints for finding the right apartment in the right neighborhood, designing your budget, screening roommates, and dealing with neighbors, **Making the Break** will show you how to live within your means. Don't end up living in a storage unit with your boyfriend, his brother, and a hot plate because you weren't prepared! You can be safe . . . and warm . . . and still live within your budget. Find out how!

Cleanliness Is Next to Godliness. You hate to clean. Got it. But unless you have a housekeeper or an anal-retentive roommate, somebody's going to have to put their nose to the grindstone if you're ever going to bring a date home. Laundry and stain removal, storage, and stinky stuff, these timeless ideas will show you how to get your place in tip-top shape and keep it that way with almost as little effort as cash. Learn to clean a toilet like a hotel maid and identify that aroma wafting from your fridge. Don't forget your karma. Make your own planet-friendly cleaning products and keep the earth and your wallet in the green.

Pretty Is as Pretty Does takes you room by room to turn that boring white box of an apartment into a one-of-a-kind, stylin' place you can be proud of. Forget spending wads of cash. Vision, ingenuity, and a little bit of muscle are all you need. Learn how to organize your space to maximize the living and minimize the clutter, buy new furniture on the cheap, and refurbish the old stuff to look like new. Set up a working kitchen that won't blow your budget and find a great mattress that won't blow your sleep. Turn found objects into lamps, furniture, and unique wall art. Use bottles for picture frames, make your own rugs, and turn books into wallpaper. Haven't made contact with your inner artist? Fear not. Necessity really *is* the mother of invention and resourcefulness breeds inspiration.

Danger, Will Robinson. It's true. Life's not always easy. Here you'll find answers to some of the most common but confusing questions. Starve a fever or feed a cold? Do greasy burgers really cure a hangover? How do I put out the fire in my oven? These helpful hints from first aid and personal safety to renter's rights and rental insurance will give you a heads-up before being held up.

Even more than living within your means, this guidebook is a testament to the idea that creativity, not money, is the key to crafting your own reality. And when you figure out how to turn a stack of redwood posts, some wagon-wheel spokes, and a can of shoe polish into a bed fit for a king, you'll have proof that you can do anything you set your mind to.

TOP 10 SIGNS
IT'S TIME TO
MOVE OUT

10. You can't get a date because the teen line you share with your fourteen-year-old sister is always busy.

9. Your parents converted your bedroom into a sewing room.

8. You have to sneak out the window to stay out past midnight.

7. Your parents charge you rent and make you split the utilities and cable bill with them.

6. Your mother greets you every morning with a glass of orange juice and the apartment listings from the classifieds.

5. You're married.

4. Your children call your parents Mom and Dad.

3. You think moving into the basement is the same as moving out on your own.

2. You're forty and you're still calling dibs on the top bunk.

1. Your parents bought this book for you.

**If this sounds familiar, your time has come.
Your preparation begins now.**

MAKING
THE BREAK

i started making the break the day I was born. In fact, it's shocking I wasn't a preemie! Fiercely independent and precocious, I began planning my escape route the moment I could make a list. Where I would go to school, when I would graduate, how long I'd stay in the chorus, and when I'd win my first Tony. It wasn't that I didn't like where I grew up, or my childhood for that matter. Quite the contrary. I loved my family and the expansive beauty of Montana. How could I not love a place whose name begat my own?! To this day, that place holds a deep and special power over me, but I always knew it wouldn't present the kinds of opportunities I desired. There were bigger skies in my eyes.

Fresh out of college, I ditched my dreams of New York and Broadway for the silver screen and a boyfriend of two whole months with whom I moved to Los Angeles on a whim. We lived in a one-room storage unit in a bank of garages equipped with a refrigerator, a hot plate, and his younger brother. It was tight, but we made it work. We'd been there two years already when, after our brutal breakup, I bolted for my own apartment and my circumstances became crystal clear: I had nothing. No furniture. No friends. No money. As I sat in the middle of my new living room, alone but for a hand-me-down kitchen table, a tattered futon mattress, and a couple remnants left over from the previous evening's all-night carpet-ripping-up project that had left my fingers blistered and my less than stellar hardwood floors exposed, I wondered: What was I going to do?

Overwhelmed by flashbacks of my failed relationship, the sadness was no doubt heightened by the dramatic soundtrack of my life, Annie Lennox's "Why" on continuous play, eventually melting the cassette. I wallowed in memories of good times:

tana's habitat

dancing in a moonlit street to Dr. John until the batteries of our jam box wore out, switching clothes in the Loews bathroom to sneak into a second movie incognito, reading James Joyce aloud in a candlelit bubble bath. I reminisced about how he used to make things for us: furniture, bread, fanny packs. That guy could build a television from tinfoil and bubble gum! I would just look on, marveled by his creativity. And that's when it hit me. If he could do it, so could I!

The next day, I spent $30 of my last $50 on a drill, found a bunch of wood in an alley, and constructed myself a desk. And it was cool! I continued to collect things and turn them into what I needed until my entire apartment was furnished with art made from the everyday.

With this new sense of pride, I threw my ego to the wolves and dug out every phone number I'd bothered to collect over the past two years and called it. "This is Tana," I'd start. "We met at so-and-so's party last year, remember? Listen, I know I said I'd call before and didn't, but it's been a rough year. I just split from my beau, I'm all alone, and I remember that we hit it off enough to save your number. Wanna have lunch?" To my surprise, every single person whose number still worked accepted my offer, and my social life was off and running.

Now all I needed was a job.

decisions, decisions

finally, you're moving out. It's your own personal Independence Day. You've waited for this for as long as you can remember. Truth be told, so have your folks. They may be pouring on the tears, but they're wiping them with the blueprints they've had drawn up to turn your bedroom into a rogue neighborhood mah-jongg parlor. Of course they'll leave some signs that you once existed in their lives, a picture here, a trophy there. And they'll welcome you home for holidays, though you'll be sleeping on the couch.

Not to worry. You're ready! With just a little preparation, forethought, and planning, you can leave home with ease.

THINGS TO THINK ABOUT BEFORE YOU LOOK

you've probably built up a pretty good fantasy over the years of what your first apartment looks like. If you're anything like me, it's in a fabulous, old building with oversize rooms and high ceilings, tons of closet space, hardwood floors, a great view, and architectural details for miles. But for most of us, *that* place isn't a realistic option. Most first apartments require some compromises to fit our budgets. Before you hit the streets, think about what you really need and what you can live without in your first nest and make a list.

WHAT'S YOUR STYLE?

Apartment buildings come in every shape and size imaginable, from small duplexes and four-plexes to medium-sized buildings with ten to fifty units to high rises and mega complexes with thousands of apartments in numerous buildings spread out over acres of land. You can find apartments with tons of character, like hardwood floors, crown molding, and beautiful tile work, or units with a more modern flair including dishwashers, garbage disposals, cable TV, swimming pools, parking, and health clubs. In many areas it's easy to find an apartment where the rent covers the cost of utilities and the landlord picks up the tab for building upkeep, including gardening, trash pickup, pool maintenance, etc.

A **house** also has a lot to offer. Besides providing you with more privacy, a yard, in-house laundry facilities, more living space, and (probably) off-street parking, it can also feel more like a home. It's a great option for people with pets or hobbies that require spreading out, and, if you plan on doing a lot of entertaining, neighbors who don't share a wall are far easier to deal with than those who do. Sure, you pay for these niceties. A house almost always means higher rent, utility bills, and increased responsibilities including yard work, maintenance, and trash duty. And a single-family unit likely doesn't offer the built-in social opportunities of an apartment. Of course a roommate or two could help offset the bigger bills, share extra household chores, and advance your social life.

The **guesthouse** is a third alternative which falls somewhere between a house and an apartment. Small, stand-alone cottages, they share property with a main house. Guesthouses can be quite charming and afford a sense of luxury that goes along with the neighborhoods they are often associated with; however, they can be expensive and extremely hard to find unless you know someone who knows someone who has one available. Because of the inherent nature of a guesthouse, they're not always built for long-term living, either. You may be stuck using the kitchen and laundry facilities in the main house. That may be great if you enjoy the people who live there. Or not so great if those grumbling seven-year-old twins won't stop hassling you for a ride on your motorcycle or eating your potato chips!

With the urban revitalization of the 1980s, **loft living** has become increasingly popular, especially in bigger cities. Inspired by the artist's ateliers of Paris in the twenties, converted office buildings, warehouses, factories, stores, reclaimed waterfronts, and historic areas are popping up everywhere as live/work spaces with wide-open floor plans. Because of the downtown and industrial locations, loft dwellers tend to have easy access to job opportunities, nightlife, theaters, museums, and cultural diversity. Higher crime, congestion, pollution, cost of living, lack of green space, and fast pace of life add to its drawbacks.

With patience and persistence, you can find the perfect situation for yourself. Ask yourself some questions and take good notes:

- How much can I afford?
- How much room do I need?
- Do I need ramps, elevators or other handicap access?
- Do I need a home office? Other kind of workspace?
- Do I need a formal dining room?
- What are my privacy concerns? Do I want a social atmosphere? Intimate atmosphere?
- Will I have a roommate who needs his or her own room? Do I want to share a bathroom?
- Do I have appliances? Do I need them?
- Do I need a full kitchen or can I live with a hot plate?
- Is it important to have an on-site manager?
- Can I live with carpet? Or do I need hardwood floors?
- Does an old building give me the creeps because too many people have lived there?
- Is a new building too sterile for me?

THE GOOD STUFF

Living quarters come with as many amenities as you can imagine. What do you have to have? What would you like to have? Make a list of your absolutes. Be realistic, but don't compromise. This will most likely be your home for at least a year, so do everything you can to make sure you'll be comfortable there right off the bat.

What do you just *have* to have?

- Dishwasher
- Garbage disposal
- Closet space
- Storage space

- Appliances (refrigerator, stove, microwave)
- Pool
- Fitness center
- Community room for entertaining
- In-unit washer and dryer
- Laundry on premises (Are there enough washers and dryers to meet the needs of the building's occupants?)
- Central air conditioning and heating
- Cable TV
- High-speed Internet
- Green space
- Views and natural light

TURN UP THE HEAT

Chances are, your new abode will have a combination of utilities. Electricity will control the lights, fridge, stereo, TV, computer, etc., while natural gas may power your furnace, water heater, and/or stove. While your landlord is usually responsible for supplying and paying for your water, you are typically responsible for heating it up.

The largest issue you're likely to face in terms of utilities will be your choice between a gas and an electric stove. Go natural. Gas offers superior cooking control (which you may or may not care about), it will save you a few bucks in the long run, *and* Mother Earth could use a breather. Check out **www.NaturalGas.org** for more info on the benefits of natural gas.

LOCATION, LOCATION, LOCATION

For me, location is a priority. I like living in a central setting, walking distance from movie theaters, museums, and other places I frequent like the dry cleaners, the gym, good restaurants, and the farmers' market. And, because I live thousands of miles away from my family, my friends are an important aspect of my community, one I always factor into my choice of neighborhoods. I mean, if there's a spur-of-the-moment grill fest, I want to be there without spending two hours fighting traffic!

Think about some of these things:

- Do I want to be in the hustle and bustle, or do I prefer being in a more secluded area?
- How long do I want my work commute to be?

tana's habitat

- Do I want to be able to walk to things?
- Is public transportation convenient?
- Can I get a good pizza delivered?
- Do I mind running errands all over town, or do I prefer being near a super center where I can do everything at once?
- Do I have any family considerations?
- Do I need to be near outdoor activities?
- Do I want to live in a culturally diverse area?

Location can make or break your living experience. Don't be afraid to ask your potential landlord and neighbors lots of questions about the area. And get out there and experience it for yourself before you sign that lease!

SAFETY RULES

Security is key. You've got to feel safe in your new place. What makes you comfortable?

- Do I need a secure building with a doorman?
- What kinds of security precautions are in place?
- Does the front door of the building stay locked?
- Is there a working security buzzer?
- Are the street and common areas of the building well lit?
- Will I feel safe walking from the car or public transit stop to my place at night?

Take a friend and check out the neighborhood at night. Walk around. Can you envision doing this alone every night? Ask questions of the people who live in the building or area. Call the police station and ask for a neighborhood report. And log on to **www.SexOffender.com** to search for convicted sex offenders living nearby.

READ THE SIGNS

"No Parking 12 noon to 2 p.m. MWF or 8 p.m. to 8 a.m. any day but Saturday without Permit 13 except Sunday which requires Permits 34 and 16 if your last name starts with letters J–P or your shoes are blue unless your mother's maiden name is O'Shea and you have two cats. Parking all other times permitted."

Look familiar? If you have a car, make parking a priority on your list.

- Do I need an assigned parking space or garage, or is there ample street parking?
- Am I willing to pay extra for a spot? How much?
- How attached am I to my paint job? Am I willing to park in an uncovered area? Under trees?
- Will my guests or I need a parking permit to park on the street or on the premises? How much does that cost? How easy are they to get?
- If I park on the street, are there time limits? Do I have to move my car every two hours or worry about street cleaners?

In my neighborhood, permit violations are $39 a pop and if you don't pay up in thirty days, they shoot up to $80. Rack up enough unpaid fines and you'll get the boot. The big, orange boot. And let me tell you, there's nothing convenient about that. Do yourself a favor. Think this one through before you have to learn the hard way.

TURN IT DOWN

If you choose an apartment, you'll have to share walls and ceilings with the people living around you. You'll hear people walking. You'll hear people talking. You'll hear people's stereos, their arguments, their dogs, their electric guitars, and their scene study rehearsals. And they'll hear you, too. That's part of apartment life and there's not much you can do to control it except to be respectful to others and hope they'll do unto you.

What you can limit are other outside noise factors by choosing where you live:

- Live on a busy street? You'll probably hear sirens, horns, car alarms, and traffic noise day and night.
- Live on an alley? You may deal with early-morning garbage trucks.
- Live near a school? Laughing children and tardy bells. Even on the weekends. Advil, anyone?
- Live in a happening neighborhood? How many partiers are you willing to hear scream, "I love you, man!" as they make the crawl from tavern to taxi?

Think about the retreat you want to create and consider your surroundings. Even living in the back of the building may do wonders.

tana's habitat

FEAR OF COMMITMENT

A lease is a rental agreement that locks you and the landlord into a specified period of time, usually a year. You agree that you'll abide by the terms of the lease and pay the rent on time; the landlord agrees that he will rent you the space at the negotiated price for the period of time you've agreed upon. During this period, the landlord cannot raise your rent or evict you unless you wreck the place or don't pay the rent. You can't disregard the tenets of the lease. If you break the lease by not paying the rent, moving out before the term is over, or ignoring some other principle of the lease, you'll lose your deposit and, most likely, get a ding on your credit report.

A month-to-month lease is just that. Month-to-month. The advantage to you is that you don't have to commit to staying in a place more than a month. The disadvantage is that the landlord can raise the rent, change the terms of the agreement, or terminate the lease every thirty days. If you're unsure of what your immediate future holds, month-to-month may be the perfect way to go.

FIDO AND FELIX

Do you have a pet? Are you thinking about getting one? Pet-friendly rentals are hard to find. Be prepared.

Most apartments that accept pets will charge an extra, nonrefundable deposit for cleaning and damage. Often times a landlord will stipulate a weight limit for your companion. So if your pooch is packing a paunch, or is even over twenty-five pounds, you could both be sleeping in your car. Some leases may require a dog to be certified in obedience, come with a Canine Good Citizen award, show proof of vaccination and medical records, or even have a letter of recommendation from a vet.

Other considerations:

- Where will my pet be comfortable? Is there enough room for him?
- Is there someplace to walk my pet? Someplace for him to be on leash? Roam about? Will he be safe?
- Is there a lawn to "water"?
- Are there children in the building or other pets that may be a conflict?
- Does Polly "want a cracker" all day long? My neighbors may not be too tolerant of my talkative toucan!

If you need help finding a pet-friendly pad, visit **www.PetRent.net**, or **www.PeopleWithPets.com**, or find your local Humane Society at **www.HSUS.org**. If you don't have a pet, this is the perfect time to stay solo.

READY-MADE

Are you testing the waters in a new city? Doing a short internship? Don't want to commit to furnishing an entire residence all at once? A furnished apartment may be just what the doctor ordered.

Totally equipped with all you need to live, furnished apartments come with everything from TVs, linens, and vacuum cleaners to ironing boards, dishes, and coffeemakers. They'll even supply you with artwork for the walls, throw rugs, and hanging plants!

Fully loaded doesn't come cheap. Furnished apartments can as much as double your rent. And for some, not having a hand in decorating can put a damper on moving to a new place.

GETTING THERE

If you rely on public transportation, be sure to give this some attention:

- Where's the closest bus or train stop? How long will it take me to walk there? Can I handle it in the winter?
- How many transfers will I need to get to where I want to go—like work? How long will it take to ride there?
- Can I get to other destinations? How easily?
- Is the bus schedule convenient to my schedule? Do the buses run on the weekends? Late nights?
- Where do I buy my pass? Is it convenient?

Don't be held hostage by a stinky subway schedule.

ZIP IT

Insurance companies are always looking for ways to stick it to us. Two ways they unfairly prejudge us is by our age and zip code. You can't do much about your age, but you can do something about the zip code in which you live. Check with you car or renter's insurance agent and ask for a list of cheaper zip codes. You might be able to save a couple hundred bucks on insurance by living just a block or two away.

tana's habitat

ROOMMATES: TO HAVE OR HAVE NOT

for as long as you can remember, you and your greatest pal have fantasized about moving in together. The constant giggle fests, the late-night heart-to-hearts, cooking and clothes swapping, popcorn and pool parties. What could be better? It's a match made in heaven!

Or is it?

Did you know that your best friend sets his alarm for 4:44 every morning to check SETI@home for the possibility that he's missing an alien invasion? Did you know that his morning shower is more to expectorate than exfoliate? Did you know he trims his toenails in the living room and saves the clippings to use as bait on his Australian Bream fishing expeditions?

No doubt, having a roommate can be a wonderful experience, but friend or foreigner, bad habits and OCD are not sold separately. As you begin pondering your potential partner, take off your rose-colored glasses and factor in the pros and cons of real life living situations. Be honest with yourself about what you want and who you are.

And never, ever forget these words: A bosom buddy does not always a bedfellow make.

MORE CASH, MORE CRIB

Financial worries can have a profound effect on your psyche, affecting everything you do from work to play. Not that having money will make you happy, but it sure can keep you from worrying about it. That's why cash is the number one reason to share a residence. Who wouldn't like to cut their living expenses in half *and* afford a better apartment? Rent, utilities, cable TV, Internet service, phone, food, it's like a 50 percent off sale on life!

On the flip side, money is also the number-one reason people end a roommateship. Discrepancies over even a few dollars can weird people out. So before you sign that lease, do yourself a favor and make sure your potential roommate can (and does) pay his bills on time. Ask him for a current credit report to check for any red flags. Offer up a copy of yours, too. You can get one for a nominal fee by visiting any of the credit bureaus at **www.Experian.com**, **www.Equifax.com**, or **www.TransUnion.com**. In fact, you're entitled by law to one free report each year. Find out more at **www.AnnualCreditReport.com**.

DOUBLE YOUR PLEASURE, DOUBLE YOUR FUN

Companionship is another great reason to live with someone. It's nice to come home to someone, to share a meal on the couch and your favorite episode of *The Simpsons*. Roommates provide the opportunity for meeting new people, making new friends, and expanding your knowledge of different cultures and backgrounds. And there's always the chicken soup factor. You're not feeling well, there's not a drop of stock to be slurped, and delivery is not an option, you've got that special someone to run out to the store and pick up the Progresso. No noodles, please.

Of course, there's a price for all this companionship. It's called companionship. There is someone home every time you walk through the door and they don't like *The Simpsons*. You don't like all of their friends and you hate chicken soup.

SAFETY IN NUMBERS

Does the thought of coming home to a dark, empty apartment scare you? When you're lying alone in bed at night does every little noise generate a Hitchcockian plot in your wandering mind? Maybe having a roommate would make you feel safer. After all, the one place you absolutely need to feel protected is your own home.

Share your concerns about safety with your potential roommate to make sure they're on the same page. Is it important for you to have the doors locked at all times? Does he like to leave the windows open when he leaves the apartment? What are your needs when it comes to alarm systems, secret codes, hiding a key or handing out spares? Does she come home from work late and need an escort from her faraway parking spot? Talk it out and decide if you meet each other's safety needs.

KNOW THYSELF

Have you decided to live with someone? Before you go roommate shopping, it's important to have a clear picture of your living habits. Be honest with yourself about how you live and what you will (and won't) tolerate in a housemate. It's hard to change your mind about letting someone smoke in the apartment once she's moved in. She may not be very understanding and your Febreze bottle is running on empty.

Fill out the **Roommate Questionnaire** (see pages 19–21) to help you assess yourself and your desires. Be sure to have your potential roommates do the same so you can compare notes.

If you think the screening is just for strangers, think again! Just because you like someone doesn't mean you're roommate compatible. Don't jeopardize a great friendship because you can't live together.

tana's habitat

WHERE TO LOOK

Start by putting the word out to everyone you know and trust to let them know you're looking for a roomie. Give them the specs of your ideal housemate and provide them with a copy of your completed **Roommate Questionnaire** so they can weed out the definite nos. If your word-of-mouth campaign falls flat, check out rental and roommate matching services in your area. Try free online want ads like **www.CraigsList.com**, **www.Yahoo.com**, or **www.RoommateLocator.com**. Check out online pay services like **www.Roommates.com** or **www.RoommateNation.com**. If you're a member of a fraternity, sorority, or club, place a roommate ad in their newsletter. Check with your alumni association or the bulletin boards at your union headquarters.

One year, upon returning to college from summer vacation, I was hit hard when I showed up at my apartment to find that my roommates had given my room away after hearing a rumor that I would not be returning to school that semester. Freaked to no end, I ran straight to the only place I could think of with a free phone, the graduate student lounge. In a heated frenzy, I dialed every number I could remember, hoping someone would take me in. Out of the blue, an angel appeared. A new grad student on a departmental tour with one of my favorite professors passed by and I overheard her mention she wasn't sure where she would be living. "I need a place to live and someone to live with!" I screamed, slamming the phone back into its cradle. "What do you say?"

"Uh, OK," she replied, unsure, as we walked arm in arm to the nearest rental service where we signed the lease we renewed three more times before our schooling was complete. Lucky for us, Carpeta, the Patron Saint of Apartments, shone her beacon brightly upon us.

INTERVIEWING THE CANDIDATES

If you can, interview any potential roommates in person. You want to be able to look them in the eye and check their body language as you get to know each other. Go in with a detailed list of questions and concerns from your **Roommate Questionnaire**. And take a parent or friend along for the ride. It never hurts to have a second opinion of someone you trust.

TOO MUCH INFORMATION

Privacy can be a sacred thing and its boundaries are different for everyone. You may not think anything of busting into the bathroom to take a shower while your roommate takes a time-out with the *Time Out*. And he may not think twice about reading the journal you accidentally left on the coffee table. Could it be you just need some me time in the apartment and she never seems to leave? Whatever the case, every-one needs some level of privacy.

This is an important issue, so think about what areas of your life are private and the things you think your roommate should also keep to themselves. Are you an exhibitionist? It may not bother you if your roommate is home while you traipse around the kitchen all nudey, but he may not be so comfortable with your nakedness. What if she shared too much about her life or you could hear him in the throes of passion? Would it be too much?

Make a list and check it twice, because when it comes to privacy, there's no going back.

CAN'T WE ALL JUST GET ALONG?

You don't have to be best friends (or even friends) with your roommate. In fact, quite often it's people who aren't great friends who make the best roommates. So, if not friendship, what else is there? Compatibility. But when compatibility and friendship fall short, you've just got yourself a mess.

In an act of desperation, I once moved into a two-bedroom apartment with a rotating occupancy of four out-of-work actors. As we all struggled to make ends meet, one of my roommates picked up a job at the Blockbuster Video around the corner. The hours weren't ideal, 4 p.m. until midnight, but he took it to another level by turning his evening post into an all-nighter.

The Swing King would return from his shift around 12:30 a.m., just as the rest of us had nestled into our sleeping bags for a good night's slumber, and proceed with his "day" as if it were high noon. On went the television, *ring* went the telephone, *clank, clank, clank* went the pots and pans as he satisfied his nightly craving for Top Ramen and peanut butter until finally he dozed off to Snoresville around six in the morning. Just in time for the rest of us to arise from our restless nights to tip-toe around our Sleeping Beauty sprawled out on the couch in front of *Good Morning America*.

Sometimes a girl just needs a place to lay her foam pad.

You can check your astrology charts and add up your numbers, draw the rune stones or consult the I Ching, but when it comes down to it, compatibility is about respect, give and take, choosing harmony, and picking your battles. Find someone whose living habits are similar to yours, don't expect too much and just work it out. If you left your sharing skills at kindergarten, maybe a roommate isn't for you. Anything in the common areas is typically fair game. At least when no one is looking. Would you mind sharing common items like kitchen supplies or the big TV in the living room? Do you want to share food or condiments? What happens when you eat the last pickle? Is your toothpaste off-limits? What about borrowing clothes or jewelry without asking? Toilet paper? Aspirin? Cleaning supplies?

This is just the tip of the iceberg when it comes to sharing your space with another. So figure out what your limits for sharing are and make sure everyone's boundaries are respected. With time, the line between yours and theirs is easily blurred. Take the time now and make a list of what belongs to whom or mark it with your initials or a symbol. You don't want to fight over who owns what skillet or who bought the copy of **tana's habitat**.

THE DIRTY TRUTH

Splitting the household chores with a roomie is a good thing, right? It's hard to see the downside. But if his idea of clean must pass a military inspection and your attitude allows for a little clutter and a few dirty dishes, you can count on some serious friction. Nobody wants to nag or be nagged. And nobody wants to find a pile of dirty dishes on top of their bed.

Examine your habits, get a handle on hers, and keep in mind that compromise is the name of this game.

GOING WITH YOUR GUT

If you're considering rooming with a stranger, you may also want to consider running a background check on them to confirm their rap sheet is as spotless as their button-down. Try **www.SafeRent.com** or **www.USSearch.com**. It's cheap and easy and may offer you some peace of mind to know the only body you're likely to find in the freezer is a chocolate bunny.

SEALING THE DEAL

You've found the perfect roommate, so now what? Before you sign a lease or even find an apartment, fill out a **Cohabitation Agreement** (see pages 24–25) to iron out just how you're going to live together. This contract covers everything from cleaning, sharing, and shopping to private time and party time. Think of it like a business plan that can grow and change as your relationship does.

Make sure you each sign it and keep a copy. Although this isn't a legal document, it can be a good tool to help resolve any conflicts down the road.

Roommates are partners and, if you're signing a lease together, you're both equally responsible for paying the rent. And not just your share. If your roomie skips out, you end up with the tab. It's not just the rent, either. There are lots of other bills involved. The real bummer is that their negligence can ruin your credit, making it next to impossible for you to do anything financially from getting a credit card or renting another apartment to buying a car or even a house. For seven years.

So wise up. Don't get stuck paying a $400 phone bill for which you aren't responsible or picking up the slack when your live-in decides to quit her day job. Put a plan into action instead and protect everyone involved with the **Roommate Contract** (see pages 22–23) *before* there's a problem. Together you can agree upon:

- How much each person pays for rent and deposit
- How you'll split other bills and expenses
- When the bills are due and how they get paid
- Bookkeeping duties
- How you'll pay for damages and late fees
- How to handle disagreements
- Who has to move out if there are irreconcilable differences

If you can, add both names to every financial obligation you share including leases and utilities. If only one name is allowed on an account, split them up, fifty-fifty, to spread the risk.

Keeping track of who pays what and when is essential. Get yourself a household ledger and use it. You never know when a discrepancy will arise, and it's always better to be safe than sorry. Especially when it comes to money.

Get in the habit of writing receipts for every transaction, *especially* with cash. Judge Judy loves documentation when there's no paper trail from the bank.

The phone bill is the statement that fuels a million and one heated roommate breakups. Don't let it burn you! Here are some options:

- Get separate lines.
- Share a landline and have your long distance company assign you each a password.
- Share a landline for Internet service and go cellular.
- Check out Voice over IP services like Vonage or Skype and get unlimited calling for a flat rate.
- Don't forget the international and 900 blocks.

roommate questionnaire

THE BASICS

1. Where do you want to live?
   _____ Apartment _____Townhouse _____Duplex _____House
   _____Other
2. How many people would you feel comfortable living with?
3. Do you want your own bedroom? Y/ N
4. Do you need a furnished or unfurnished place?
5. Do you have or are planning on getting a pet? Y/ N
   If so what?

MONEY

6. Do you have a job? Y/ N
7. How much can you spend on rent/utilities including: gas, electric, cable, phone, DSL, and any shared miscellaneous expenses?
8. Do you have much debt? (school loans, credit card, car note) Y/ N
9. Do you have a car? Y/ N Do you need parking? Y/ N
10. How do you prefer to pay bills?
    _____ The first of the month _____ The first and fifteenth of the
    month
    _____ Every week _____ As soon as they come in

HABITS

11. Each person should be responsible for his or her own:
    _____ Bills _____ Cleaning _____ Cleaning supplies
    _____ Cooking _____ Groceries _____ Toiletries _____ Other
12. I enjoy cooking. Y/N
13. I will do my dishes every night? Y/ N
14. I eat (breakfast, lunch, dinner) in the apartment. Y/ N
15. I clean up after myself in a timely manner. Y/ N
16. I smoke . . . (what and how much). Y/ N
17. I don't mind if others smoke around me. Y/ N
18. Concerning alcohol, I drink . . . (what and how much?)

19. I don't mind if others drink around me. Y/ N
20. Concerning drugs, I . . .
21. I am: Neat 1 2 3 4 5 Messy
22. I expect my roommate to be: Neat 1 2 3 4 5 Messy
23. I work best with a set schedule of housekeeping chores. Y/ N
24. I am: Quiet 1 2 3 4 5 Loud
25. When it comes to time alone in the apartment, I need:
A lot 1 2 3 4 5 Very little

PROBLEMS AND CONFLICTS

26. When I have a concern, I . . .
27. When I am upset about something that does not directly concern my roommate, I expect my roommate to . . .
28. When I am upset about something that directly concerns my roommate, I expect my roommate to . . .
29. When my roommate is upset about something that does not directly concern me, I will . . .
30. When my roommate is upset about something that directly concerns me, I will . . .

SHARING

31. I'm willing to share small items like clothes, CDs, dishes, food, etc. (List items that can be shared.)
32. Furniture and electronic items I have and will be bringing with me are:
33. I am okay with my roommate borrowing my stuff without asking. Y/ N
34. When it comes to lending money . . .

FRIENDS AND PARTIES

35. My friends could best be characterized as . . .
36. I often have overnight guests. Y/ N
37. My significant other visits . . .
38. Out of town guests are . . .
39. Giving parties is . . .

40. Beginning and ending party times for me are: _____ to _____

41. I generally party on (days of the week) . . .

ROOMMATES

42. A good roommate for me is . . .

43. A bad roommate for me is . . .

PERSONAL

44. I consider myself to be . . .

45. I hope others consider me as . . .

OTHER

If there are any other topics that you feel are important to a roommate relationship, be sure to discuss them.

roommate contract

This agreement made on _____ (date) is a contract between
_____ and _____,
co-tenants, for the rental premises located at _____
_____
_____(address)

This agreement is to last for the same term as our lease agreement, which runs
from _____ to _____.
I understand that I am entering into a legally binding agreement that is
enforceable by and between my roommates. I understand that this agreement
is not enforceable with regard to my landlord, and will not protect me against
any claims that my landlord may have against me or my roommates under our
lease agreement.

SECURITY DEPOSIT

The security deposit for the rental premises is $_____. My share
amounts to $_____. I accept responsibility for damages, which I, my
pet(s), or my guests cause, and I will reimburse my roommate(s) for the part
of their security deposit withheld for these damages.

RENT

The total rent according to the lease agreement is $_____ per month.
I promise to pay $_____ per month on or before the due date set forth
in the lease agreement. My payments will be made (directly to the landlord)
or (to _____, my co-tenant, who will
pay the landlord) [circle one]. I understand that we as a group and I as an
individual am responsible to the landlord for the total rent due for the full term
of the lease agreement. I understand that the landlord can evict all of the
tenants if the landlord does not receive the rental payments in full and on time
each month.

UTILITIES

I promise to pay 1/___ of the deposits and/or hookup charges for all utilities.

I promise to pay 1/___ of the monthly utilities (water, gas, and electric).

I promise to pay 1/___ of the monthly phone service charge, plus all long distance calls which I make.

I promise to place the following utilities in my name and to ensure that monthly payments are collected and made in full and on time: _____
_____

I promise to pay as follows for any additional utilities or services (cable, Internet access, security system, etc.):_____

MOVING OUT

If, for any reason, I move out of the rental premises before term of lease is completed, I realize that it is my responsibility to find a replacement tenant. I promise to take reasonable steps to find a replacement roommate who is acceptable to my present roommates. If one of my roommates moves out, I understand that it is my responsibility to take reasonable steps to find a replacement tenant. I understand that it is in the best interests of all roommates to replace any departing tenants as quickly as possible because all of the roommates still remain liable to the landlord for the full amount of the rent.

COHABITATION AGREEMENT

Attached is a description of additional agreements that are incorporated into this contract, including: house cleaning; groceries and food shopping; sharing of personal items; privacy and quiet times; guests and overnight guests; etc.

The roommates have executed this agreement on _____ (date).

Signed by:

_____   _____
(Name)   (Name)

_____   _____
(Name)   (Name)

cohabitation agreement

This agreement is to preestablish ground rules that will ensure a peaceful coexistence as roommates in all areas of cohabitation.

HOUSE CLEANING

We agree to share the following responsibilities of cleaning including: sweeping/vacuuming, dusting, emptying the trash, picking up/tidying common living areas, dishes, defrosting the refrigerator, etc.

Daily chores:_____

    To be split up as follows: _____

    _____

Weekly chores:_____

    To be split up as follows: _____

    _____

As needed chores:_____

    To be handled in the following manner:_____

    _____

Shared cleaning supplies such as:_____

    To be shopped and paid for in the following manner:_____

    _____

GROCERIES & FOOD SHOPPING

The following list of food and nonfood items to be shared by all roommates (such as condiments, spices, toilet paper, toothpaste, etc.):_____
_____
_____
_____

Shopping and food cost to be handled in the following manner: _____
_____
_____

I agree to share my personal food and food-related items. Y/ N Yes, but ask. Those agreed-upon food and food related items to be shared without asking are:_____

SHARING OF PERSONAL ITEMS

The following is a list of my personal items I will share: _____

_____

You need to ask before using. Y/ N

PRIVACY & QUIET TIME

My bedroom is:_____

I need _____ of private alone time in the apartment, and I ask you respect my wishes in this matter by:

As for quiet time in the apartment, I need it to be quiet between the hours of _____ and _____ on M T W T F S S.

GUESTS & OVERNIGHT GUESTS

Ground rules for guests are as follows:_____

Ground rules for overnight guests are as follows:_____

_____

FINAL REMARKS

_____

_____

_____

_____

The roommates have executed this agreement on _____ (date).

Signed by:

_____   _____
(Name)   (Name)

_____   _____
(Signature)   (Signature)

These agreements are provided for the mutual benefit of roommates, but do not constitute legal advice. If you need legal advice, you must contact an attorney.

MAYDAY, MAYDAY

you've taken every precaution. You've filled out all the questionnaires. You've signed the contracts and agreements to ensure the ideal living companion and situation. But there's no guarantee that your relationship won't sour. Personalities change and people don't always live up to their responsibilities.

Whatever the case, it's important to remedy your problems ASAP. The longer you wait, the tougher it will be to rectify a bad situation, especially if it's financial.

WHEN GOOD ROOMMATES GO BAD

If you're having minor problems like personality or lifestyle clashes, sit your roommate down and have a heart-to-heart. If you filled out the **Cohabitation Agreement** together, chances are, with a gentle reminder, she'll see the error of her ways and step up the respect. After all, she did agree on the rules once.

But respect works both ways. Don't antagonize your roommate or you may end up the victim of roommate revenge. On the upside, Jerry Springer and Dr. Phil are holding auditions at an auditorium near you.

Anything that jeopardizes your health or safety is a serious infraction of your living agreement and must be dealt with immediately. If you are in danger, getting hurt or abused in any way, leave. Get out and get help. You may even need to call the cops.

If you are not physically threatened, sit your roommate down and ask him to stop the offending behavior. Offer to help work out a solution. If that doesn't work, you may need to take a more formal approach by documenting the problem.

Keep a detailed record of your roommate's behavioral offenses and the conflicts you've had with him. This should include who said what, witnesses, dates, and times of said events. You may need this info if it escalates into something that calls for legal action.

If their activity is criminal, report them to the police.

WHEN ROOMMATES DON'T PAY

Even though both of your names are on the lease, you're equally responsible for paying the rent—all of it. And your landlord won't care about the drama that's keeping them from cashing your check. In most states, if your roommate is on the lease and can't come up with the rent, he's obligated to replace himself with an acceptable roommate or keep paying until you are able to replace him. However, you can't get blood from a turnip.

If your roomie no longer pays his share, try to convince him to move out immediately and find a replacement to limit your financial burden. Keep your landlord in the loop about what's going on so he won't feel so blindsided if you have to move out suddenly and break the lease. If you show some good faith about paying your rent, your landlord may be lenient with you until the situation is resolved. At the very least, he could abstain from chinking away at your credit report after the door's hit you in the butt.

Never take the law into your own hands by changing the locks, locking someone out of the apartment, or holding your roommate's possessions for ransom. It's against the law and you could go to jail. Instead, get thee to small claims court. Take your **Roommate Contract**, your household ledger, your lease, and your unpaid bills and let the judge do his job.

But don't be afraid to have a roommate. Be prepared, do your homework, and it can turn into one of the most fulfilling friendships you'll ever have.

money matters

with setting out on your own comes financial responsibility. Know what you can afford and prepare for the unknown so there's never too much month left at the end of your money.

IN AND OUT

how much you can spend on rent is directly related to how much you earn and owe. If you were trying to buy a house, a bank would only qualify you for a loan if they could prove that you can pay all your bills on time on your salary, with some left over for a rainy day. They call it a **debt-to-income ratio**. It's a great guideline for renters to follow, too, to make sure you'll always be able to pay the piper. The general rules of thumb:

- Keep your housing expense below 30 percent of your pretax income.

- Housing expense plus recurring debt should equal no more than 36 percent of your pretax income.
- Save 10 percent of your pretax income.
- The rest is up to you.

How much apartment can you afford? Figure out your debt-to-income ratio and you're well on your way to finding out.

INCOMING

Grab a clean pad of paper and a calculator or a spreadsheet application like Excel, Microsoft Money, or QuickBooks and start with the good stuff. Take all your income sources into account and list your gross earnings, what you earn before tax. If you have one job, simply take a look at your last pay stub. If you have multiple sources of income, make a list. Check your bank statements for deposits if you need a refresher.

INCOME	WEEKLY	MONTHLY	YEARLY	TOTAL
main income				
secondary income				
other income				
TOTAL INCOME				

OUTGOING

Now that you know what's coming in, it's time to figure out how much is sneaking out the door. Realizing your actual expenses can be an overwhelming task, but it doesn't have to hurt as much as a root canal. Start slow, breathe deep, and, most important, be honest with yourself.

Start by listing the steadies: Car payment, health and car insurance, student loans, Internet service, Netflix, gym membership—all the payments you know will be the same every month.

Next, list the swingers—the bills with varying amounts you know you pay every month: cell phone and land line, credit cards, and any other outstanding, recurring debt. Refer back to old bills or your checkbook to find the average monthly payment for each.

tana's habitat

Finally, go for the dribblers and drabblers: food, toiletries, entertainment, clothing, nails, haircuts, car maintenance, transportation, birthday gifts, etc. Be realistic with yourself about how much you spend and don't forget to add some cushion for emergencies.

Use this budget form to get started. There may be some items that don't pertain to your situation.

EXPENSE BREAKDOWN	WEEKLY	MONTHLY	YEARLY	TOTAL
CURRENT UTILITIES				
electricity				
natural gas				
phone				
cell phone				
internet				
cable/satellite tv				
other				
TRANSPORTATION				
car payment				
insurance				
gas				
maintenance				
licensing				
other				
FOOD AND FOOD-RELATED ITEMS				
groceries				
meals outside the home				
cleaning supplies				

EXPENSE BREAKDOWN	WEEKLY	MONTHLY	YEARLY	TOTAL
toiletries				
other				
PERSONAL EXPENSES				
hair				
manicure/pedicure				
gym membership				
clothing				
laundry				
dry cleaning				
pet expenses				
health insurance				
other				
other				
CREDIT DEBT				
credit card 1				
credit card 2				
credit card 3				
student loan 1				
student loan 2				
student loan 3				
other				
other				
other				

EXPENSE BREAKDOWN	WEEKLY	MONTHLY	YEARLY	TOTAL
ENTERTAINMENT AND TRAVEL				
movies				
dining out				
sporting events				
concerts				
travel				
gifts				
other				
other				
PROFESSIONAL FEES				
doctor				
dentist				
eye care				
chiropractor				
veterinarian				
other				
TOTAL EXPENSES				

What do you have left over for rent and utilities? Subtract your total expenses from your total income and find out. Don't forget the recommended dose of (dare I say?) savings! 10 percent of your gross income.

my total income x .10 = suggested savings

IN AND OUT	WEEKLY	MONTHLY	YEARLY	TOTAL
total income				
minus total expenses				
minus savings				
equals rent				

HOW DO YOU RATE?

Compare yourself to a bank's idea of how your income is best spent, fill in the blanks, and see how you measure up.

my total income x .36 = bank's ideal debt-to-income

COMPARISON	BANK'S IDEAL	MY REALITY
my total expenses plus rent		
my savings		

CUT THE FAT

coming up a little short? Take a good, hard look at those dribblers and drabblers. It's easy to fritter away lots of dough in the gray area between need and desire, so figure out where you might be able to trim a little off the top.

YOU'RE A D.I.N.K.

Consider making your household Dual Income No Kids by getting a roommate to split the cost of rent and utilities. No-brainer.

NO FUMAR

Are you insane? If you don't quit smoking for your health, do it for your wallet!

The average pack of cigarettes sells for $5 in most states and, in some, for as much as $7.50! That pack-a-day habit will cost you $1,825 every year, minimum. Pay off your school loans in just a few years instead. And don't forget to cash in on those auto and health insurance discounts for nonsmokers.

Breathe easier with more money in your pocket and less tar in your lungs. Quit smoking.

CAFÉ NO WAY

Stop the Starbucks! Even if you only buy a no-frills cup of joe, those $2 a day add up to $730 a year. And if your habit's highbrow, those cafés au lait will easily skyrocket your bill to upwards of $1,500 per year. On coffee! Are you cuckoo for cappuccino? Treat yourself once a week if you must and learn to brew a good pot at home . . . in that new apartment you can finally afford.

BROWN-BAG IT

Take your lunch to work and save over $100 a month!

CABLE ACCESS

Cable TV is a costly habit. That $50 to $100 a month can easily be spent on something less frivolous or more fun. Read a book, watch regular TV, rent your favorite show's season on DVD, or spend time with friends. Spend $1,200 a year to watch television after your next raise . . . if you're not on vacation.

TRANSPORT ME

Walk, carpool, or take public transportation! Save the planet and your pennies. Trade hubcaps for spokes. If you dump your car and buy a bike, you'll save on car payments, insurance, gas, and parking. And you can take a bike lots of places you can't take a car. Including a bus!

STICK TO IT

you know what you earn, you know what you spend, you know what you save, and you know how much rent you can afford. You've even figured out how to cut back to ensure ends will meet month after month. Congratulations! You've created a budget.

Now comes the hard part: sticking to it.

PACK THE PAXIL

Living on a budget isn't easy, no matter how big it is. There are always more places to go, more people to see, more things to do, more bucks to be spent, so existing within your means is a real triumph. There is no greater sense of accomplishment than knowing you can take care of yourself. Prioritize and come up with creative ways to follow your financial plan and you can step away from the black hole of debt, knowing you're at least $90 a month richer without your antianxiety meds and Tylenol PM habit.

- Use coupons for restaurants, dry cleaners, car washes, and other services you frequent.
- Take care of the things you already have and repair them instead of throwing them out and replacing them with something new.
- Comparison shop. Take the time to find lower rates for insurance coverage and credit cards. Look for the best phone and cellular plans that fit your usage. Log on to **www.LowerMyBills.com** and see how much you can save.

tana's habitat

- Make businesses compete for your business. Don't be afraid to say that you "saw it for less" somewhere else. You just might get the discount you want. Make sure you've done your homework, though, and have the documentation to back up your claim.
- Find specials at local nightspots. A lot of bars offer happy hours, cheap drink specials, and deals on munchies. Twenty-five-cent wings anyone?
- Party in the park with friends. Hang out and play Frisbee-golf, badminton, or croquet. It's cheap, easy, and fun.
- Have cocktails at home. Invite friends over for a movie night or game night and keep the bar tab low. Who wants to spend $7.50 for one drink? Have everyone pitch in for snacks and booze and it won't cost much. No drunk driving, please.
- Only buy clothes that are on sale. Think twice about spending your money on a trendy item you may only get to wear a couple of times before it goes out of style.
- How often do you cut or color your hair? Every four to six weeks? Can you go less often? Even if you cut back to six to eight weeks between treatments, you can easily save $300 a year. Teach yourself to touch up or do it with a friend. Have a mani/pedi party and forgo the spa chair for savings.
- Any meal you can prepare and eat at home saves money. No tipping, no driving, no parking, and no time wasted. Plus, at home you can eat barefoot or in your pajamas. Make a bit extra and take the leftovers to work the next day for lunch.
- Recycle for cash. You'll feel good about the environment and pocketing the pennies.
- Find friends or family to shop with you at warehouse stores like Costco and Sam's Club and split bulk items.

EAT MORE FOR LESS

It's easy to go hog wild at the Piggly Wiggly. Use some common sense and you'll find lots of ways to save at the supermarket.

- Don't shop hungry. Everything looks good and ends up in your cart.
- Do make a grocery list and stick to it. No need to wander up and down each aisle, just get in, get out, and get on with your life.
- Clip coupons, it's free money! Some markets even double their value, which makes it well worth the cost of the Sunday *Times*.

- Shop sales and compare prices in the comfort of your home instead of crowded stores. You can find grocery store ads and department store booklets in your mailbox.
- Only buy the groceries you'll use. Spoiled foods like fruits, veggies, and meat equal cash in the trash.
- Most markets have value clubs; in-house discount cards you swipe for additional savings. Use them and save a bundle.
- Go generic. The labels aren't glossy, but check 'em out, anyway. You may find the store brand is offering the same ingredients for a lot less money.
- Always check your receipt while you're still at the cash register. Make sure you were charged the correct amount, all coupons were accounted for, and all discounts were applied to the total sale. Most of us are too lazy or too embarrassed to go back to fight for discounts. Do it anyway. You work hard for the money!

HABIT FORMING

"Habits are at first cobwebs, then cables," says the old Spanish proverb. Build your budgeting habits by setting up a monthly routine. Follow some rules to make following your budget *más fácil* (that means easy).

- Pay bills as soon as they arrive. Get them out of your life as quickly as they came in. Pay them on time, skip the late fee.
- Pay off your credit card debt and keep it off. Use credit cards for emergencies only. Two CDs and five DVDs do not an emergency make.
- Compare prices. Do the research and drop spending on a whim and you'll never have buyer's remorse.
- Make an impulse fund. Set aside a few bucks every week to buy a little something crazy every couple of months.

INSTITUTIONALIZED

how are you going to manage this budget? Where are you going to keep all this cash?

I know what you're thinking. You hate banks. All they do is bombard you with service charges and extra fees for doing absolutely nothing. They're so impersonal, they never remember your name, and they make you feel like you're just a number, especially the big banks. And you're right. Banks are not our friends.

So what are you gonna do? Bury cash in your backyard? Hide it under your mattress? No. You're going to do the bank thing, just like everybody else. But it doesn't have to be miserable and it doesn't have to cost you a fortune. In fact, you can actually get one over on your bank. Become the customer the bank despises! The customer who pays no fees, keeps a low monthly balance, and gobbles up every convenient service they offer.

BIG AND BIGGER

Banks are for-profit institutions owned by stockholders who want to make a big profit on their investment. One way they increase those already hefty profit margins is by charging you loan-shark rates for everything from maintaining basic checking accounts, making deposits, and writing checks to talking to a teller and using your ATM card, as well as charging exorbitant credit card interest.

Not-for-profit cooperatives, **credit unions** are financial institutions that are owned and collectively controlled by their members, groups that share something in common such as a workplace or union organization. They accept deposits from members, pay interest on those deposits in the form of dividends from earnings and use other profits to provide the same basic functions as a bank. Account fees and loan rates are much lower than those charged by banks. That means you pay less fees, but you earn less interest, too. Just like a bank, the federal government insures your money.

The one big drawback to a credit union is the lack of ATM machines. And paying $1.50 or more in fees to another institution to borrow $20 of your own money is a variation on an old loan-shark trick! Don't be a sucker. If you join a credit union, plan ahead to make sure you're flush with cash when you need it. If you're really desperate, make a grocery run and buy something you need like toilet paper and get cash back for free. You can never have too much toilet paper.

Credit unions aren't for everyone, and not just anyone can participate. Find out if you're eligible or interested in participating by visiting CU Match Up at **www .HowToJoinaCU.org** or America's Credit Unions at **www.CreditUnion.coop**.

SIZE MATTERS

Open a checking account and do it at a big bank. The bigger the better. "But which big bank?" you may be asking yourself. The one with lots and lots of ATM machines. If you travel all over your state, find out which bank has carpeted your state with ATMs. If you travel nationwide, think about opening an account at one of the behemoth banks, like Bank of America, Citibank, or JPMorgan Chase. The money you save on ATM charges will make up for the monthly service charge, which you're not going to pay anyway.

All you need is a valid driver's license or state-issued photo ID, Social Security number, and enough cash or a check to meet the minimum requirement needed to open the account you desire.

TOTALLY FREE CHECKING

Most big banks offer free checking these days. According to the law, "free checking" means the bank cannot charge you a recurring maintenance fee, require a minimum balance, or charge an excessive check-writing fee, a per-check fee, or a deposit fee. What they can charge you is a sizable administrative fee for setting up your account.

So how do you get that monthly fee waived? Many banks waive the fee if you directly deposit your check. And thanks to the growing popularity of payroll service companies, more and more businesses, even small companies and temp firms, offer this service.

Other banks offer free checking for customers who don't employ the services of a teller. Hello. If you're waiting in line to see a teller, you better be at least ninety years old and signing your checks with a quill pen! This is the lost and ancient art of banking. Negotiate for free online banking, bill pay, and banking by phone.

HIDDEN (AND NOT SO HIDDEN) FEES

When opening an account, make sure you ask for a list of all the fees before you sign the banking contract. Some banks will charge you a fee for:

- Closing the account soon after opening it
- Lack of activity
- Calling to check your balance
- Issuing a debit card
- Use of a debit card
- Dropping below your minimum balance on an interest-bearing account

Some fees you just can't avoid:

- NSF: Insufficient funds aka bouncing a check
- Depositing a check from someone else that bounces

- Stopping payment on a check
- Bounce protection

The best way to avoid these fees it to keep track of how much money is in your account and never overdraw on it.

ONLINE NOT IN LINE

Use online bill pay and save yourself the time of writing checks, waiting in line to buy stamps, and other unnecessary hassles and expenses. Money is removed from your account instantly so you don't have to wait five to seven days for your balance to reflect the payments, which reduces your chance of bouncing a check and paying $30 in NSF fees to your favorite financial institution. Do it online and you'll always know how much money you have in your account because you'll never have a dozen checks floating in and out of our nation's post offices.

BALANCING ACT

Just because you have blank checks doesn't mean you have unlimited access to money. You need to balance your checkbook regularly and keep track of it.

If you're unsure of how to balance your checkbook, I'll go slowly. The register is the flippy book with all the blank lines inside they gave you with your checks. Turn to the cover and it should show you how to keep your account in balance. It doesn't? Don't sweat it. It's easy.

- Enter your balance.
- Every time you write a check, write down the number of the check, to whom you made the check out, and for how much on one of those blank lines.
- Subtract that amount from the balance, giving you your new balance.
- When you make a deposit, add it to the balance.
- Keep receipts for your ATM withdrawals and deduct them as soon as possible.

Every month your bank will send you a statement. It's a record of every transaction you made on the account for the last month. Compare this statement to the register you've been keeping. They should match up. If they don't, figure out where you have gained or lost money, account for it, and correct your check register.

Resolve any problems or discrepancies immediately. Can't figure it out on your own? Think the bank owes you money? Get thee to a teller and get it figured out.

SAVE ME

Do not, I repeat, do not open a savings account at the same bank as your checking account. Why? Pure psychology. You want these two entities to remain separate. If you can easily dump money from your savings account into your checking account every time you're a little low on cash, you'll never save!

Your savings account should have two main features. Easy entry. Difficult exit. Find a painless way to funnel 10 percent of every paycheck into that account no matter what! And reduce the options for withdrawing that money. In fact, don't withdraw it. Forget about it. When you have enough to open a CD, money market account, or money market fund then do it.

CERTIFICATE OF DEPOSIT (CD)

A CD is very similar to a savings account. When you park your money there, you get a higher interest rate, but you can't withdraw any funds for a set amount of time, anywhere from three months to six years. If you do, you pay a penalty, and lose some of that hard-earned cash.

MONEY MARKET ACCOUNT

Think of a money market account as a checking account on steroids. After establishing your account with a minimum balance, you can still get at your money by writing checks or visiting the ATM. What's more, you'll make money through interest, though probably not as much as you'll make from more restricted accounts like a CD.

MONEY MARKET FUND

Take a dash of CD and a dollop of money market account, and you've got yourself a money market fund. With this investing tool, brokerages invest your money in a variety of ways, such as in CDs and government securities. Your take will be a little better than in a regular ol' money market account, but you'll still be able to write checks and use the ATM.

WHAT YOU'LL NEED TO SAVE FOR

freedom has a color: It's green. And you'll need lots of it to get settled in your first place.

MOVIN' IN COSTS

Most landlords will require first and last month's rent plus **security deposit** to be paid before you move in. The deposit serves as insurance against any damages you inflict upon the property. It can also be used to safeguard against unpaid rent or a broken lease or to clean the apartment when you move out.

The maximum amount a landlord can legally charge varies from state to state, but should never be more than two times the monthly rent for an unfurnished apartment, three times the rent for a furnished apartment. With that said, I've never paid more than $500 for a security deposit. It depends a lot on your credit history.

In some states, landlords are required by law to keep your security deposit in an interest-bearing account. This means any interest made off your deposit is to be paid to you either annually or at the termination of your lease. Don't get too excited. It'll barely cover the cost of one Saturday morning McGriddle.

CLEANING DEPOSIT

Some landlords will hit you up for a **cleaning deposit**. This is to cover the costs of cleaning the apartment when you move out. Even if you leave your apartment cleaner than the day you moved in, you'll still have to pay for it. And don't think you'll get even by leaving your apartment in a dirty, filthy mess when you move out. If you do, you'll have to pay *extra* to have it cleaned. And that comes out of your security deposit. Yeah, it's a scam.

Cleaning deposits usually run $50 to $100, fair market value for a housecleaner to come in and whip the place into shape.

PETS

Do you have a pet? The average **pet deposit** ranges between $100 to $300 per pet. If your little buddy causes any dings or dents to the apartment like "water damage," it'll come out of the pet deposit. If the damage repairs cost more than the pet deposit, the balance will come out of your, say it with me, now, "security deposit."

BROKER FEES

A broker is someone who handles all the work of finding an apartment, scheduling showings, and negotiating the deal for you. If you hire a broker, expect to pay a hefty fee. Most agents' charge equals one month's rent or more. Unless you're moving to a new city far away, trying to find an apartment in New York or San Francisco, loaded, or lazy, you won't need to use a service like this. Save your bucks for a new couch.

UTILITIES

if you've never had utilities in your name or you have bad credit, you may have to put down a deposit for gas, electric, or phone. If you have a roommate, you can split the deposits, but make sure you have a written plan for how those monies get repaid when one or both of you move out.

Set-up fees and deposits will vary state to state, but these figures are in the ballpark.

UTILITY	SET UP FEE	DEPOSIT
GAS	$25.00	2 x monthly bill average in zip code
ELECTRIC	$12.00	2 x monthly bill average in zip code
PHONE	$33.01	$25–$100 depending on credit history
CABLE TV	$29.95	first month's payment
CABLE INTERNET	free if you install the software; $49.95 if they do	no additional deposit if you already have have cable; if you don't, first month's payment
SATELLITE TV	$49.95 activation fee credited to future service	$0–$150 depending on credit history
SATELLITE INTERNET	limited availability, rates vary	$0–$150 depending on credit history
DIGITAL TV	$49.95 activation fee credited to future service.	$0–$150 depending on credit history
DIGITAL INTERNET	limited availability, rates vary	$0–$150 depending on credit history

tana's habitat

BATTLE OF THE BUNDLES

Sure, the foot bone's connected to the anklebone. The anklebone's connected to the shinbone. But your phone line connected to your TV set? That's a new one!

The advent of new technologies has brought a dizzying array of choices for services including local, long-distance, and cellular-phone plans, television, and Internet options. As titans like Comcast, the Baby Bells, AOL Time Warner, and Cox go head-to-head to offer consumers everything under one umbrella, bundled services are emerging as the way of the future.

The advantage? You get all the services you want or need, competitively priced, without the hassle of having to pay five different companies at the end of the month. The disadvantage? It's still expensive and, like many things in life, the discounts only rack up with additional services: spend more, save more.[1]

SHOULD I STAY OR SHOULD I GO?

Bundled packages are built on broadband. The best way to shop for one is to start by looking at where your money goes now and focus on getting the best version of the service that's most important to you.

- What are my Internet needs?
- Do I make enough long-distance phone calls to justify $40 to $60 a month for unlimited calls? If you make less than six hours worth, probably not.
- Do I make international calls? Most of the time, you'll need a separate plan to cover these.
- Do I have a cell phone? How do I use it?
- What can I afford?

WHAT ARE MY BROADBAND OPTIONS?

DSL

Digital Subscriber Line (DSL) is a digital technology that sends high-bandwidth over copper telephone lines. It allows data to be sent twenty times faster than a 56K modem and ten times faster than ISDN. DSL offers "always on" service, increased security, and doesn't interfere with your ability to make and receive phone calls.

DSL can be complicated to install and may need extra equipment, phone jacks, and other complicated configuring that your provider may or may not supply.

CABLE

Cable Internet is an "always on" connection that delivers considerably faster speeds than dial-up and DSL without interfering with your ability to make and receive telephone calls. It uses the same fiber optic wiring used to provide cable television and is especially useful for online gamers, downloading music, instant messaging, and surfing graphic-intensive websites.

However, the more people who use your cable network, the slower the service.

SATELLITE

Satellite Internet uses a space satellite to send broadband, which makes it a great option for people living in the boonies where DSL or cable are not yet available. Of course, that access comes at a price. Satellite Internet is one of the steepest Internet alternatives.

In order to receive satellite service, you must have a clear, unobstructed view of the southern sky to receive the signal. And because the signal has so far to go, you may notice lags in the time between clicking on a link and receiving the data.

VOIP

With Voice over Internet Protocol (VoIP), your telephone calls are routed over the Internet through your broadband service of choice: DSL, cable, or satellite. You plug a standard phone into a little black box called an Analogue Telephone Adaptor (ATA), which plugs into your existing broadband Internet connection. The ATA simulates a dial tone when you pick up the phone to make a call, rings when you receive a call and, as far as you can tell, works exactly the same way a telephone does. But because your calls are being sent and received over broadband, the cost is low, low, low.

What's particularly cool is that, because the phone is plugged into the Internet, it can be anywhere. So you can take your phone and ATA to Europe or South America, plug it into a broadband connection in your hotel room or Internet café, and still make and receive local and long distance calls just like you were at home because the area code never changes![2]

On the downside, if your cable or satellite happens to go out, you're stuck without a telephone, an Internet connection, and, probably, a television. Also, VoIP does not provide a direct connection to 911.

For more information on VoIP, visit **www.Vonage.com** or **www .Skype.com**.

Because every individual's needs vary as greatly as the infinite configurations of service bundles, it's impossible to recommend any one plan. Even consumer advocate groups are having trouble figuring out a way to rate and review. Put your nose to the grindstone and compare plans on websites like **www.LowerMyBills.com** and **www.SaveOnPhone.com**. Review the reviewers at **www.Consumer Search.com** and find others.

PROMISES, PROMISES

In their fervor to prevail, companies are sometimes guilty of over-promising by selling packages that don't even exist yet! If it sounds too good to be true, it may be.[3]

WORD TO THE WISE

Know what you're getting into when you sign that service agreement. Know what the setup fees are, how many months you have to pay up front to get the discount you're applying for, if there's any equipment you need to buy or lease, and if there are any hidden fees in that teeny, tiny print. You can guarantee there's something in there that will increase your monthly payments by 10 to 15 percent. Gulp.

HOT AND COLD

some places have appliances, some places don't. A stove and fridge are necessities unless you want to rely on a hot plate and an ice chest, so BYO or keep looking for an apartment that includes them.

Before you buy, be sure it will fit in your place! Measure the height, width, and depth of the space and make sure the numbers add up.

USED ME

Put the word out! Someone you know may know someone who knows someone who has the used appliance of your dreams sitting idly in their garage. They might even give it away for the extra garage space! Check the classifieds and community newspapers, secondhand shops, or **www.CraigsList.com** if there's one in your area. Try **www.FreeCycle.org**. These folks *give* stuff away. Lots of appliance stores also sell used appliances or floor models. You can find a great used refrigerator for $150 to $250, a used stove for $100 to $200, and a used washer and dryer for $100 to $300.

Wherever you buy, make sure you know the refund/return and repair policies. Nobody likes a lemon.

STAY COOL

What to look for when shopping for a used fridge:

WHAT'S YOUR STYLE?

Side by side, freezer on the top, or freezer on the bottom? Make sure the doors will open in the space you place it.

IS IT EXPENSIVE TO RUN?

If the fridge you're buying is more than ten years old, it may use more electricity, which costs you mo' money. Look into energy-efficient models and save yourself $20 to $30 a year on power.

HOW DOES IT LOOK?

Did the previous owners care for this fridge well? Is it clean? Mold free? Check for dents, rust, funny noises, or anything that may say to you, "Don't buy me."

HOW DOES IT WORK?

Plug it in before you buy. Does the light turn on? Does the temperature control knob work? Is the freezer frost-free? Or does it need to be manually defrosted? Let it run for a bit to make sure it gets cool. The refrigerator section needs to cool to between 35° to 40° F. The freezer should be 0° F.

GASKET

It's the rubber piece that runs around the perimeter of the door. Check for mold and make sure it's sealing properly. Shut the door on a piece of paper and try to pull it out. If it slips out easily, the gasket's not keeping the cold in. It may need to be replaced or the door hinges adjusted. Don't forget to check the freezer door's gasket, too.

SHELVES, DRAWERS, AND RACKS

Are all the parts there? Are any of them broken or cracked? Do they slide and move smoothly? Can they be removed for easy cleaning?

WARRANTY

Is it still under warranty?

tana's habitat

HOT STUFF

What to look for when shopping for a used stove:

WHAT'S YOUR STYLE?

Gas or electric? Make sure you have a gas hookup before buying a gas stove. Is it self-cleaning? Or am I willing to Easy-Off?

HOW DOES IT LOOK?

Has the stove been taken care of or are there rust spots, dents, and broken knobs and burners?

BURNERS

If it's electric, plug it in and check each burner to make sure it heats up. If it's gas and still hooked up, fire her up. Not hooked up? Test it out as soon as possible and make sure it can be returned for a full refund if she's a dud.

OVEN AND BROILER

Test it. Make sure it gets hot and that a couple of racks and a broiler pan are included. If it's a self-cleaning oven, does it get the job done?

GASKET

It's the rubber piece that runs around the perimeter of the oven door. Test the conditions to confirm the heat stays in the oven, not in the kitchen.

HOSES

If you're buying a gas stove, look at the hoses for cracks or other damage. If it needs new ones, they can be had for $10 to $20 bucks at the hardware store. Beats a gas leak.

WARRANTY

Is it still under warranty?

If any used appliance you buy doesn't come with a user's manual, look online, check eBay, or call the manufacturer for a guide.

SPIN CYCLE

Heads up! If you're buying a washer and dryer, make sure your apartment has a washer/dryer hookup.

WHAT'S YOUR STYLE?

Top load? Front load? Side by side, stacked, or portable? Front loaders are more energy efficient and will save you $60 to $100 a year in electrical bills. Portable washers can be attached to the sink and wheeled into a closet for easy storage!

HOW DO THEY LOOK?

Have they been well cared for or are there rust spots, dents, mold, and broken knobs? Are the basins clean?

HOW DO THEY WORK?

Test-drive before you buy. Does the washer fill with water? Does the spin cycle spin? Does the temperature control knob work? Does the dryer door close? Is there a lint trap? Is there actually any difference between high heat and cool down? How long do the cycles take?

WARRANTY

Is it still under warranty?

OTHER APPLIANCES

think you need a dishwasher? Don't sweat it. Look for a newer apartment that has one built in.

How about that microwave? Do yourself a favor and just buy a new one. You can find a stylin' nuker for under $40 at Target, Best Buy, or Wal-Mart. Vacuum cleaner? If you don't need the style of a Dyson, you can get yourself a brand-new Dirt Devil for around $50 to start sucking up those dust bunnies.

BELLS AND WHISTLES

With so many opportunities to get a great deal on used appliances, why would you ever buy new? Choice. Get the extras, get it delivered, and get it brand, spankin' clean.

tana's habitat

Over time, what you save on electricity with energy-efficient models can add up, too, and that steel-clad warranty may offer you some peace of mind.

WARRANTIES

A warranty is a promise made by a manufacturer to stand behind their product. Federal law requires that warranties be available for your reading pleasure before you buy, even if you're shopping by catalog or online. Just as you compare style, price, and characteristics of products before you buy one, you can also evaluate the warranty's coverage.

HOW LONG?

Check the warranty to see when it begins and when it expires, as well as any conditions that may void coverage.

HOW DO I GET SERVICE?

You've got to contact someone if there's a problem. Find out if it's the seller or the manufacturer.

WHAT HAPPENS IF MY PRODUCT FAILS?

Know whether the company will repair the item, replace it, or refund your money.

WHAT'S COVERED?

See if any parts or types of repair problems are excluded from coverage? Do they require you to pay for labor charges? Do you have to pay to ship the item to a factory for service or return it in its original packaging? Some conditions of the warranty may prove expensive and inconvenient.

WHAT ABOUT CONSEQUENTIAL DAMAGES?

What if your dishwasher breaks and the flood ruins your linoleum? Who's fixing the floor? Many warranties don't cover your time or expense repairing damages caused by the product.

ARE THERE CONDITIONS OR LIMITATIONS?

Some warranties provide coverage only if you maintain or use the product as directed. If a product designed for personal use breaks at the office, you may be out of luck.

GET IT IN WRITING

Did the sales guy tell you his company would provide free repairs or ongoing maintenance? Get it in writing or you may be up the creek without a paddle when it slips his mind, he quits his job, or just plays dumb.

EXTENDED WARRANTIES

There's no such thing as an extended warranty! It's often called that, but what you're really getting is a service contract. Like a warranty, service contracts provide service and/or maintenance for a specified time. Warranties, however, are included in the price of the product; service contracts cost extra and are sold separately.

Are you considering purchasing a service contract?

- Confirm that the warranty doesn't already cover the repairs and the time period of coverage that you're buying with the service contract.
- Is the product likely to need repairs? What are the potential costs of those repairs?
- How long is the product covered?
- Who's offering the service contract? Are they on the up and up?

FURNISHINGS

unless you're paris Hilton, your furnishing budget will probably be slim. You don't have to have everything at once. Invest the most in the pieces you know you'll want to keep and compromise on the others. It's not forever.

SET PRIORITIES

Decide what you can't live without. Your list will most likely include a bed, couch or living room chairs, kitchen table and chairs, TV, stereo, and DVD player.

KNOW THY BALANCE

Make purchases based on your budget. Know what you can afford and when you can afford it to limit impulse buys. Add a furnishings allowance to your monthly budget so you can save for big-ticket items.

HAND-ME-DOWNS

Not everything has to be new! Ask Mom for castoffs, check the want ads, garage sales, estate sales, flea markets, thrift shops, and eBay.

MAKE IT

Lots of places sell ready-to-assemble furniture. Try Ikea, Target, and Wal-Mart for stylish, inexpensive pieces that will get you through the long or short haul, or consider getting unfinished stuff to pretty-up yourself.

MAKE IT A CLASSIC

Just like clothes, there are some classic pieces of furniture that never go out of style. Look for accessories like lamps and pillows that will fit with anything. Mission, arts and crafts, Danish modern, and Shaker styles will never lose their cool.

ASK AND YE SHALL RECEIVE

Have you got a graduation or birthday coming up? Register for gifts at your favorite discount department store and get all the things you need for your new home.

PACKING AND MOVING EXPENSES

if you're lucky, you can get away with as little as a tank of gas for a borrowed truck, a couple of six packs of beer, and a pizza. Give yourself $100 to cover the cost of moving day. But if you've got to shell out the big bucks, look for bargains.

BOXES

Don't pay for boxes. Ask for them at grocery or department stores. Find out when they unpack their goods and see if you can pick them up before they toss them into the crusher. Make sure they're in good shape, though. You don't need to contaminate your stuff with bacteria or use flimsy boxes that were wet.

NEWSPAPER

You'll need lots of it for wrapping your fragiles. Don't just throw fifty cents into a machine and grab all the issues the day you start to pack. It's bad karma and it's against the law. Collect it or use paper bags from the supermarket. People leave their previously read papers at restaurants and coffeehouses, too. Ask there.

PACKING TAPE

Grab a couple rolls. You'll be bummed if you run out with one more box to seal.

BOX CUTTER

You'll need something to open the boxes with when you start to unpack, and a box cutter works better than teeth. Scissors work, too. Razor blade, utility knife, X-Acto. You choose.

MARKER

One felt-tip marker to label your boxes will make it easier when unloading the truck. Be specific in your labeling. Try "Kitchen: Fragile" or "Kitchen: Cleaning supplies. Poison" instead of just "Kitchen."

TRUCK

If you can, borrow a friend or family member's truck. Just fill up the tank and wash the windows before you bring it back.

If you have to rent a truck, it'll cost you. Usually about $20 a day plus mileage for most average apartment-sized trucks. Check rental companies like U-Haul and Ryder and price compare.

FRIENDS AND MOVERS

Good friends will help you move. Great friends will also help you unpack. Give them some beverages and food for their hard work. A hug and a thank-you note never hurt. And never forget karmic retribution. When it's your turn to help with a move, step up to the plate.

Movers will increase your costs considerably. These hulks charge anywhere from $80 bucks an hour and up. Who can blame them? See if you can find some guys from the high school around the corner or the community college on the other side of town to do it for $50 for the day. Or try **www.SSMovers.com** for a free quote.

ADD IT UP

if the place you're moving into is $750 per month for a one bedroom, your move may be as much as $3,075 depending on the deposits you'll be required to put down. And that's without furniture!

FIRST MONTH'S RENT	$750
LAST MONTH'S RENT	$750
SECURITY DEPOSIT	$500
CLEANING DEPOSIT	$75
PET DEPOSIT	$200 per pet
UTILITIES SETUP AND DEPOSITS	$300
APPLIANCES	$400
THE MOVE	$100
TOTAL	$3,075

SAVINGS PLAN

you've seen how the approximate costs can add up. Now it's time to get crackin' with some concrete ways to save before you move. Make it a priority and you'll be amazed at how quickly you'll rack up the numbers and be flying solo.

LIVE ON YOUR BUDGET

Live on your budget as if you're already living on your own. Put everything that's not a real living expense yet like rent, utilities, and food into a savings account. This is a great test to make sure you can live within your means, so it's important not to cheat. Think of it as financial training.

TIME RICH, CASH POOR

If living on a trimmed-down budget is still leaving you with an empty wallet, then put your spare time to work. There are lots of ways to make extra cash without resorting to age-old professions or money laundering.

GET A SECOND JOB

Choose your employer wisely and you may get an employee discount in addition to your salary. Get a job at Ikea and furnish your living room with that 25 percent off!

THAT'S ODD

Don't want to commit to a second job? Think you lack creative skills? There's still no reason to waste those lazy Saturday afternoons. Fill up your time, and your apartment fund, with odd jobs.

- Spend the day whipping foam for cappuccinos at a craft fair booth. (Yes, I've done this.)
- Help a rich dowager transcribe notes from a committee meeting. (Ditto.)
- Clean houses. (This, too.)
- Yard work. (Yep.)
- Entertain at themed children's parties. (Mmm-hmmmm.)
- Wash cars, pets, or windows. (*The Apprentice* did it, why not you?)
- Rob a convenience store. (On second thought, skip that one.)
- Paint houses.
- Move furniture.
- Clean pools.
- Deliver food.
- Babysit.
- Be a handyperson.

Think about what you like to do and what you're good at and put those talents to work. Check the classifieds or cruise **www.CraigsList.com** for a chance to earn some short-term cash. Look for a temp agency that specializes in odd jobs. They're out there! Need some inspiration? Visit Odd Job Jack at **www.OddJobJack.com**.

Put your computer to work. Depending on your skills, you could:

- Design websites.
- Copy music collections to computers for easy iPod uploads.
- Organize desktops and clean up hard drives.
- Tutor MS Word, Final Cut Pro, etc.
- Typeset.
- Set up a home network.

Any way you can think of to use your computer, you can bet someone will want the service. Put an ad in the paper, put up flyers, check the want ads online, and tell your friends to tell their friends. Get the word out.

SELL IT

Think creatively and make money in home-based sales.

- Have a yard sale. Clothes, books, magazines, old computers, tools, games, furniture, jewelry, half empty cosmetics. Whatever you've got lying around, people will buy. I've even sold used deodorant sticks! Before you trash it, turf it.
- Get your friends together and have a combination sale. More sellers, more searchers.
- Turn your closet into cash by selling your clothes to a resale store. If you haven't worn it for a year, give it a new home and make room for the riches.
- eBay. If people can make their living auctioning breast milk online, you can certainly sell your stuff for a quick buck. Buy low at garage or estate sales and put treasures up for bid. Be a broker and sell things for other people who don't have the time. Find folks with big-ticket items and charge 10 to 15 percent commission on the entire sale. Need some leads? Try assisted-living facilities or senior centers where you'll find lots of folks downsizing.
- Make stuff. Design greeting cards, sew purses, or make jewelry and sell your wares at a flea market or farmer's market. Target holidays and align yourself with everyone's inner gift giver.

Take it from me. No matter how desperate you think you are, no matter how good of an idea it seems at the time, never, ever, under *any* circumstances, even if you think you never really liked her anyway, sell your dead grandmother's jewelry. It's a regrettably bad idea.

MOUTH OFF

Lots of companies are dying to know what you think of their products. It's called focus testing, and a lot of marketing firms will pay big bucks just to hear your opinion. To find focus groups in your area, check the ads in the weeklies and keep your eyes peeled around the campus near you. The 18 to 24 set is a favorite marketing demographic, so you're bound to see one eventually. If the paper chase doesn't pan out, try going online. A Google search on "focus groups" and your city can turn up companies looking for participants.

Does showing up to a focus group seem too taxing? Earn your pay and have your say with online surveys at sites like **www.PaidSurveysOnline.com** and **www.SurveyMania.com**. You may as well check out **www.Volition.com**, too; the oldest free-stuff site on the Internet. There you can browse for odd jobs, freebies, and other cool ways to save and earn cash while surfing the Net.

LAB RAT

As a last resort, you can always sniff around the psychology department on a nearby campus. Grad students are dying for test subjects to help further their research. Sometimes they'll even compensate you for your time. If you're not squeamish about being a human guinea pig, you could really clean up. Craigslist also advertises for study groups for depression, smoking cessations, etc., that may pay up to a few hundred dollars for participating.

ENTERTAINMENT

Find some cost-saving alternatives to spending for fun.

- Think about what you're ordering when you eat out. Do you really love iced tea or just order it out of habit? Shave a couple of bucks off your bill by sticking with water. Not too hungry? Skip an entrée and get an appetizer instead.
- Rent movies instead of going to the movie theater. Going once a month instead of every week makes it more special.
- If you're catching a flick, hit the multiplex before 2 p.m. on a Saturday and you can save big bucks on your tickets. Sneak your own snacks. Who needs to blow $10 on a Coke and popcorn?

- Lots of cities have free concerts in the park or other citywide events. Seek them out.
- Go gallery hopping. They're free! And the openings usually serve snacks!

BUDGETING FOR LIFE

"At my age, are you kidding me?
Why do I need to budget for life? I'm just a kid!"

if this is your attitude, it's time for a reality check. Now is the time to pump up your economic IQ, before your life kicks into high gear. Learn a few things about credit history, debt management, and financial planning before your future becomes your today.

DON'T KNOW MUCH ABOUT HISTORY

Credit history is an account of your bill-paying capabilities and habits that allows potential lenders to assess the level of risk they would take on by loaning you money. Do you pay your bills on time? Do you pay them in full or make partial payments? Are your payments perpetually late or have you ever not paid at all? All this info gets logged in your credit history report. Chances are, you've already got one.

Credit reports are used for every major purchase you make in your life. Cars, houses, apartments, even cell phones. Having a bad credit history won't necessarily preclude you from being able to make these purchases, but you'll certainly pay way higher interest rates and deposits than someone with a good credit rating. If you have really bad credit, you may actually get blacklisted from getting loans or renting an apartment altogether. At least until you clean up your act.

Getting a good credit rating isn't easy. It takes time, discipline, and desire. Keeping a good credit rating is even harder.

CHECK YOU OUT

Do you even have a credit report yet? Contact the credit bureaus and get a copy of your personal credit report to find out. You may be surprised at how much information they've already collected about you!

- Name, Social Security number, birth date, current and previous addresses, and employment history
- Account information including loan amounts, debt amounts, credit limits, and payment history
- Public records like tax liens, bankruptcies, or other monetary judgments
- A listing of anyone who's viewed your credit report and why

Look at what the landlords will see to make sure it's correct before you start applying for apartments. Be sure to get print-outs from all three of the major bureaus, **www.Experian.com**, **www.TransUnion.com**, and **www.Equifax.com**. Because they each collect specifics independently of each other, the information on each report may differ.

SIGN ME UP

Start proving your financial worthiness by establishing your credit.

- Set up a checking account at a bank.
- Get a Visa debit card.
- Put your apartment and utilities under your name.
- Apply for a credit card at your bank and use a co-signer.
- Get a secured credit card.
- Apply for a retail or gasoline credit card.

DEBIT CARD

This ATM or check card lets merchants deduct money straight from your bank account. Debit cards with Visa or MasterCard logos are accepted by anyone that also accepts Visa or MasterCard credit cards; the difference is there's no float time. The purchase is deducted from your account immediately so you can only spend as much as you've got.

CREDIT CARD

A credit card can be used to buy goods, services, or cash up to a preapproved limit. You make a purchase, the credit card company pays the bill, and you reimburse them at the end of the credit period. Don't pay the bill all at once? You'll be charged a hefty interest rate on the remaining balance for the privilege.

CO-SIGNER

If you can't get a credit card all on your lonesome, try a co-signer. Parents or guardians are sometimes good ones. This person is responsible for repaying a debt if you default. It's the bank's way of making sure that if you don't foot the bill, your someone will.

SECURED CREDIT CARD

These cards are secured by a savings account. The amount in the savings account is directly related to the limit on the secured credit card. You make a purchase, the credit card company pays the bill out of the money from your savings account, and you reimburse your savings account when you pay your statement. The interest rates (for borrowing your own money) are much lower, and within a year you could be eligible for an unsecured line of credit.

RETAIL CARD

Many retailers will offer you credit to shop with them. Department stores, home improvement stores, and gasoline stations are all good places to look. They work just like a credit card, but you can only use them at the issuer's establishment. FYI, these bad boys come with dangerously high interest rates.

YOU BETTER SHOP AROUND

Since you're just starting out, most banks or credit card companies will stick you with a 20 to 25 percent interest rate to compensate for the risk. Negotiate! Get them down to something reasonable, if possible. If your parents are co-signing, try to get the same rate they're getting. It never hurts to ask! Keep in mind—you can always take your business somewhere else. They're not the only bank in town.

NOW WHAT?

regardless of how you get credit, you're going to need to use it to establish a payment history. But this is not gratis! You have to pay it back right away or you'll be establishing bad credit!

- Make one small purchase on your card—$10 or less.
- When the bill comes, pay it in full right away.
- Repeat and you're on your way to establishing great credit.

KEEP THAT CREDIT RATING SQUEAKY CLEAN!

Say no to missed payments and large outstanding balances. Pay your bills as soon as they arrive to avoid late fees and higher interest. It takes time to build a good credit rating, but it only takes one missed payment to ruin it. Don't count on the U.S. Postal Service to get your payment to the bank on time. Manage your bills online and make sure they get there early!

A CAUTIONARY TALE

Trust me, using your credit cards like they're free money is cancerous to your financial health. Credit cards are not free money. Repeat, "*Not free money.*" In fact, they make for very expensive money. And twenty-somethings are the prime targets for banks looking to make a buck. These debt pushers love you because they think you're inexperienced and impulsive.

Prove them wrong! Don't be a part of the scam. Don't let them take advantage of you. Don't help them rake in billions of dollars every year on your naïveté. Think twice or thrice before pulling out the plastic for little purchases like a $10 T-shirt or sale-priced belt. Pay for it with cash or let it go. Those little numbers add up fast. And because it compounds daily, interest adds up even faster.

If you're not convinced, take a look:

BALANCE	PAYMENT	INTEREST RATE	TIME TO PAY OFF	INTEREST PAID
$2,500	$250/ month	22%	1 year	$287
$2,500	$100/ month	22%	2 years, 10 months	$875
$2,500	$50/ month	22%	11 years, 5 months	$4,339
$5,000	$500/ month	22%	1 year	$574
$5,000	$200/ month.	22%	2 years, 10 months	$1,750
$5,000	$100/ month	22%	11 years, 5 months	$8,678

tana's habitat

Every time you apply for credit, your report is pulled. Every time your report is pulled, you are assigned a score to rate your creditworthiness as excellent, good, or poor. This number, or credit rating, is called different things by different credit bureaus (Equifax calls it a Beacon Score, Experian calls it a FICO Score, and Trans-Union calls it an Empirica Score), and predicts the likelihood that you will pay back a loan or make payments to a lender according to the agreed-upon terms.

Beware of those credit checks! Every time someone pulls your score, it's lowered. The more your credit is checked, the lower your score is.

Some credit checks are nonnegotiable, like applying for a credit card or insurance, renting an apartment, or turning on your utilities. But others you can live without, like car salesmen. Ever wonder why these Corvair corsairs collect your driver's license before you take a test drive? They're not perusing your DMV records, they're checking your credit. And not just once, but several times, with multiple agencies. Before you buckle up, be clear that they're not allowed to check your credit. If you don't tell them, they assume that it's OK.

FEEDING THE MONSTER

it's hard to be debt free. The best tool you have is to manage your debt. Don't let it manage you.

HANDLE IT

- Set up an easy-to-use filing system.
- Keep accurate records.
- Stick to your budget .
- Pay all bills on time.
- If you can't pay the entire bill, make a partial payment of 10 percent or more.
- Pay with cash, not plastic.
- Make a plan to pay off your debt as quickly as possible.

SCHOOL DAYS

Start managing your student loans the day you apply for them.

- Set up an easy-to-use filing system
- Keep separate files for each student loan, not one big one for all those different loans.
- Keep all paperwork. This includes your application, disbursement and disclosure statements, loan transfer notices, and promissory notes.
- Make sure you have correct, up-to-date info such as telephone numbers and addresses of all loan holders.
- Keep detailed notes of all phone conversations including the name of the person with whom you spoke, the date, and a summary of what you discussed.
- Keep all of this information until you have the loan paid off.

If you don't stay on top of your loans, they can easily overwhelm you. As long as you're in charge of the situation, it will be much easier to manage.

CONSOLIDATE

Most students have loans from many companies, which can get confusing when you start to pay them off. Do yourself a favor and consolidate them.

Student loan consolidation simply means you take out one loan for the exact amount of all your outstanding student loans. You use the money from the new loan to pay off all the others, leaving you with only one large loan with a low interest rate.

Typically, the term on the new loan is longer, making your monthly payment smaller and easier to handle when you're first starting out. Unfortunately, because you're paying over a longer period of time, you will end up paying a bit more over the long run.

Some lenders will give you a discount for consolidating, paying on time, and using direct debiting. Never hurts to ask.

WHERE TO APPLY

Check with your current lenders to find out if they have consolidation programs, check out the "Manage Your Loans" section of **www.SallieMae.com**, or visit Uncle Sam at **www.StudentAid.ed.gov**.

INVESTING IN FUTURES

financial planning is more than saving for your retirement. It includes every-thing you need to save for from purchasing a home, going on vacation, and buying a car to paying for your children's college, paying for your parents' sixtieth wedding anniversary, and having an emergency fund in case of medical problems, unem-ployment, or even unexpected car repairs.

It's very important to start early. Every dollar you save in your twenties is worth about ten times that of a dollar saved in your forties. Check it out:

Jane saves $25,000 by age twenty-five (probably an inheritance) and never saves another penny of her income. At age sixty-five, she'll be worth $1,131,481 if it grows at an average of rate of 10 percent annually.

Dick doesn't start saving until age thirty-five when he gets that big promo-tion. To reach the same amount as Jane by age sixty-five, Dick is going to need to save $6,880 each year assuming that he gets the same 10 percent return as Jane. That's a total of $206,400 Dick has to save when Jane only set aside $25,000. Gulp.

Start now.

the hunt

with your list of apartment requirements, budget limit, and perhaps even a roommate, it's time to hit the streets.

Finding an apartment isn't easy. You're going to be covering lots of space and making tons of phone calls. If you don't have a local phone number or a cell phone, search the Yellow Pages or online for a cheap voicemail box so people can return your messages. Try **www.fecg.net/voicemail.asp** to see if you're eligible for free voicemail service. Landlords are notorious for not calling back, so if you don't hear from someone, don't be afraid to keep on calling.

Arm yourself with a competitive attitude and let the games begin!

KNOW WHAT'S WHAT

rental properties have a language all their own. These code words are the key to your success. Here are some of the most common ones:

Efficiency (EFF): A large room, which serves as a combination living room/bedroom with a separate bath. It may or may not have a separate kitchen.

Studio (STU) also known as **Bachelor (BACH)** or **Single (SNG):** These typically have one large room, which serves as a combination living room/bedroom with a separate bath and kitchen.

Junior (JR): These small units have a living room and a small (read supersmall) adjacent room just big enough to hold a single bed, a dresser, and, if you're lucky, a nightstand.

One bedroom (1 BD; BDR; BDRM): These units have a bedroom, kitchen, and living room and vary in size.

Loft: A big open apartment with few walls to partition off rooms. Often in older, industrial-type buildings found in downtown areas.

Duplex (DUPL): Any building containing two dwelling units. Most commonly refers to side-by-side units with a common wall and roof.

House (HS): A stand-alone, single-family dwelling.

Guest House / Cottage (GHS; COT; CTG): From a small, scary, rustic box above a garage to a charming one-bedroom detached unit next to a beautiful pool. Ask for specific details when you call.

Townhouse (TNHSE): A two-story rental unit with more than two units located on either side but not on top. Usually has a private entry.

Condominium (CONDO): An apartment building where the tenants own their own unit but not the building itself. You may have a different landlord than your neighbor, but are still required to follow the common laws of the organization.

Garden apartment (GDN APT; GRDN APT): An apartment development consisting of two or more structures surrounded by an abundance of lawns, plants, flowers, etc., giving it a gardenlike atmosphere. These buildings are usually one or two stories tall with anywhere from a few apartments to twenty or thirty. Unit sizes will range from studios to three bedrooms. Often times they have a pool.

Mid-Rise: Approximately three to ten stories tall with elevators. Apartment sizes vary.

Mega complex: The buildings in a mega-plex could be garden style to mid-rise or a mixture of both. They typically have a pool(s), gym, tennis courts, and other amenities. There could be a few hundred to as many as several thousand apartments in the mega-plex. Some are so large they even have their own zip code, shopping, and concierge service.

High-Rise: A building ten or more stories tall. It may have a doorman, underground parking, and security. Some even have a pool or garden on the rooftop.

Penthouse (PH): A luxury apartment on the top floor of a high-rise building.

Walk-up: Just what the name implies, this building is three to five stories tall, without an elevator. Apartment sizes will vary.

Doorman Building (DM; DRMN): A very nice building with expensive apartments and all amenities including a doorman. He's a pleasant man who opens the door to the building for you, hails cabs, and does all sorts of other niceties. Don't forget, they expect a Christmas tip.

Brownstone: An early twentieth-century brick row house (mostly) found in New York City or other older large cities, usually three or four stories tall. These babies are swank.

Prewar: A New York City term for a high-rise apartment building built between 1890 and 1940. Lots of character including hardwood floors, high ceilings, crown molding, and other architectural details.

Rent Control (RNTCTL): Laws that limit how much a landlord can charge for a property, including the amount and conditions under which he can raise that rent.

Section 8 (SECT 8): Federally subsidized, low income housing administered by the Department of Housing and Urban Development (HUD). The tenant pays up to 30 percent of his or her adjusted monthly income, HUD pays the difference to make the rent. Visit **www.hud.gov/offices/pih/programs/ ph/index.cfm** for more information on public housing and other programs offered by HUD.

CHARACTERISTICS

2 + 2: The first number represents the number of bedrooms. The second number equals the number of bathrooms.

Adjacent (ADJ): A term used to describe a not-so-nice neighborhood next to a nice neighborhood. For example: Beverly Hills adjacent elevates the status of a neighborhood to garner higher rents.

Alcove (ALC): An area not usable for much more than a desk or a reading area. They'll want you to think it's a bonus room. It isn't.

Air-conditioning (A/C; AC)

Amenities (AMEN): Some luxuries like a dishwasher, microwave, pool, gym, or a host of other good things. Ask for specifics when you call about the place.

Appliances (APPLS): Refrigerator and stove are included. Might also include dishwasher **(DW)** and microwave **(MCRWV)**.

Balcony (BALC): A small deck that might hold a chair and a couple of plants.

Bonus Room (BON): A big alcove.

Bedroom (BR; BDR; BDRM)

Central Air / Heat (C/A; CAC; CAH): A cooling and heating unit for the entire building with in-apartment temperature control.

Character / Charm: This usually implies that the apartment has architectural details like crown moldings, wood floors, high ceilings, and other details you rarely get with a newer apartment.

Controlled Access (ACS; SEC): You'll have to use a key to get into your building. It's a safety thing and keeps the crazies from just wandering into your building. Your friends will have to get buzzed into the building.

Cozy: The implication is intimate charm, but the truth is that it's probably small, cramped, and not for the claustrophobic.

Den: An extra room, probably big enough for a home office.

Deposit (DEP)

Dining room; Formal dining room; Separate dining room (DR; FDR; SEP DIN): A decent-sized room to put a table that will comfortably seat six for all those mixers you'll be throwing.

Dishwasher (DW)

Eat-in kitchen (EIK): A tiny place for a table and two chairs.

Excellent (XLCT)

Fireplace (F/P, FRPL)

Free cable (CBL; TV INCL)

Furnished (FURN): The basics: couch, kitchen table, a few pots, pans, dishes, silverware, bed, and dresser. Most likely outdated and beaten up. Think rental car.

Garage (GRG): A designated parking spot in a large parking structure.

2-Car Garage (2CGRG): A doublewide garage for parking or storage.

Gated / Secured Parking (GTD; SCRD PRKG): A good safety feature, you'll need a garage door opener, code, or pass card to enter parking area.

Hardwood floors (HDWD)

Hardwood + Carpet (HD + CRPT): Hardwood floors in the living area and carpet in the bedrooms.

Hot water (HW)

Kitchen (KIT)

Kitchenette (K'ETTE): It has a tiny refrigerator and tiny stove with a few cabinets and almost no counter space.

Laundry (LNDRY): Either in the unit or on site.

Lease (LSE)

Living room (LR)

Loft Space (LOFT): A small, elevated space above another room just large enough for a bed or desk.

Luxurious (LUX): Not rustic.

Microwave (MCRWV)

New (NU)

On-Site Management (OSMGR; MGR): A manager lives on-site to handle any problems or emergencies you may have.

Pool (PL)

Quiet building: Quiet people only may live here. It may also imply no kids or seniors only.

Refrigerator (FRIDG): Usually means it comes with the apartment.

Renovation / Renovated (RENO): Some landlords think this means changing drawer pulls. See it to believe it.

Reserved Parking (RSVD PRKG): An assigned parking space.

Rustic: A beat-up old cabin with holes in the roof.

Spacious (SPAC): A normal- to good-sized room, but not palatial.

Square Footage (SF or Sq Ft)

Stove (STV): Comes with the apartment.

Subterranean Parking (SUB PRKG): Underground parking.

Utilities included (UTIL INCL)

View (VU): Some sort of desirable view is available from the unit whether you have to hang off your balcony to see it or it's right out your living room window. If it's a really great view the ad will say **incredible** or **dramatic view**.

Walk-in closet (WIC): Sure, you can walk in, but do you have to back out?

Wall-to-wall carpeting (WW)

Washer/Dryer (W/D)

Washer/Dryer Hookups (W/D hook up, LNDRY hook-up): You supply the washer and dryer; they supply the hookup.

Washer/Dryer on-site (W/D on-site): Coin-operated washers and dryers on the premises.

Yard (YD; YRD)

FIND THE RIGHT PLACE FOR YOU

there are several viable ways in which to find an apartment.

HOOF IT

Drive or walk around your preferred neighborhoods and look for "For Rent" signs. If you can, call the number on the sign immediately. The landlord may live on the premises or could have left the unit open for potential renters' convenience. "Do not disturb occupants" means just that.

WORD UP

Put the word out to everyone you know—friends, family members, and others. Give them details of the type of place you want so they know what to keep their eyes peeled for.

READ IT

Scour the want ads in your newspaper and local weekly. Drive the Internet highway and search sites like **www.CraigsList.com**, **www.RentNet.com**, **www.Rent.com**, or **www.ApartmentGuide.com**. Don't forget to check out the classifieds in your local college's paper or look for the free rental guides outside the grocery store.

PAY FOR IT

Use an apartment rental service. These are almost always pay services, but the small membership fee is often worth the exclusive listings they offer. You won't find these places advertised anywhere else *and* the apartments are categorized by neighborhood to help your search stay focused.

SKIP THE BROKER

Brokers are a different animal altogether. Although they will do the brunt of the work for you, they'll charge you an arm and a leg for it, the equivalent of one month's rent or more! Brokers are often a necessity in high-dollar areas where bidding wars on rentals are a way of life, like NYC.

tana's habitat

MEET AND GREET

so you found a few places you want to check out. Call to set up some appointments and, if possible, try to schedule them all on the same day.

WHAT SHOULD I BRING?

- A copy of your credit history if you have it. If you supply it, you may not have to pay for one each time you apply for an apartment.
- Your checkbook. If you find a place you like, act fast and put down that deposit.
- Tape measure to make sure your furniture will fit.
- An apartment checklist and landlord questionnaire.
- A pen to take notes and fill out the application.
- Personal info for the rental application.
- Current address and how long you've lived there.
- Social Security and driver's license numbers
- The names, addresses, contact names, and phone numbers of your current and past employers.
- The names, addresses, contact names, and phone numbers of your current and past landlords (if any).
- Bank account info.
- Three references: name, phone number and relationship to you. Make sure to use people who will say kind things about you! Don't forget to let them know you're using them as a reference so they're not caught off guard if a potential landlord actually calls.

APPLY YOURSELF

You'll have to complete an application for every apartment you'd like to rent. Print out a sheet with all your personal info and make copies to bring so you don't inflict yourself with carpal tunnel. Better yet, download a standard residential rental application from **www.nolo.com**, fill it out, and make a bunch of copies. It will save time and exude maturity. But don't lose any of them. Everything anyone needs to steal your identity is right there.

THE VIEWING

Schedule your appointments during the day, if you can. It's a lot easier to see flaws in the light.

- Are the closets big enough for your shoe collection?
- Will your furniture fit? You can't stuff your king-size bed in a bedroom the size of large closet.
- Check for water damage and cracks on the ceilings and walls.
- Look for mold and mildew in the bathroom, shower, and kitchen. If you can, look behind the fridge.
- Are the counter surfaces in good condition or are they nasty?
- What condition are the appliances in? Don't forget to look inside.
- Check out the sink, garbage disposal, and cabinets.
- What is the condition of the paint? Is it a new paint job or does it need a fresh coat?
- Do all the light fixtures and switches work?
- Are there enough electrical outlets? Where are they?
- Try every door and lock. Do they work and close properly?
- What is the condition of the flooring? Are there stains on the carpet? Does it smell?
- Check out the water pressure in the shower and sinks.
- Flush the toilet. Does it work properly, or do you have to jiggle the handle to stop the flow?
- Are there enough cabinets and drawers in the kitchen and bath?
- What condition are the window coverings in?
- Is the building clean and well maintained?
- Where are the phone jacks and cable access?

DOG EAT DOG

Getting the perfect place can be extremely competitive. You're not the only one looking! Step it up and elevate yourself from the crowd to increase your chances.

DRESS TO IMPRESS

If you have a suit and tie, it couldn't hurt, but at least dress like you have a job. This is not the time to show off your nipple piercings, your skull and crossbones jewelry collection, or your propensity to sweat.

tana's habitat

WATCH THE CLOCK

Always keep your appointments and be on time. There's nothing that says responsibility more than punctuality.

BE PREPARED

Arrive with all your ducks in a row. Bring that filled-out application and your checkbook and let every landlord know you're serious!

FLATTERY WORKS

If you love the place, let the landlord know! There's no need to be shy about how much you'd enjoy living there. Just keep that effusiveness in check if you want to negotiate for a lower rent.

NO SUCH THING AS A STUPID QUESTION

make copies of the landlord questionnaire and apartment checklist to fill out at each interview so you can separate the winners from the losers.

landlord questionnaire

1. Building address _____

2. Contact name and phone number _____

3. How much is rent? _____

4. When is the apartment available? _____

5. How much is the security deposit? _____

6. Will it be placed in an interest earning account? _____

7. What is the lease term? _____

8. What happens when the lease is up? Will my rent go to month-to-month? Will I have to sign a new lease? _____

9. Is this a rent-controlled apartment? How much can rent be raised each year? _____

10. When is rent due? _____

11. Will the apartment be rekeyed before I move in? _____

12. What utilities do you provide? _____

13. Is there an on-site manager? _____

14. Who should I contact with problems? _____

15. When was the building built? Do I need to worry about asbestos, lead paint, or any other toxic elements? _____

16. What, if any, improvements to the apartment can I make? Paint? Who pays for it? _____

17. Is the water heater large enough to accommodate the number of people who will be living in the apartment? _____

18. Can I have pets? If so, what species are allowed? _____

19. Do you have special rules about BBQs, guests, and garage sales? _____

20. Do you allow subletting? Under what conditions? _____

21. What are the other tenants like? Neighbors? Young, old, loud, students, working professionals, kids, pets? _____

APARTMENT CHECKLIST	UNIT 1	UNIT 2	UNIT 3	UNIT 4
address				
air-conditioning				
ample outlets				
bedroom privacy				
blinds/curtains				
cable tv connection				
carpet				
hardwood floors				
closet space				
fireplace				
furniture: will mine fit?				
light fixtures				
natural light				
paint/wall conditions				
patio/balcony				
pet-friendly				
phone jack in each room				
storage				
upstairs/downstairs				
view				
KITCHEN				
age of refrigerator				
frost-free freezer				

tana's habitat

APARTMENT CHECKLIST	UNIT 1	UNIT 2	UNIT 3	UNIT 4
counter space				
dishwasher				
garbage disposal				
gas/electric stove				
microwave				
water pressure				
drawer and cupboard space				
BATHROOM				
shower/shower curtain				
bath				
toilet				
storage				
COMMON AREAS				
general cleanliness				
laundry facilities on-site/nearby				
noise level/garbage chutes/ alleys/hallways				
parking: secured/garage/ permit/street/guest				
bike racks				
elevators/stairs proximity				
mailbox				
privacy				
atmosphere: social/intimate				

APARTMENT CHECKLIST	UNIT 1	UNIT 2	UNIT 3	UNIT 4
amenities: pool/gym/etc.				
SAFETY				
emergency exits				
fire extinguishers				
functioning windows				
gated entrance				
intercom				
lead hazards				
locks on all doors				
outside lighting				
screens				
smoke detectors				
NEIGHBORHOOD				
average community age				
public transportation				
distance from school/work/ freeway accessible				
proximity of grocery/bank/ post office/fun				
safety				
street noise/traffic				
club and bar proximity/ nighttime noise				

SCREEN ME

A landlord is allowed to charge a fee to screen your rental application, though there are no national laws governing the practice or regulating the amount. Each state is different. Generally, the landlord cannot charge you more than the actual cost of the screening and is required to give you an itemized receipt documenting those out-of-pocket expenses. It's illegal for him to charge you an application fee if there are no vacancies, and, if he does obtain your credit report, he is obligated to provide you with a copy of it at your request. You have sixty days to ask.

BEFORE YOU PAY ANY APPLICATION FEES, ASK:

- How long will it take you to get a copy of my credit history, review it, and get back to me with an answer?
- Is the fee refundable if it takes too long and I have to go elsewhere?
- I already have a copy of my credit report. Will you accept it?

AND ANOTHER THING

Remember, there are lots of places to live out there, so you don't have to jump at the first place you see. Try to talk to other tenants in the building or neighbors for the inside scoop, and don't be dazzled and agree to a lease beyond your budget. Nothing will make you hate an apartment more than being held hostage by the rent.

SIGN HERE

finally, you're approved! The only thing left before unpacking those boxes is to read and sign the lease. And yes, you do have to read it. All of it.

WHAT'S A LEASE?

A lease is a written agreement between a landlord and tenant that specifies the terms under which a tenant can occupy a property. It is a legal document, so once you provide your John Hancock, the apartment is yours for the duration of the lease.

What you'll see:

- The names of the landlord and tenant.
- The address of the rental unit.
- The amount of rent.
- When, where, and to whom you must pay your rent. For example: Rent is due no later than the first of every month. Mail your check payable to (landlord) at (this address).
- Penalty for late payments and what constitutes late. It might say something like: "Tenant will be assessed a late fee of $25 for any rent paid after the 5th of the month." My landlord charges 6 percent of the rent amount. Not that I know.
- The amount and purpose of the security deposit, how it will be held, and how it will be returned. Try and get them to hold it in an interest-earning account and agree to an itemized receipt for any monies withheld from the deposit at the end of your term.
- Who is responsible for paying the utilities.
- How much advance notice you'll have to give your landlord before you move out. It's usually thirty days once you've completed the term of your lease.
- What happens at the end of your lease. Will you need to sign another lease or will your rent go month-to-month?
- Penalty for breaking the lease.
- How often and how much they can raise your rent. It's usually only once a year and something like a 2 to 3 percent increase. The increase will be the maximum allowed in your state or county, so check with your local housing authority to make sure you're getting a fair and legal deal.
- Under what conditions a landlord may enter the apartment with or without you present.
- Any restrictions like pets, overnight guests, additional roommates, or loud music after ten p.m. Every landlord has his own set of rules. Make sure you know and understand them before you sign.

Landlord tenant laws are different in every state. Visit **www.hud.gov/local/index.cfm** or **www.Tenant.net** to find out what landlords are required to provide in your state and make sure those things are reflected in your lease.

SAY CHEESE

Take a camera and document anything in the apartment in disrepair. Go over the pictures with your landlord and attach copies to the lease so there are no discrepancies about damages when you move out.

Don't have a camera? Spend the $6 on a disposable. It's worth it.

PARLEY

This is the time to get your landlord to fix any problems before you move in. Pull out your droopiest puppy dog eyes and ask to get those hardwoods refinished, stained carpets and linoleum cleaned or replaced, and a fresh coat of paint in the color of your choice. Get it in writing, including a completion date, so that it's ready to move into when you're ready to move in.

DENIED

If your rental application is rejected due to bad credit, don't ignore the situation. Contact the credit bureaus immediately and find out what you can do to remedy the situation.

- **Experian:** (800) 397-3742
- **Equifax:** (800) 685-1111
- **TransUnion:** (800) 916-8800

ARE YOU BEING DISCRIMINATED AGAINST?

According to the Fair Housing Act, you cannot be denied a roof over your head because of race, color, religion, sex, sexual orientation, disability, marital status, familial status, ancestry, or national origin. If you think you've been unfairly treated, tell it to the judge. Visit **www.FairHousing.com** or **www.hud.gov/ renting/index.cfm** to file a complaint.

YOU'VE BEEN VERY NAUGHTY

If your rental application is turned down, it may not be discrimination at all. Tenant Screening Services collect and sell information on bad tenants, so anyone who's ever skipped out on their lease or torn their place to shreds may find themselves on this list of undesirables. He's no Santa Claus, but you can be sure your landlord is checking this list twice.

MOVING TO A GALAXY, FAR, FAR AWAY

it's tough enough to find an apartment in a city you know well. Imagine finding a place from the other side of the country! Do your research, ask a lot of questions, and be careful. Approach it from a business angle, and you'll be surprised by your success rate. You can do it!

MAP IT OUT

Buy a street map of your destination and start familiarizing yourself with the city. If you've already been there, you may have a general idea of what neighborhood you'd like to live in. If not, use the map for some pointers. Locate parks, lakes, rivers, historical markers, and local attractions to get an idea of what's where.

MAKE A LIST

Know what you require from your new neighborhood. Think about:

- Commute time
- Schools
- Community demographics like age, education, lifestyle
- Population density desires like urban, suburban, or rural
- Other things that are important to you like being close to entertainment, places of worship, etc.

Jump online to discover the ins and outs of different neighborhoods. Try **www.CitySearch.com** or MSN Cityguides at **http://local.msn.com** to find out about the social scene. Look up zip codes on **www.NeighborhoodScout.com** and get information on everything from crime rates and languages spoken to median education level, popular occupations, and income. Might as well **www.MapQuest.com** your route to work while you're at the keyboard.

tana's habitat

CALL THE COPS

Don't be afraid to call neighborhood police stations to get the crime blotter.

YOU'RE HIRED

If you're moving for a job, ask your employer for help. Some companies keep apartments just for new hires. They may have good contacts in the rental market.

HIT THE BOOKS

Contact your alumni association to get access to their bulletin boards and online apartment listings. A lot of times these opportunities are more affordable and offer a built-in connection through your affiliation with the university.

ON AND OFF

Try the usual suspects online, **www.CraigsList.com**, **www.RentNet.com**, **www.Rent.com**, or **www.ApartmentGuide.com**, or Google "Apartment Rentals" plus your destination to find rental listings or services specific to that locale. Go online or visit the newsstand and pick up that city's newspaper or area magazines that may have apartment listings in the classifieds.

FRIENDS

Any pair of eyes, ears, and legs you can use on the other side will be of great help. Get on the horn and start connecting the dots.

MAKE THE CALLS

You've lined up a list of apartments to call about, so grab your landlord questionnaire and your apartment checklist and start dialing. Ask lots of questions and try to get pictures. If you've got a friend in the area, have them stop by a few places to take a look-see.

ON A LIMB

Just go! Figure it out when you get there!

- Stay with a relative, friend, or a friend of a friend while you look for a place to live. You'll compensate them for their generosity, of course.
- Let your employer foot the bill until you can find a suitable place to live.
- Couch hop.
- Sublet an apartment for a couple months through **www.Sublet.com**.
- Or find someone with a room to rent. Try **www.EasyRoommate.com** or **www.RoommateClick.com**. Set up a temporary situation. Agree to a month or two. If it works out, even better!
- Try your hand at house-sitting. Find a gig online at **www.House Carers.com** or **www.CraigsList.com**.

SITE UNSEEN

Signing a rental agreement on a property you've never seen probably isn't the smoothest move. If you absolutely have to, at least find a friend or acquaintance in the area to take a look for you and report back. Not an option? Include a clause in your lease that extricates you from the terms if the apartment is unsuitable for you.

make a move

they say that, in terms of stress, moving rates right up there with looking for a job, getting a divorce, and being a dentist. Limit your suicidal tendencies with planning and preparation.

UNENCUMBERED

before you even consider packing, take a look at what you've got and purge, purge, purge. There's no reason to move a bunch of junk you're just going to scrap (or pile up) when you get to your new place.

CATEGORIZE

Get yourself three large boxes and label them: **Keep**, **Sell**, **Trash**.

   Go through everything you own, room-by-room, leaving no junk drawer unturned, no plastic bag unopened, and catalog your possessions. Anything you want to hang on to goes in the **Keep** box. If you don't want it but think someone might pay money for it at a yard sale, toss it in the **Sell** box. If it's junk, **Trash** it.

Not so sure? If you haven't seen it, worn it, or used it in a year, give it a new home. No questions asked.

SCHEMATIC

Start in a closet or a dresser and *do not move on* until everything in that area is in a **Keep**, **Sell**, or **Trash** box. Don't put anything away, just sort. By the time you finish separating trash from treasure, everything you own will be in one container or another.

NO SECOND THOUGHTS

Immediately unload the items from the trash box into the Dumpster. Don't give yourself any room to change your mind! Move the **Sell** box out of the way for your yard sale.

BREAK IT DOWN

Relabel two large boxes **Need** and **Pack**. Go through the items in your **Keep** box and separate the things you will need on hand before you make your move: clothes, linens, a couple dishes, medications, etc. Put that stuff in the **Need** box to put away. Everything else, like books, decorations, extra linens, and kitchen stuff, can go in the **Pack** box to be boxed and put aside for the move.

PACK IT UP

anything you can pack up ahead of time will eliminate stress on moving day. If it's summer, get your winter clothes out of the way. Box up all your extra electronics, food, and cosmetics and live on the bare essentials.[4]

WHAT YOU'LL NEED

- Packing tape
- Boxes
- Plastic trash bags

tana's habitat

- Felt-tip marker
- Scissors
- Newspaper or other packing material
- Notebook and pen

SUPPLIES SURPRISE

You're going to need lots of boxes. Getting more than you think you need will inevitably make your move more simple.[5] If you buy your boxes from a moving company, you can always return the unused ones for a refund. If you got them free from the grocery, just toss the leftovers into the recycle bin. Keep a few empties set aside for last minute stuff like bedding, clothing, and cleaning supplies. You'll need strong packing tape to close up the boxes securely. This is an instance when less is not more.

HOW MANY BOXES WILL I NEED?				
I AM MOVING:	1–2 ROOMS	2–3 ROOMS	4–5 ROOMS	6–8 ROOMS
wardrobe boxes	2	3	6	10
large boxes	4	8	15	25
medium boxes	3	6	12	18
small boxes	6	10	18	25
dish pack boxes	1	2	3	4
bubble wrap	1	1	1	1
packing tape	1	2	4	5

Keep all your packing supplies in one central area. It's easy to lose markers, scissors, and notes to yourself amidst the mess.

MAKE A LIST

Write everything down! Number every single box and list its contents in a notebook. Be specific about what's inside. Don't lose the list!

CONTAIN ME

- Use wardrobe boxes for bulky, lightweight items like comforters, pillows, and blankets, and clothes that need to stay on the hanger. But don't make the boxes too heavy to lift!
- Use empty trashcans to pack things in.
- Take advantage of your luggage and fill it to the rim. Especially if it has wheels!
- Use lawn and leaf bags to pack clothing, towels, and sheets.
- Designate a *color* for each room in your new place; green for the bathroom, blue for the living room, etc. Apply colored stickers on the box near the box number. Put a matching sticker on the door to each room in your apartment so everyone will know where to put everything when they arrive.

OTHER PACKING TIPS

- Pack boxes to capacity, but don't overpack. Underpacked boxes tend to get crushed in the move and overpacked boxes will leave you with a hernia.
- Label each box and indicate when it needs to be loaded on the truck. If you need it first, load it last.
- Clothing, linens, and towels make great packing material for breakable items like glasses.
- Use paper plates between china and dishes to add cushioning.
- Pack stereo and TV equipment, kitchen appliances, and anything with a cord attached in its original box or wrapped in a blanket. Bubble wrap can produce static electricity and damage electronics.
- Remove toner or ink cartridges before moving a printer or copier. They could get damaged and break open during the move. What a mess.
- Use small boxes for books to avoid overpacking those heavy suckers. And definitely use extra tape on the bottoms.
- Small artwork, framed pictures, and mirrors can be wrapped in newspaper, clothing, blankets, or sheets. Transport them in the truck between the mattress and the box spring for extra protection.

IT'S PERSONAL

Gather your important papers. Birth certificate, school records, mover estimates, new job contacts, utility company numbers, recent bank records, current bills, address book, car title, maps, etc. Keep them with you!

tana's habitat

FIRST NIGHT

Be prepared to spend the first night in your new digs without unpacking. Set up this ten-item survival kit ahead of time and keep it easily accessible.

1. A full change of clothes: pants, shirt, socks, underwear, and jammies— that is, unless you sleep au natural
2. Toiletries: toilet paper, toothbrush, toothpaste, soap, hairbrush, moisturizer, medication, makeup, and towel
3. Toolbox: hammer, screwdrivers (Phillips and regular), and box cutter to open boxes
4. Cell phone if you have one
5. Bedding
6. Alarm clock
7. Radio
8. Bottle/wine opener, can opener, paper plates, napkins, and glasses
9. Food for the morning
10. A little cash so you can order take-out

CLEAN UP YOUR ACT

You'll probably want to clean your old place after moving out, and your new place before moving in. Put together a kit of basic cleaning supplies, rags, and a vacuum and keep it handy.

LEAVE IT BEHIND

Take a few precautions to ensure a safe move. Forget packing:

- Old car batteries
- Fuels
- Aerosol cans
- Paint/mineral spirits
- Flammable liquids or corrosive acids
- Bleach
- Firearms and ammo
- Matches
- Perishables

Find the Household Hazardous Waste collection facility in your neighborhood and dump them there instead. Look in the government listings in the phone book to find the one closest to you.

PUT IT ON THE LAWN

yard sales, tag sales, garage sales; whatever you call them, I've paid for more than one move by having one. It's not easy, but if you do it with friends, it can be a profitable and fun way to spend a day. Pull out that **Sell** box and get your money mojo moving.

RULES

Some communities don't allow private sales of any kind. Check with the city before you set up shop or you may be spending your proceeds on fines!

SAY IT LOUD

Set the date and start advertising two weeks before the sale. Spend a couple extra bucks and place an ad in the newspaper to get the word out. Be sure to include the hours of the sale, your address, and any hot-ticket items in the copy so people will know you've got good stuff and where they can get it. Don't forget to post the sale on bulletin boards around the neighborhood. Some of the usual suspects include grocery stores, Laundromats, gyms, and dry cleaners.

GET IT TOGETHER

Give yourself a week or so to learn your product before the sale.

- Clean and repair anything that needs work.
- Price everything. Charge 10 to 30 percent of the original cost depending on condition, then write the price on masking tape. Stick it to each item so that you won't be confused on sale day. Do yourself a favor and round the numbers to quarters. Dealing with nickels, dimes, and pennies in the afternoon rush may drive you to drink.

- Know how far you're willing to haggle. Remember, this is stuff you don't want to keep, so be flexible.
- Organize like-priced items together in a convenient place.
- Make signs, and lots of them.

IT'S A SIGN

Signs are a *very* important part of a successful sale. Make sure you clearly mark the date, time, and location of the sale on every sign, and, if you're using arrows, confirm they're pointing in the right direction! Use bright colors and list some of your better merchandise.

- Paint your signs on paper grocery bags filled with rocks and staple at the top. Place them around the neighborhood like sandwich boards!
- Mount poster board on stakes to hammer into lawns like "For Rent" signs.
- Take down the signs after the sale or you'll have bargain hunters on your lawn for days. At the least, you'll be a litterbug.

CALL AHEAD

Besides making money, the yard sale is about getting rid of stuff. Have a plan for what you'll do with leftovers before you even begin selling. Call Goodwill or Salvation Army and make an appointment for them to pick everything up at the end of the day. Or borrow a friend's truck and haul it to a drop-off yourself. Don't let anything sneak back into the house!

PRESALE JITTERS

Avoid sale time scares by preparing everything the day before.

- Get change. Go for $100 worth of fives, tens, ones, and quarters. Lots of customers will be coming straight from the ATM with their crisp twenties. Be sure you can accommodate their $2.50 purchase.
- Dig out that fanny pack or a cigar box to handle all your money. Something other than your pocket to help keep your cash organized. And never leave it unattended.
- If you can, organize the sale area. Set out your merchandise and get everything in order.

- Post signs everywhere in the neighborhood, but keep them off of utility poles. All those staples are dangerous for the phone man.
- Gather any supplies you need, like bags and newspaper for wrapping fragile things, paper and pen to write receipts, a calculator, and an extension cord to test any electrical items.
- Make sure the sprinkler timer is turned off so the lawn's not soaked before your sale. (Or during, for that matter!) Gather some blankets and sheets to display your merchandise on just in case.
- Pick up some bagels, cream cheese, and fruit for an easy morning nosh.

SALE DAY

The early bird gets the worm, so brew yourself a big pot of joe, slather yourself with sunscreen, and get on out there and sell, sell, sell.

- Invite your friends to help! Turn up some tunes to make it social *and* financially successful.
- Take Polaroids of everyone who buys something and turn it into a collage for your new place!
- Don't forget to count your money before you start so you know how much you've earned at the end of the day.

BEFORE YOU MOVE

it takes a long time for information to get processed, so start your address changes early to make sure you get what you've got coming.

- Fill out a change-of-address card. Pick one up at any post office or go to **www.USPS.com/moversguide** to do it online.
- Register to vote at any post office or online at **www.DeclareYourself.com** or **www.RockTheVote.org**.
- Cancel or reroute newspaper and magazine subscriptions.
- Alert your car and health insurance companies, doctors' offices, and DMV of your new address.
- Don't forget to update your credit card companies, student loan holders, or other debt carriers. They'll find you anyway.

- Let your bank know, too. Order new checks while you're at it.
- And, finally, update your library card!

A REAL TURN-ON

call ahead to have your utilities scheduled to go on the day before you move in to keep you out of the dark. Check your local Yellow Pages online for the web address of your local utilities and register online or by telephone.

- Gas
- Electric
- Land line
- Cell phone
- Internet
- Television

Compare plans and set up your utilities in one fell swoop by visiting **www .ConnectUtilities.com**, **www.MoveEngine.com**, or **www.AllConnect.com**.

INSURE ME

It's doubtful that most renters have renter's insurance, but since your landlord's insurance won't cover your household goods in case of loss, you might as well check into it before you move in. Depending on where you live, your age, the crime rate, and how much stuff you have, you can get it for as little as $10 a month. Ask your auto insurance company and get a deal with an insurance bundle.

- Find insurance companies that offer renter's insurance in the Yellow Pages or online.
- Contact an agent and ask them to explain their standard policies. Do you need extra protection to insure valuables like jewelry, art, or other collectibles?
- You'll need to provide them with your new address, a description of your household possessions, and an estimated value.
- They'll provide you with estimates to provide coverage for your personal property against theft, fire, and wind damage; personal liability for accidents

of others on your premises; damage to property of others in your care; and living expenses if you're forced to leave your apartment during emergencies or repairs.

- Get an estimate for a replacement value policy that will reimburse you for the actual cost of replacing your goods instead of a depreciated value.
- Choose the insurer based on their ability to protect you as you desire, their reputation, and the cost of the policy . . . in that order.

If you decide renter's insurance just isn't for you, you can always change your mind.

MOVE IT

if you're not borrowing a friend's pickup or cramming boxes in your Corolla for a cross-town crusade, reserve a moving truck at least a week in advance. Try for two. Do not put it off until the last minute, or you'll get stuck with a semi when all you need is a van.

Plan your move midweek instead of a weekend. This ensures better truck availability, and usually a better price, too.

HOW BIG OF A TRUCK DO I NEED?		
TRUCK SIZE	NUMBER OF ROOMS TO MOVE	SIZE
10-Footer	Small 1-bedroom apartment	Approx. 350 cubic feet
15-Footer	2-bedroom house or apartment	Approx. 750 cubic feet
20-Footer	3–4 bedroom house	Approx. 1205 cubic feet
25-Footer	Large 5–8 bedroom house	Approx. 1550 cubic feet

Comparison shop and ask questions.

- How much is the basic rental charge for the number of days I need the truck?
- What's the deposit?
- Is it cheaper midweek rather than on weekends?
- Is it cheaper midmonth rather than at the beginning or end of the month?

- Do you charge for miles?
- What's the gas mileage like? Do I need to refuel?
- Where do I pick it up? Drop it off? Are there time restrictions?
- What if I'm only going one-way? Are there penalties?
- Are there any age restrictions?
- Do you have to check my driving record?
- Can I have more than one driver?
- What's the cancellation policy?
- Do you include any moving supplies like dollies, ropes, or furniture pads? If not, how much extra are they?
- Will my auto or credit card insurance cover me in case of an accident? If not, how much is extra insurance? What happens if I'm not insured?
- What happens if the truck breaks down? Do you have roadside assistance? Who pays for that?
- Any specials?

Visit **www.Uhaul.com**, **www.PenskeTruckRental.com**, **www.Ryder.com**, and **www.BudgetTruck.com** for starters.

If you feel uncomfortable driving a large truck, practice in a vacant parking lot until you're a master.

HELLO, DOLLY

If you're moving anything big, include a dolly in your reservation. Refrigerators, appliances, big dressers, and pianos all move easier on wheels.

PADS

Throw a couple furniture pads and blankets in with your rental, too, to make sure your bedroom set doesn't get dinged when you're sailing over the speed bumps.

U-PACK, WE DRIVE

Whether you're moving across town or across the country, several companies offer options that will keep you out of the driver's seat. They drop off a trailer or crate, you fill 'er up, and they pick it back up and deliver it to your destination. After you've unloaded, they come haul it away.

These services can be great values for the money. Some of them offer movers to assist in loading and unloading at an additional cost. And, if you don't have a place to live yet, they'll even store your stuff in secure units with easy access until you do. Try **www.PSPickup.com**, **www.Upack.com**, and **www.Mayflower.com**.

THE LONG HAUL

If you're moving across country and are planning on shipping just a few boxes, your three best avenues are:

- **United States Postal Service**. It's the cheapest, but slowest.
- **UPS**. Ground should be able to get anywhere in the United States in about seven working days.
- **FedEx**. They have several options including overnight, but you'll pay through the nose.

If you've got a lot of stuff to transport, think about hiring a moving company if you don't want to drive it yourself. It'll cost you.

- Ask for referrals. Query friends and relatives. If you're moving for work, your employer may have a company they like to use. They're probably paying for it anyway, so check with them.
- Go with the big boys. It's your stuff and you want it to arrive in prime condition. Look into **www.UnitedVanlines.com**, **www.PSPickup.com**, **www.Upack.com**, and **www.Mayflower.com**.
- Be sure you read the fine print. Know how much extra you pay for labor, gas, and insurance.

RESERVATIONS

If you're moving into an elevator building, call your landlord and schedule the use of the service elevator before you move. It sure beats the stairs!

CLEAN IT

your new apartment should already be sparking clean, but give it a quick once-over before you drag your stuff in anyway. Vacuum the carpets, sweep and mop the

tana's habitat

floors, wipe down all the kitchen cabinets, drawers, countertops, fridge (inside and out), and stove. Don't forget the closets. And you just never know who's been in your bathroom, so disinfect the toilet, tub, and shower.

SHELVE IT

Are you planning on using shelf or contact paper? This is a good time to lay it down. Look for fun styles at Target or your local hardware store. The dollar store usually has a pretty good selection, too. Don't want to spend the extra cash? Cut paper grocery bags to size instead.

YOU'RE WALKING ON IT

The carpets should be deep-cleaned before you move in, so check with your landlord to make sure that's been done. If not, get him to schedule it before you move in. It'll take a day or two for the carpets to dry, so ask well in advance.

If you're doing anything more drastic to your floors, like ripping up the carpet and refinishing the hardwoods, do it now to avoid a really big mess and an even bigger hassle.

COLOR YOUR WORLD

One of the easiest ways to add life to an otherwise dull, white room is to paint it. You OK'd it with your landlord before you signed the lease and, hopefully, even got him to agree to foot the bill and the labor! But no matter who's doing the work, get it done before you move in. Painting around furniture is a sure way to ruin it.

- Try painting a wall or two or even the ceiling to add a splash of color.
- Paint a series of various-sized dots or squares on your walls. Use one or multiple colors.
  - Lay out some painter's tape in a circle on your wall.
  - Draw a circle on top of the tape and cut it out with an X-Acto knife;
  - Peel away the inside of the circle and paint.
  - Overlap them, put them in the corners or even on the ceiling.

- Use a similar technique for stripes.
  - Place a few strips of painters tape on your wall in a striped configuration you like. Horizontal, vertical, mix and match.
  - Paint over them.
  - Let the paint dry and carefully peel back the tape!

Employ these top 5 ways to get your friends to help you move.

1. Beer
2. Beer
3. Beer
4. Atkins-approved paninis
5. Beer

Reserve the date and time with your friends in advance and call to confirm. And remember, if you ever want your friends to help you move again, you'll be packed and ready to go when they arrive.

MOVING DAY

now your bags are packed; you're ready to go. Your friends are waiting outside your door. Make your move easier and safer by planning how to pack the truck.

WHAT YOU'LL NEED

- Dolly
- Plenty of rope
- Furniture pads and blankets

- Load the heaviest items, such as furniture and major appliances first. Place them on the front wall of the truck and make sure the weight is distributed evenly from side to side. Cover the furniture and any appliances with a blanket or sheet to keep them from getting scratched.
- When loading dressers and chests, remove the drawers before you load them. It will lighten the load and you won't have to worry about them sliding out as you haul. Once on the truck, replace the drawers and secure with them with rope for transit.
- Load the truck a fourth at a time and pack it securely from floor to ceiling. Tie down each quarter load with rope.
- Long items like mattresses and box springs should be loaded along the side or back wall of the truck. Pack them in mattress bags or lay a blanket down to prevent them from getting dirty.
- Once the larger items are loaded, start putting the heavier boxes down low and lighter boxes on top. Stack similar-sized boxes on top of one another and place the odd-shaped and fragile items on top of the pile.
- Roll and tie rugs with rope or strong twine.
- If you're moving in an open truck, make sure everything is tied down and secure. If it's a closed truck, pack everything at a uniform height. If there's extra room in the back, be sure to secure the load with rope to keep it from shifting while you drive.
- If you need it first, pack it last. Including your cleaning supplies, tool kit, and ten-item survival pack!
- Always lift with your legs, not your back.

UNLOAD

If your boxes are properly marked and you've packed everything well, unloading should be a piece of cake. Make the effort to do it before you call it a night. Nothing screams "Steal me!" more than a truck filled with unknown wonders.

- Crank the tunes, dude!
- Deliver each box to its designated room and drop it in an out-of-the-way corner.
- Bring in the furniture.
- Call for take-out and celebrate!

UNPACK

Although it's great to wake up in your new place with everything unpacked and in order, your moving day may leave you too pooped to pop. Wake up in the morning refreshed and have at it then.

- Start in the kitchen and wash all your dishes before putting them away. There's a good chance they have newspaper ink on them.
- Arrange the furniture. Function before form gives you a couch to crash on when you've just had enough.
- Put it away. Do your best to make logical choices in storing your things, but keep in mind you can always change it later. Sometimes it's better to get it out of your hair and get living!
- Recycle your packing supplies. Remove tape from your boxes, break them down, and put them in the paper bin. Newsprint, too. Any bubble wrap or plastic packing materials can be tossed in the plastics bin.
- Make it pretty.

SETTLING DOWN

get into the groove of flying solo.

- Call your mom! Let her know you made it.
- If you're moving across country and don't have a permanent place to stay, get a P.O. Box to eliminate any confusion between temporary residences.
- Let everyone know you've moved! Send out change-of-address cards to all your friends and family. Don't forget to include your new phone number and mailing address. Go to **www.usps.com/mailingonline/ postcard.htm** to find out how you can send custom postcards for cheap. All you have to do is fill out the info and upload your address book. Simple.
- Throw yourself a housewarming party.
- Explore your new neighborhood!
- If you've moved to a new city, don't forget to set up that bank account.

WRITE IT OFF

Moving's tax deductible! Save all your receipts and fill out **IRS Form 3903** while all the expenses are still fresh in your mind.

HI, MY NAME IS . . .

Moving out on your own to a new neighborhood or city can be a lonely experience. Especially if you're coming from an atmosphere filled with social stimulation or familial ties. But if you're going to make new friends, you're going to have to put yourself out there. The Welcome Wagon's route has long been paved over.

DO SOMETHING

Find an activity you like or have always wanted to do and do it. Take a pottery or cooking class, join a softball league or museum group. Whatever interests you. It will automatically give you common ground in which to start a conversation with other participants.

INTRODUCE YOURSELF

Don't be shy. A simple "Hi" and a smile works wonders. Let people know you're new in town and ask them what's fun to do or see around there.

SMILE

Walking around with a smile makes you much more approachable.

REMEMBER NAMES

Nothing is more endearing than remembering someone's name. Not good at it? Learn how at **www.LearnThat.com/courses/lifestyle/names**.

INTERESTED IS INTERESTING

People love to talk about themselves. If you want to make friends, ask people all about their life. Listen up and look them in the eye. A good conversationalist is a good listener.

IT'S ABOUT YOU, TOO

Tell people about yourself. Your hobbies, interests, or talents are all things that are important to you and say a lot about your personality. But remember, nobody likes a braggart.

WHINING AND COMPLAINING

Shy away from the drama. People tend to be drawn to those who are upbeat and happy rather than someone burdened with negativity.

INSTIGATE

Don't depend on your new friends to call you or make plans. Have an idea or plan in mind and make the call to invite them to join you.

EVERYONE'S DIFFERENT

Not everyone will be exactly like you. Be accepting and appreciate the differences in people. You may just discover something new in you along the way.

DON'T RUSH

It takes time to develop and nourish friendships. You'll be fine.

CLEANLINESS IS NEXT TO GODLINESS

i guess you could say ours is a sordid affair: a love-hate relationship. I love things clean. I just hate cleaning them. The roots of my dysfunction run deep, traced back to my childhood. I suppose it's my mother's fault. (Isn't it always?) Or maybe it would be fairer to blame it on my internal mantra that pleads with me to take the easy way out.

Out of sight, out of mind, I thought as I jammed my drawers with junk and stuffed my closet to the gills with shoes and stuffed animals, school assignments, sack lunches, and record sleeves, the doors nearly bursting at the seams. You'd never know it to walk into the room. My bed was neatly made, hospital corners and all, the book shelves were organized, the furniture dusted. Nothing but carpet was under the bed. Every "easily spied by Mom" space was picture perfect. It was behind closed doors where I kept my little secret, my system.

What was I thinking? It was a question I asked myself over and over again the afternoon I returned home from school to find the entire contents of my closet, two dressers, a nightstand, and three backpacks piled high on top of my bed. Hangars and drawers, clothes and books, all my personal possessions reduced to a giant heap in the middle of the room. I guess Mom didn't approve of my system.

I cried and mumbled expletives under my breath for the next few hours as I separated my clothes into categories: to hang, to fold, pants, skirts, tees, and undies. Quietly and methodically, I put my belongings in order, back in their proper places so that I might find my bed to slip into before morning.

tana's habitat

As traumatic as that was for me, I managed to muster up enough strength to handle a repeat performance. And not just one or two, but several, each as violating as the last. What was I thinking? That wasn't easy!

I'm no neat freak, but I've cleaned up my act considerably over the years. My rebellion is over and yet the theme persists. Just last month I was in Montana visiting my Mom and I threw some darks in the wash. A mixed load. When I peeled my favorite, freshly cleaned, white linen pants from the basin of the washer, it hit me. "Oh no!" I moaned.

"What happened?" Mom asked as she raced into the laundry room. I held up my pants, no longer white, but a dingy, chalky blue. I'd done it again. Washed my brand-new jean jacket with the lights. "Tana? Why do you do stuff like that?" she asked, dumbfounded.

"I know, Mom. I know. What was I thinking?"

clean house, happy planet

housework sucks. there's no doubt about it. But with a little knowledge and some strategizing, you can stay on top of the clutter.

THE EVERYDAY ARSENAL

arm yourself with these basic tools. No home is clean without them.

Broom and dustpan: Get a broom with frayed edges. It's good for getting all the bits and crumbs.

Mop: Try one with a microfiber cloth covering that can be thrown in the wash. They're good for all sorts of surfaces including floors, walls, and countertops.

Vacuum: The type of vacuum cleaner you need depends on the surfaces you'll be cleaning. Go to **www.WhatsTheBest-Vacuum.com** to find out will work for you, or get a multipurpose cleaner with a brush roller for carpets and rugs and a soft head for hardwoods and vinyl flooring.

Cotton rags: For dusting, cleaning windows, and mirrors. Old T-shirts work great.

Sponges: Some for dishes and some for general cleaning. Don't mix them up or you'll make yourself sick.

Steel wool: Very fine for cleaning pots and pans.

Toothbrushes: Great for getting hard to reach spots. Make sure to mark them as hazardous or assign a specific color to those you use for cleaning. Toothpaste and tile grout do not a good combination make.

Toilet brush and plunger

A TREASURY OF TOOLS

the essential toolbox.

- Toolbox
- Claw hammer
- Screwdrivers
    - Slotted: This is the flat kind.
    - Phillips head: This is the pointy kind that forms an X.
- 25' Tape measure
- Needle nose (with wire cutter) and regular pliers
- 2' Level
- Stud finder
- Utility knife
- Cordless drill and bits
- Pencil and pencil sharpener
- Safety goggles: Eyes are precious.
- Assortment of screws and nails
- Spackle and putty knife

- Paint key
- Wood glue
- Electrical, blue painter's, and duct tape
- Stepladder

SECRET AGENTS

store bought cleaning supplies work great, but many contain hazardous chemicals that harm the earth, our health, and our wallets. Make your own detergents from earth friendly ingredients and you'll save the environment *and* your assets. You'll be amazed by their efficacy, too.

KEY INGREDIENTS

What comes from your fridge can clean it!

Baking soda (bicarbonate of soda): Cleans, deodorizes, softens water, and is a good scouring powder.

Washing soda (carbonate of soda): Think baking soda on acid. Found at most grocery stores in the laundry aisle, it's caustic and should be used while wearing rubber gloves. It's great for really tough stains like that nasty grease buildup in your oven.

White vinegar: Cuts grease, deodorizes, and disinfects everything from laundry to linoleum. It's the great panacea.

Pure / liquid soap: A general all-purpose cleaner that biodegrades completely. Try Dr. Bronner's in liquid or cake. Clairol Herbal Essences Shampoo is a good one, too.

Lemon juice: Mild bleach, a deodorant, and a cleaning agent.

Borax: A naturally occurring mineral salt. It cleans, deodorizes, bleaches, and disinfects, and is used to control pests such as ants and cockroaches.

GENERAL ALL-PURPOSE CLEANERS

Pick up a bunch of spray bottles to keep your mixtures. Mark them well with indelible ink on a piece of tape. Add a couple drops of essential oils like lavender, eucalyptus, or lemon for that fresh scent of clean.

REGULAR STRENGTH (FOR COUNTERTOPS, TABLES, WALLS, FIXTURES)
½ teaspoon baking soda
2 teaspoons borax
½ teaspoon liquid soap
2 cups hot water

EXTRA STRENGTH (FOR WHEN THINGS HAVE GOTTEN OUT OF HAND!)
1 teaspoon washing soda
2 teaspoons borax
½ teaspoon liquid soap
2 cups hot water

SUPER-DUPER STRENGTH (FOR TOUGH STAINS AND GREASY MESSES)
2 teaspoons washing soda
2 teaspoons borax
½ teaspoon liquid soap
1 cup hot water

CAVEATS

Rinse surfaces well with water to avoid white residue. And remember, marble and fiberglass surfaces are both easily scratched. Only use the regular-strength formulation, and try it on a hidden area first, just to be sure.

SITE SPECIFIC

Don't trust that an all-purpose cleaner lives up to its name? Try some of these concoctions on your special tasks.

Dishwasher detergent: Use pure soap to wash dishes and add white vinegar to the rinse water to give glasses an extra shine.

Pot cleaner: To remove burnt-on food, cover the damage with water, add two teaspoons of baking soda, and bring to the boil. Leave to cool and scrape off.

Silver cleaner: Line a bowl with aluminum foil, fill with hot water, and add a quarter cup of salt. Put the silver in and leave until tarnish disappears.

Silver and metal polish: Make a paste with lemon juice and baking soda. Rub it on with a soft cloth, rinse with water, dry, and buff.

Toilet cleaner: Make a paste from borax and lemon juice for cleaning toilet bowls.

Grout and mildew cleaner: Dip an old toothbrush in vinegar and scrub the tile grout to remove mildew and mold. Helps to prevent new growth, too.

Window cleaner: Use a solution of 1 part white vinegar to 2 parts warm water. Wipe windows with a damp cloth and use wads of newspaper to dry and polish.

Furniture polish: Mix 1 cup olive oil with a half cup lemon juice in a spray bottle. Spray a soft cloth and wipe over furniture. Shake it, shake it, baby. A lot.

Air freshener: Simmer vinegar or herb mixtures in water, or try cinnamon and cloves.

CLEAN ENOUGH

the key to a clean apartment is to keep it picked up. Build some simple habits into your daily routine, and the deep clean won't feel like such a chore.

- Wash your dishes and wipe down the countertops before you go to bed.
- Put your dirty clothes in the hamper, not on the floor.
- When the trashcan is full, take it out.
- Clean up spills right away to avoid stains, bugs, and smells.
- Don't leave food out.

- Use something, put it away.
- Keep your makeup contained.
- Hang up those predate clothing discards. You'll save time on laundry and leave room on your bed to, uh, sleep!
- Trash the magazines and newspapers. Clip unread articles to save in a folder.
- Place a mat at the door and wipe your shoes before you come in the house to keep the carpets clean. Or better yet—take of your shoes!

ON SCHEDULE

Once a week, come rain or come shine, clean the big stuff. If you've kept your place surface clean throughout the week, you won't have to pick up, so it shouldn't take you more than a couple hours. Do it every Saturday morning and treat yourself with a latte for a job well done. Hang a chart on the refrigerator and give yourself a gold star for every task you complete. Give yourself an incentive if a job well done just isn't enough.

- Vacuum and mop your floors.
- Dust your furniture and electronics.
- Scrub down the kitchen.
- Clean your bathroom including shower, tub, toilet, sink, and floor.

These cleaning basics will get you started:

GET INTO THE GROOVE

Hardwood floors can scratch easily, so use a broom or a vacuum with a soft head attachment. Keep in mind that water warps wood, so a dry mop is the only way to go.

- Pick furniture up to move it or use a felt pad under the feet to slide without scratching.
- Use a pencil eraser to remove black heel marks.
- Use a catch pan under plants to avoid any water damage.
- Never use a wet mop.

LOVE MY CARPET

Life happens, but your carpets and rugs don't need to tell the tale. Try these stain-removal tactics to keep your floors looking their finest, even after the fact. Always work from the outer edges in so you don't spread the stain. Blot, don't rub, and, just in case, test your method on a small, hidden corner to make sure it won't cause more damage.

Coffee

Consider switching to decaf. Combine 1 teaspoon of clear, liquid soap with a cup of lukewarm water and work it gently into the carpet with a sponge. Blot dry. Next, mix 1 part vinegar with 2 parts lukewarm water. Work gently into the carpet again. Blot. Sponge the area with clean water one final time.

Blood, red wine, beer, vomit

Start asking questions and step away from the bottle. Blot the stain with a dry cloth. Work in some liquid soap with a toothbrush. Blot dry. Pour on some hydrogen peroxide and let it sit a bit before blotting dry. Flush with water and blot. Kill the smell with baking soda. Pour a bunch on, let it dry, then vacuum.

LEAVE 'EM IN THE DUST

If you need instruction on dusting your furniture, you're in serious trouble. Old T-shirts, dryer sheets, and pantyhose work the best.

I CAN SEE CLEARLY NOW

Wash your windows a few times a year, just for the feng shui of it. Getting streaks? Try wiping horizontally on the inside of the window and vertically on the outside so you can easily tell on which side the streak is occurring.

ALLERGIC TO CLEANING?

There are two types of allergy sufferers when it comes to cleaning: the allergic and the lazy. If you're a true sufferer, breathe easier with these simple ideas:

- Get a dehumidifier and keep the humidity at 50 or below to reduce dust mites (asthma-triggering, microscopic, eight-legged creatures that live in our beds and carpets) and mold.
- Clean often and wear a filter/dust mask when vacuuming or dusting.
- Use a vacuum with a high-filtration or HEPA filter.
- Wash your bedding in hot water at a temperature of 130 degrees or more to kill dust mites.
- Wash and comb your pets weekly.
- Use exhaust fans in the kitchen and bath to prevent condensation.

GREEN LIVING

don't know much about sustainability or renewable energy? Think recycling is a bogus pain in the rear? Take a look at these shocking statistics and you may think again:

- Every *single* American tosses just shy of 1 ton of waste into our landfills *every year*.[7]
- Americans use 30 percent of the world's oil supply, only 2 percent of which comes from our own soil.
- Renewable energy and conservation projects create 300 percent more jobs than the construction and operation of new traditional power plants of equal costs.
- With every mile we drive our gas-powered cars, we send 1 pound of CO_2 into the atmosphere.[8]

And that's just the United States.

Whether or not you believe in the effects of global warming, ozone depletion, or the link between oil and environmental catastrophe, there's no doubt that we are over-populated with waste. By embracing renewable energy and paying attention to what we consume, we can be a part of the solution rather than the problem. With all the information, opportunity, and resources available, there's no reason not to.

REDUCE

it's not your fault you use too much of everything. Advertisers trick us into using more than we need. It's their way of getting us to buy more. Start thinking about how you use things, and it'll be easy to see how much product, water, energy, and money you waste every day.

HOW MUCH DO YOU REALLY NEED?

Toothpaste: A dab about the size of a pea. As long as it's still foaming, you have enough.

Laundry detergent: Try half the recommended amount.

Shampoo and conditioner: Forget lather, rinse, repeat. From now on, lather, rinse, move on.

Dishwashing liquid: No need to soak. Use just a bit and when it stops foaming add a bit more.

What else?

- Reduce paper waste by using cloth napkins, dishtowels, and bringing your own cloth bags to the grocery store.
- Reduce plastic waste by using a water filter pitcher or tap system instead of buying bottled.
- How many times do you wear a pair of jeans before you wash them? Give them one more wear.
- Give your towels another shower.

REDUCE ENERGY CONSUMPTION

Snuggle up to the idea of winterizing your apartment. Even in the summer. Keep your climate as controlled as your cash flow. Take a good look at your windows and doors. If you're in an older building, you'll probably see where the windows don't quite close or huge gaps around the doorframes. If it's a newer building, it may be harder to tell. Hold a lit candle up around the perimeter of all your windows and doors. If the flame flickers, you've got yourself a gap.

PROTECT YOURSELF FROM THE ELEMENTS

EXTERIOR DOORS

Apply weather stripping around the edges of the door(s). Adhesive-backed foam strips work great for gaps that vary in width. Felt stripping is cheaper, but isn't very durable. Get it at the hardware store.

SNAKE

Get these at a discount department or bed-and-bath store for $8 to $10 or make your own. Cut off a leg from a pair of pantyhose, fill it with rice, sand, beans, or cat litter and knot the end. Wrap it in a piece of decorative fabric tied off with yarn at the ends. Works great for doors and drafty windowsills.

WINDOWS

Use weather stripping on the top and bottom, and foam between the sash and jambs where the top and bottom windows meet. Or try an easy-to-use insulator kit from the hardware store. It includes double stick tape and clear plastic that shrinks to your window under the heat of a hair dryer.

WINDOW AIR CONDITIONER

If you can, remove your air conditioner and store it for the winter. Otherwise, turn the vent off and cover the unit with a window air conditioner bag or other plastic. If you live upstairs and cannot cover the unit from the outside, wrap it in plastic from the inside.

FIREPLACE

Keep the damper tightly closed when not in use to keep the cold air out.

THERMOSTAT

Set your thermostat for savings:

	HEAT	A/C
when you wake up	68°	75°
while you're at work	60°	80°
when you get home from work	68°	75°
while you're sleeping	60°	80°

More ideas for the long, cold winter:

- Lower the thermostat and dress warmer. Put on your sweats and thick, fuzzy socks around the apartment.
- Wrap up in a blanket or cuddle with someone special.
- Run a humidifier. It helps hold in the heat and keeps your skin from drying out from the dry winter air.
- Sleep on flannel sheets and use lots of blankets.
- Hang heavy curtains instead of sheers on your windows.
- If you have bare floors, get some throw rugs.
- Move the furniture away from heating vents, radiators, and registers. This

tana's habitat

will allow the heat to circulate in the room much better instead of it congregating behind furniture where you aren't.

Find more energy-saving ideas at the U.S. Department of Energy, **www.eren.doe.gov**.

REUSE

reusing an item for its intended purpose or creating new ways to use it is a great way to conserve. And by not sending it to a recycling center, you're saving all the energy it would cost to haul it away, break it down, and mold it into a new product. For instance, the energy used in recycling one glass bottle could light a 100-watt light bulb for four hours! So before you throw something in the trash or recycling bin, ask yourself if it has an alternative use. Soon you'll get your creative juices flowing and find endless ways to reuse most any product.

WAYS TO REUSE

- Buy reusable products like rechargeable batteries instead of single-use items.
- Reuse newspapers to clean windows and mirrors.
- Reuse discarded bottles as picture frames and vases.
- Reuse all bags and containers. Brown bags make great wrapping paper or receptacles for recyclables.
- Reuse plastic grocery bags as packing material, to carry wet clothes home from the gym, or pick up after your dog.
- Borrow or rent something you may use only one time.
- Sell or donate clothes, furniture, and any item you're inclined to throw out because you're done with it. It may be perfect for a friend or a neighbor, or to sell at your next yard sale.
- Reuse plastic containers for leftovers and storing small, loose items.
- Resealable plastic bags can be washed and reused countless times.
- Printer paper has two sides. Use both. Try proofing documents on the computer instead.
- Buy products made from recycled products.

The Freecycle Network is made up of many individual groups across the globe. It's a grassroots movement of people who are giving (and getting) stuff for free in their own towns. Check out your local group or become a moderator yourself by visiting **www.FreeCycle.org**.

RECYCLE

you've exhausted ways to reuse your solid waste. But before you chuck it in the trash, ask yourself, "Can I recycle this?" The answer will, most likely, be yes, since as much as 60 to 65 percent of all trash is recyclable. These days, most neighborhood sanitation departments have a recycling pickup as well. I'll bet if you check by your trash bin, you'll find containers for paper, metal, and plastic. Recycling and buying recycled is easy. There's no excuse not to do it.

WHAT'S RECYCLABLE?

It only takes a minute to learn what types of plastic, paper, glass, and metal your area will recycle. Call your city municipal department or Google the name of your town and "recycle" to find out what they'll accept, then start pausing at the trashcan to check for those recycle symbols on the bottom of whatever you're about to toss.

Set up an easy-to-use recycling center in your kitchen, and don't forget to put a "No Junk Mail" sign on your mailbox.

PAPER

Most paper and paper products you use every day can be recycled: newspapers, magazines, printer paper, cardboard, telephone books, mixed colored paper, pizza boxes, and cereal boxes. They can only recycle clean items so make sure to wipe any food particles from the containers before you throw them into the bin.

WHY RECYCLE PAPER?

Because to produce 1 ton of new paper . . .

- Takes approximately 7,000 gallons of water
- Takes 17 to 31 trees

- Takes 4,000 KWh of electricity, enough energy to run a three-bedroom home for one year
- Produces 60 pounds of pollution
- Produces a greenhouse gas twenty times more potent than carbon dioxide when broken down in a landfill

GLASS

Green, clear, or brown, recycle it down. Rinse it out, but feel free to leave the labels on. Ceramics, heat-resistant cookware like Pyrex, windows, lightbulbs, leaded glass, and mirrors are not recyclable.

PLASTIC

Water and soda bottles, orange juice and dip containers, plastic condiment bottles, shampoo, conditioner, and lotion bottles are all recyclable.

METAL

Most of the metals you use every day can be recycled, from steel and tin cans to soda cans, empty aerosol cans, and aluminum foil. You can also recycle brass, copper, and nickel alloy products, though you may have to take them to a special metal recycling center.

E-WASTE

Electronics are not biodegradable and must be taken to a special recycling center for drop-off. If they still work, find them a new home, donate them to charity, or give them to a local thrift store. If not, check with your local sanitation department for details. Electronics include:

- Cell phones/regular phones
- Computers and computer components
- Office machines
- Printer/toner cartridges
- TV
- Stereos
- Videotapes
- CDs

Get a free ream of paper when you recycle an ink cartridge at Office Depot or return your empty cartridges for discounts at **www.123inkjets.com**.

TOXIC WASTE

Don't contaminate our earth by throwing toxic waste into the garbage. It's actually illegal. Call your sanitation department and find out where the drop-off center is. They may even come and pick it up for you. It's that important.

- Paint and solvents
- Glue
- Drain, kitchen, and oven cleaners
- Bleach, detergents, and disinfectants
- Batteries
- Furniture and shoe polish
- Nail polish and nail polish remover

COMPOSTING

composting is the controlled decomposition of organic materials, like leaves, grass, and food scraps resulting in a soil-like material rich in nutrients and minerals. Yes, there are worms involved. And, yes, it can be stinky, but only if you don't do it right. But because organic matter makes up 25 percent of the waste U.S. households produce, composting can really reduce what ends up in landfills.[9] Besides, it's great fertilizer!

HOW TO BUILD A WORM BIN

Easily adapt a plastic storage bin for composting. It should be eight to twelve inches deep, have a tight-fitting lid, and be opaque in nature to keep the conditions warm and damp.

- Drill ten quarter-inch holes in the lid and three around the top of each side of the bin for air circulation.

- Shred newspaper into one-inch strips and soak them in water. Pile the wet paper in the bin until it reaches eight inches. You could also use potting soil or leaves.
- Before adding any organic material like fruit or vegetable scraps to your new bin, give them a good wash to cut down on the possibility of fruit flies.
- The best things to add to your bin are washed fruit and vegetable scraps, coffee grounds and filters, eggshells, paper napkins and towels, and dead plants and flowers. You can throw in tea bags, too, but remove the staples. They're no good for worms' stomachs.
- Add two pounds of red worms (*Eisenia fetida* or *Lumbricus rubellus*) to your bin. Not night crawlers or anything you've found in the yard, they don't work. Find them at the bait and tackle shop, on eBay, or from The Worms Wrangler at **www.WormsWrangler.com**.
- Cover all the food scraps and worms with your bedding material. Each time you throw in new scraps, cover them up and make sure the bin stays moist. Use a spray bottle to give it a mist.
- In one to four months the bedding will start to get dark and crumbly, like dirt. It's harvest time!
- Move all the bedding over to one side of the worm bin. Add new, damp-ened bedding to the empty side, and start placing food scraps on that side. In about a month, most of the worms move to the new bedding, allowing you to scoop out the relatively worm-free compost. Put it in your garden! Throw some on your plants! Or toss it on the lawn!

WHAT DO WORMS EAT?

Feed worms a varied diet, but don't overload the bin with fruit or you'll attract fruit flies.

MATERIALS TO INCLUDE	MATERIALS TO EXCLUDE
Fruit and vegetable scraps	Meats
Eggshells	Dairy foods
Coffee grounds with filters	Fats
Tea bags (remove staples)	Oils (including peanut butter and mayonnaise)
Fireplace ash	
Leaves	Grease
Grass	Pet excrement

MATERIALS TO INCLUDE	MATERIALS TO EXCLUDE
Yard clippings	Fish scraps
Vacuum cleaner lint	Diseased plants
Wool and cotton rags	Bones
Sawdust	
Nonrecyclable paper	

For more information about the New York City Composting Project, visit them online at **www.NYCCompost.org**. And try **www.NRDC.org/cities/living/gover.asp** for more ideas about green living.

MAYDAY, MAYDAY

stuff happens. Whatcha gonna do?

Broken lightbulb: If you break a lightbulb while it's still in the socket, you could panic and run screaming into the streets. Or, turn off the switch, cut a potato in half, shove it onto the broken bulb, and twist to pull out the shattered bulb.

Fuse box / circuit breaker: Locate that breaker box as soon as you move in and label all the switches so you know which one powers which room. When you lose power, which you will, flip the switch back and forth. If it doesn't work, you may need a new fuse. Just call the landlord.

Sticky drawers: Remove the offending drawer, rub a bar of soap along the underside of the drawer, giving it a light waxy coating. Replace the drawer. You may need to open and close a few times before it starts to move freely and quietly.

Squeaky doors: WD-40, my friend. WD-40. Move the door back and forth as you spray to work in the oil.

6

take stock

before you clean it, you're gonna have to equip it. Outfitting a kitchen doesn't have to be intimidating. Get the basics, and as your cooking skills and appetite change, you can add on.

THE LIST

this list of gadgets, cookware, and appliances has everything you might need to cook up a storm in your first kitchen. And if a recipe calls for a tool you don't have, this assortment will certainly give you enough options to punt.

POTS AND PANS

- 1-, 2-, and 4-quart saucepans
- 8" and 12" or 14" skillets for frying and sautéing
- 8-quart stockpot for soups, stews, and pastas
- Roasting pan

Heavy-gauge aluminum is probably your best bet for starters. And lots of times you can get a great deal on pots and pans in a set. But, before you buy, *read the box!* Find out how they're made, what they're made of, and how to take care of them. Are you willing to do what it takes to keep them in good condition? If you're a frittata fan, are the handles heat resistant enough to withstand an oven over 350°? Test the weight and make sure they're heavy enough to stay on your burners but not so heavy that you have to go to the gym six times a week in order to lift a pot of rice off the stove.

BAKEWARE

- 2 8" or 9" round cake pans
- 2 cookie/baking sheets
- 13" x 9" x 2" baking pan
- 8", 9", or 10" springform pan
- 9" x 5" x 3" loaf pan
- 12 cup muffin tin
- Cooling racks

You'll find bakeware made out of aluminum, steel, nonstick, silicone, and glass. Heavy aluminum is great because it is an efficient heat conductor and its weight keeps the pans from warping. Plus, it's easy to clean! And, although it's a little more expensive, silicon's nonstick surface and flexibility make it a winner, too.

APPLIANCES

- Blender
- Food processor (Don't bother with the two cup jobbers. They never have enough room, even if you're just cooking for one.)
- Hand-held mixer

KNIVES

- 6", 8", or 10" chef's knife for chopping and slicing
- 3" or 4" paring knife for peeling and other small stuff
- Serrated knife for bread and tomatoes
- Sharpening stone or steel

You'll notice a big price discrepancy here. Knives can range in price to $5 to $150 or more . . . per knife. If cash is an issue, buy a set for $20 from Target. They'll last you a few years and will do you just fine. If you can afford it, spend the bank and get the good ones. They'll last forever and increase your cooking pleasure by a million.

THE PLAYERS

If you're going for the quality knives, know what you're looking at:

Chef's knife: It's 6" to 12" long with a curved blade so that you can do that rocking motion all the *Iron Chef* contestants do when chopping the food of the day. A pointy tip allows you to get around bones or other tight spots, and the flat surface is good for crushing garlic. The ideal chef's knife will weigh over 7 ounces and have an 8" to 10" blade. If you only buy one knife, this is the one. Super-versatile.

Utility knife: The utility knife is 4" to 5" long with a straight blade. Though longer than a paring knife, it's really easy to handle, making it good for peeling and cutting small fruits and veggies.

Serrated knife: Like Ruffles, they have ridges. These guys come in lots of sizes and are great for cutting tomatoes and fresh bread without smashing the entire loaf. They last a long, long time, but, since they cannot be sharpened, when they die, they're dead. Thankfully, they're less expensive than the others.

SUPPORT STAFF

There's a knife for pretty much everything you might ever want to cut. They come with lots of funny names and compelling reasons for you to want them, but these are some other basics that you might want to consider adding down the line.

Paring knife: 4" blade for peeling, chopping, slicing.
Slicing knife: 10" to 12" blade for slicing anything from meat to bread to poultry.
Boning knife: 5" blade, the name gives it away. It has a thin blade for flexibility to, say it with me, "Get around the bones!"
Fillet knife: 7" blade for, you guessed it, boning and cutting really thin meat/fish/poultry.
Cleaver: 6" to 10" blade for cutting the heads off of chickens . . . or whatever.

Choose a blade made of **high-carbon stainless steel**. Some blades are *forged* (cast in a mold) and some are *stamped* (cut from a sheet of metal). Forged blades are thin at the edge and widen at the back, making them much stronger than stamped blades that are thin and flexible all the way through. For this reason, forging is the best and most durable method, but also the most expensive.

High carbon allows the blade to keep its edge and the **stainless steel** keeps it, well, stainless. Free from rust.

High-quality knives will also have a **tang**, a solid extension of the blade that runs through the handle. Look for a tang that runs the entire length of the handle.

ON THE EDGE

The part of the knife you actually cut with is called the *edge* and is formed by grinding. **Tapered grinds** are found on most forged knives. **Flat grinds** are cheaper to produce and, thusly, are found more often on stamped blades. **Hollow grinds** are very sharp, but very thin and can break easily.

GET A GRIP

Handles are for more than just the look of your knife. Make sure the grip is comfortable and that it's not going to slip and slide and chop off your fingers if it gets wet.

Handles can be made from wood or plastic. Certainly wood can look really nice, but be aware that, just like a deck, wood deteriorates over time. You could even get splinters! Bacteria buildup is common as the handle starts to loosen from the tang. Plastics are super-durable and, often times, ergonomically designed, making them more comfortable.

CONSIDER YOURSELF

The most important thing when buying a knife is how it feels in your hand. Only you can be the judge of that, but make sure the handle and blade feel balanced and that it feels macho enough to cut through everything you might want to cut with it.

HERE'S THE DEAL

How much do you need to spend? A really good forged chef's knife will probably run you around $70 to $90. Don't spend less than $40 to $50. It's really worth it, though. Put them on your Christmas list and get someone else to buy them for you or look for bargains at after-holiday clearance sales. And don't forget Mother's/Father's Day sales.

You are going to pay through the nose for these knives, but if you take care of them properly, you'll never have to buy another one again. Thankfully, you don't have to buy the entire set. Just buy one or two, test them out, and buy more when you need more.

I'M GONNA LOVE YOU FOREVER

Protect your investment!

- Get your knives professionally sharpened a couple times a year. Try asking your butcher to do it for you or take them to a kitchen store like Sur La Table that offers sharpening services.
- Sharpen the blades regularly with steel. Lots of chefs sharpen their knives every time they use them . . . even while they're cutting!
- Wash and dry the knife right away after every use.
- Keep your knives in a knife block or on a magnetic rack.
- Never cut on anything except a cutting board. Hardwood and self-healing rubber are the best.
- Don't put your knives in the dishwasher! You might chip the blade or damage the handles.

OTHER GIZMOS FOR YOUR KITCHEN

- Stainless-steel colander
- Four-sided grater
- Steaming rack
- Pepper mill
- Hardwood spoons
- Slotted spoons
- Tongs
- Measuring cups
- Measuring spoons
- Cutting board
- Rubber and metal spatulas
- Meat thermometer

TAKE THE HEAT

you'll notice that elements repeat themselves in a household. From aluminum to stainless steel, porcelain to plastic, if you focus on learning how to clean a few specific surfaces, you'll have the kitchen licked spotless.

ALUMINUM

Because it's a good heat conductor and, at heavy gauges, tends to cook quite evenly, aluminum is used for everything from kettles, saucepans, and skillets to baking pans, molds, and measuring cups.

Soak burned-on food in soapy water before scouring with very fine steel wool. Sometimes the acids in foods like tomatoes and apples can discolor aluminum. Wipe or soak in white vinegar, or two teaspoons of cream of tartar mixed with a quart of water.

COPPER AND BRASS

Copper and brass are often used for utensils that are used for slow cooking, like teakettles, saucepans, and baking pans.

Soak burned-on food in soapy water before scouring with a nylon scrub pad, never with steel wool or scouring powder. Although tarnish doesn't affect the outcome of what's being cooked, you may not like the look of it. Rub it off with a paste made of equal parts salt, flour, and vinegar or a half a lemon dipped in salt. Pickle juice works, too!

CAST IRON

These heavy dutch ovens, frying pans, skillets, and griddles are excellent for browning, braising, and stew making. And, because they season with use, they make everything taste delicious. Even better? They're a snap to clean.

Warm soapy water and a stiff brush will remove burned-on food. Other than that, just wipe them clean with a paper towel.

CERAMICS, CHINA, PORCELAIN, AND TERRA-COTTA

These heat resistant substances are used in everything from everyday dishes, clay pots, casserole dishes, and roasting pans.

Use hot water and a stiff brush to clean, but avoid using soap on unglazed earthenware.

GLASS

Although it heats up unevenly, glass absorbs and retains heat well. You'll find it used in numerous applications including coffeepots, teakettles, saucepans, skillets, pie plates, bakeware, serving dishes, mixing bowls, and barware.

Use soapy water and a plastic mesh pad to remove burned-on food. But scrub carefully. Once glass is scratched, it gets harder to clean. Getting streaks? Try wiping with some white vinegar.

NONSTICK COATING

These pots and pans are a modern miracle. But beware: scratching and overheating can give off a potentially toxic gas!

Always use wooden utensils on nonstick cookware and wash with soapy water and a synthetic sponge. To remove stains, add a cup of water, two tablespoons of baking soda, and half cup white vinegar in the pan and boil until the stain subsides.

STAINLESS STEEL

Stainless steel itself is not great at conducting or retaining heat. So in cookware, other metals, like copper, aluminum, iron, and carbon steel are added. You'll find it in all sorts of kitchen utensils including cookware, bakeware, silverware, sinks, and fixtures like showerheads, water spouts, and handles.

Just use a soapy sponge or synthetic scrubber and dry with a cotton towel to eliminate water spots. If you find yourself with a burned-on mess, try using a baking soda and vinegar concoction to scrub it clean, but never use harsh chemicals or metal scrubbers. To remove calcification like lime and other minerals found on bathroom and kitchen fixtures, ye old white vinegar does the trick.

TIN

You'll find this lightweight material used mostly in baking utensils and molds. It's actually just a coating over a base metal like copper, iron, or steel.

To clean, sprinkle some baking soda or washing soda on a damp cloth and rub. Then rinse and dry. To get rid of the burned-on gunk, just soak it in warm water with baking soda. Be careful not to scratch the coating or you may find the base metal rusting and corroding soon.

WOOD

The best wooden kitchen utensils are made from hardwoods like beech, boxwood, oak, and maple. Wood's uses vary from cutting boards, meat tenderizers, salad bowls, rolling pins, and, of course, spoons.

A wooden implement needs only a brisk rubbing with a damp cloth, and an occasional rinsing with warm water. Scrub with the grain and wipe dry immediately. Too much soaking in detergents will dry out natural oils and warp wood.[10]

To sanitize your wood, pop it in the microwave for five minutes on high and eliminate any moldy odors by rubbing on salt and lemon.[11]

PLASTIC

Soap and hot water works on these guys. Minimize stains by spraying your Tupperware with cooking oil before storing tomato sauce, beets, or other colored food. And wipe with white vinegar or lemon and salt to make the smell go away.

COUNTERTOPS

Use your homemade all-purpose cleaner on most any countertop. Spritz and wipe dry with a cloth. Follow with a damp sponge and a dry cloth.

If you have stone, marble, or Corian countertops or have any apprehension about using cleanser, just use mild dish soap and water. No need to risk it.

Do you have grungy grout in your tile? Dip an old toothbrush in vinegar and scrub the tile grout to remove mildew and mold. Helps to prevent new growth, too.

SINKS

Make a paste with borax and lemon juice to clean porcelain sinks, baking soda and vinegar for stainless steel. Rinse well and dry with a cotton cloth.

GARBAGE DISPOSAL

Clean by crushing ice in the disposal. Throw a citrus peel and some baking soda in and grind with cold running water to deodorize.

STOVE

Take a minute and wipe the stovetop clean after each use. It keeps food from building up and baking on. Don't use a scouring pad or abrasive cleaners or you'll scratch the enamel. A little baking soda and water paste will do the trick just fine.

Most stoves have removable drip pans under the burners. Just flip the burners up and pull the drip pans out for easy cleaning. Also, the entire stovetop can be lifted to clean underneath the cooking surface. You'll be surprised by how much food and grease ends up here.

OVEN

No one likes to clean an oven. So keep yours clean by placing a piece of foil or a broiler pan under your cooking to catch the drips. You'll find lots of people lining the bottom of their ovens with foil. Resist. It impedes the heat circulation, which is important for proper cooking and the life of your oven.

Don't have a self-cleaning oven? Throw the racks in the bathtub to soak in some warm, soapy water while you scrub. Dissolve three tablespoons of washing soda in four cups of warm water. Spray or wipe on, wait twenty minutes, and clean. For the tough stuff, use some baking soda and steel wool.

REFRIGERATOR

Pull everything out including shelves and drawers. Drop 1 to 2 tablespoons of baking soda in a bucket of warm water and use it to wipe down the insides of the fridge, the drawers, and the shelves.

Most people don't even know about the drain pan at the base of the fridge. It collects the condensation run off from the fridge as well as what's drained when the freezer is defrosted. To empty and clean yours, you may have to remove a panel located either on the front or back of the unit. Check your manual for details if you are not able to locate the pan. While you're down there, sweep or vacuum out the front grill that covers the condenser.

If you have an automatic icemaker or water dispenser, be sure to clean around the pipes and connections. Also, be sure to thoroughly clean the gasket around the door. An old toothbrush dipped in a baking soda and water solution is a good way to get in between the folds of the casing. To prevent mildew from growing in these dark crevices, follow up with a rinse of white vinegar. Potent, but effective.

Make sure the outsides match the insides by wiping the exterior with a soapy detergent solution.

Pull out the fridge and vacuum behind it for a final touch or dust underneath the unit by attaching a cleaning rag to a yardstick or a broom handle.

Take the time to wipe off food jars and containers as you reassemble.

WHAT'S THAT SMELL?

If the smells emanating from your kitchen are not the kinds that cause your guests to compliment your culinary skills, your fridge may not be clean enough.

INVENTORY REDUCTION

Pop the tops on those storage containers, peak inside the foil wraps, and slide open the crisper drawers. Forgotten food that has long passed its peak lurks in most refrigerators and freezers. Open up a big black bag and clean out anything suspicious or dated.

AN OUNCE OF PREVENTION

Place an opened box of baking soda on one of the shelves to prevent odors. Other options include whole coffee beans stored in a brown paper lunch bag or activated charcoal like what is used to filter water in fish tanks and water filter pitchers.

Facing a super-sized smell that just won't go away? Time to take drastic action. Clear your fridge completely and try one of these odor-eliminating options.

- Open a loaf of store-bought white bread and place it on a paper towel in the fridge. Leave it overnight where it will soak up the smells. The next morning dispose of the bread and wipe down the entire inside surface again before putting any food back inside.
- Soak some cotton balls in pure vanilla extract and leave at the back of every other shelf inside.

FREEZER

Hopefully you have a frost-free fridge. But if not, don't fret. Defrosting is a cold snap.

- Unplug your refrigerator and remove all the food. If you have a cooler, store the food in there; if not put it in a sink or tub and cover with ice and a blanket to keep it cool.

- Put a pot of warm to hot water in the freezer to speed up the defrosting process.
- Use a wooden spoon or other un-sharp object to loosen the ice and break it off the walls of the freezer.
- Once the ice has been removed, wipe down the freezer with warm soapy water, rinse, and towel dry.
- Put the food back and plug in the fridge.
- By the way, if you don't unplug your fridge, your motor will have to work double time, which may cause it to blow. Doh.

MICROWAVE

Throw two tablespoons of lemon juice or vinegar and two cups of water in a large, microwave-safe bowl and zap on high for two or three minutes. Take out the bowl and wipe that nasty Nelly down.

DISHWASHER

One more of the greatest inventions of the twentieth century—you load it, turn it on, and a short time later you have clean dishes. It's genius in its simplicity. And yet a proper loading technique remains a mystery for many.

One of the biggest sins when using the dishwasher is overcrowding. If the water can't get to the dirt, it can't very well clean the dishes! Make sure dishes and silverware aren't nesting or piled on top of each other, and that the spray arms can move about freely.

Other things to consider:

- Plastic stuff goes on top or it will melt.
- Place items like glasses, cups, and pots upside down so the dirty water doesn't get caught inside.
- Load tall to short, outside to inside.
- To avoid chipping, don't let stemware touch other items.
- Mix silverware in each section of the basket, with some ends pointing up and some pointing down to avoid nesting.
- Load sharp knives pointing down!

If you have a problem with a white or foggy film residue on your glasses, you may have hard water. Get rid of the spots by adding a little vinegar to the wash.

COFFEEPOT

Clean your coffeemaker every few weeks by filling the water reservoir with equal parts white vinegar and water and putting it through the brew cycle. Rinse by brewing three more pots of fresh water.

BLENDER AND FOOD PROCESSOR

Squirt a little liquid soap in the canister, fill half way with water, and put the lid on. Then just blend the mess away and rinse!

FLOOR

Forget the sponge mop and kick the bucket. Microfiber is your new best friend. These washable and reusable pads fit onto a flat mop head on a telescoping pole, kind of like a Swiffer. The pole is adjustable so you don't have to kill your back, and the swivel makes it easy to get into tight corners.

But what makes microfiber really great? Strong, lint free, and synthetic, every fiber is split during the manufacturing process to make it ultra-absorbent and able to hold just enough water to clean well without dripping. The positive-charged fibers attract negative-charged dust and suck up the dirt instead of redistributing it wherever you mop. And your floor is left virtually dry! Because of their efficiency and superior cleaning ability without the use of harsh chemicals, microfiber is becoming the preferred mopping method of hospitals![12]

Find one online at **www.ActNatural.net**, **www.AsSeenOnTV.com**, **www.MicroFiber.org**, or try **www.eBay.com** for a good deal.

Make this your last step in cleaning the kitchen. Start by getting every object off the ground and out of the way. Pick up the rug, take it outside to shake it, and toss it in the laundry hamper. Put chairs up on top of the table or remove them from the room entirely. Don't forget the garbage can.

With a dry microfiber mop, begin in the most remote corner of the room and work your way out. Use a dragging motion rather than a pushing motion to pile up the crumbs and try to keep the mop on the ground as much as you can. Pick up the pile with a dustpan and trash it.

Remove the microfiber pad from the mop, and shake it outside. Rinse it in hot water with a little dish soap, and wring it out well before replacing it onto the head. It should be damp, not dripping.

Repeat the mopping process. For tough spots, add a little scrubbing pressure with your foot. And be careful not to box yourself in or you'll have to walk across your clean floor to get out of the kitchen!

Wash your microfiber pad in the machine with a warm or hot load. No need to dry it, use harsh chemicals, or fabric softener.

KEEP IT UP

set some day-to-day habits to keep your weekly kitchen cleaning from getting unruly:

- End each day with an empty sink. Run the dishwasher or hand-clean the dishes before you go to bed and put them away in the morning while the coffee's brewing.
- Give everything in your kitchen a home and keep it there. Take the time to file the piles.
- Wash as you go. Rinse and wash pots and pans as you finish cooking with them. And keep a bucket of water in the sink to drop used utensils in before food dries on solid.

TO YOUR HEALTH

The kitchen is a haven for germs and bacteria. In fact, 50 to 80 percent of common illnesses like colds and food poisoning are caused by household crud. It's even said that, hold your breath, your cutting board is liable to have two hundred times more fecal matter on it than your toilet seat![13] Eeewwww! Use some caution and some common sense to stay healthy.

- Wash your hands with hot water and soap after you go to the bathroom, before food preparation, and after handling raw meat, poultry, or fish. Sing "Happy Birthday" to yourself twice and you've hit the timing mark.
- Wash fruits and vegetables with hot water and a nylon scrub brush.
- Don't cross-contaminate by cutting raw meat and vegetables on the same cutting board. Designate a different board for each task. Differentiate them by color or use a Sharpie to name them.
- Clean cutting boards immediately after each use, *especially* if you've cut up

raw meat, fish, or poultry. Use an antibacterial soap with hot water and a scrub brush. Disinfect often with white vinegar.

- Refrigerate your leftovers within two hours. Mark the date on the container so you know when they've gone toxic (two to four days).
- Replace kitchen sponges and dish towels often. Wash sponges in the dishwasher to disinfect, towels in a hot laundry cycle.
- If you use your dishtowel to wipe meat juice off your hands, put it in the hamper immediately. You don't want to contaminate everything else in the kitchen or use it to dry the dishes later.
- Don't overlook water faucets, handles, and drains as potential bacteria sources. Use baking soda and an old toothbrush to get rid of stains, grit, and grime and run a couple pieces of lemon or lime with hot, running water through the disposal.
- Doorknobs and refrigerator handles are prime targets and should be disinfected often, too.
- Remember the garbage can! Antibacterial soap, hot water, and white vinegar are your superheroes. Be sure to check the walls around the can, too, in case your aim is as bad as mine.

FRESH AIR

Simmer vinegar or your favorite herbs in water on the stovetop for a natural, clean scent around the house. Cinnamon and cloves are yummy.

MAYDAY, MAYDAY

stuff happens. Whatcha gonna do?

CLOGGED DRAIN

There are countless drain cleaners out there, almost all of them toxic to the environment and corrosive to pipes. Try an earth-friendly recipe. Remove any standing water. Then pour a ½ cup of baking soda followed by a cup of white vinegar into the drain and let it foam for a few minutes. Follow by pouring very hot or boiling water down the drain. If that doesn't work, call your landlord. Say "no" to Drano.

GARBAGE DISPOSAL

If your garbage disposal poops out, try the reset button located on the bottom of the unit under the kitchen sink.

Keep fingers, silverware, and fibrous foods like cornhusks out of your disposal. If it jams, turn the motor off immediately. Squeeze a tablespoon of dish soap into the disposal and try to loosen the jam with the handle of a wooden spoon. Turn off the circuit breaker to the disposal and use a pair of needle-nose pliers to remove the offending item, then turn the circuit breaker back on.

WATER LEAKS

Call your landlord.

GAS LEAKS

Natural gas doesn't smell of its own accord. Because this stuff is deadly, a distinctive odor is added for your protection. If you think you smell it, do not hesitate. Follow these steps to save yourself and your apartment:

- Get everyone out of the house immediately.
- Call your gas company using a neighbor's phone, a cell phone from outside your home, or a pay phone.
- Call the Fire Department if you can't reach your gas company.
- Don't turn any electrical appliances or lights on or off. Static can cause a spark big enough to ignite.
- Don't smoke or light a match or a candle.

FIRE

There are three types of common kitchen fires: dry, grease, and oven.

DRY FIRE

Boiling the moisture out of a pan is most often the culprit of these kinds of fires, so pay attention when you're cooking. Turn the burner off and cover the pan with a lid. If this doesn't immediately extinguish the fire, use a fire extinguisher and call 911.

Turn off the oven and leave the door closed until the flame is out. Opening the door will fuel the fire with an influx of oxygen, which could cause a back draft. If the fire doesn't go out immediately, call 911 from a neighbor's house.

GREASE FIRE

These are scary and marked by heavy flames shooting into the air. If you can, put a lid on the pot and turn the burner off. Use a fire extinguisher or douse the flame with baking soda and call 911. And know when it's time to abandon ship.

Warning: Never, *ever* throw water on a grease fire. This will only fuel the fire, causing it to get bigger and possibly spread to the walls or cabinets. Also never try to carry a grease fire in its pot or pan out of the house; you'll run the risk of transferring the fire to other parts of your apartment.

YOU GOT BURNED

I'll never forget the day my neighbor caught on fire. There, under the window, I cat-napped lazily in the cool breeze when a thunderous *bang* and a bloodcurdling scream jolted me out of my daydream. What the . . . ?

I ran upstairs with my broom (just in case I would be called upon to fend off murderous thugs) to find my neighbor nearly motionless in a stench of burning flesh, her hair and eyebrows still sizzling. She got distracted while lighting the pilot in her oven, forgetting to open the door before turning on the gas. The oven filled and blew up like a fireball when she put the match to it.

To the emergency room we went, and she was lucky to heal with only minor scarring.

The moral? Use caution in the kitchen! Everyone gets burned, but it doesn't have to be a tragedy. Minor burns are easy to treat at home by soaking them in cool water, treating with aloe vera cream or antibiotic ointment, and covering with gauze, but if you have any question about the severity of your injury, leave it alone and get to urgent care.

FYI, lay off the ice. It will traumatize more than help.

DOROTHY, YOU HAVE BUGS

From swanky uptown condos to artsy downtown lofts to houses in the hills, everybody has something crawling underneath those faux finishes. The trick is to handle the situation with grace and keep those critters in the walls and off the countertops.

What are you going to do? Beyond moving out, you can litter your place with little, black bug motels that you'll inevitably step on and vacuum up. You can have a guy spray dubious ingredients around your place every month. Or you can try something very, very inexpensive and simple. Boric acid.

BORIC ACID

Sounds a lot more sinister than it really is. It's a white powder that you can get for pennies at any decent hardware store. The way it works is, bugs get the acid powder on their tiny little feet and when they lick it off, as they are prone to do, it not only kills them, but it does it in a manner that sends them scurrying out of your apartment. And one application lasts for years!

HOW DO I USE IT?

Pretty simple. Spread the powder around the perimeter of your kitchen, particularly where the floor meets the wall. Use a putty knife to spread and jam it into the gaps and crevices behind all the baseboards, cabinets, etc. Use a lot, get it in as deep as possible, and wipe away the excess with a dry cloth.

Remember, this product is safe to use, but it is a form of poison (like most bug-killing products), so read all the instructions on the package before you begin. Wear rubber gloves, avoid getting it in your eyes or handling excessive amounts, and use common sense when it comes to pets and children.

HOW ABOUT THOSE FLYING VARMINTS?

Rid yourself of flies and moths. Use citronella candles or oil and keep some basil and pennyroyal plants around the kitchen.

DETOX

If for some reason you find yourself with ammonia and bleach in your cleaning routine, never mix them together. This makes for deadly toxic fumes.

bathroom basics

cleaning the john doesn't have to be a messy job. Take your knowledge of surfaces from the kitchen to the bathroom to make this job more gratifying than gross.

SINK

---

make a paste with borax and lemon juice to clean porcelain sinks, baking soda and vinegar for fiberglass or acrylic. Scrub with a wet sponge, rinse well, and dry with a cotton cloth. Apply vinegar to chrome or stainless-steel faucets and handles and use a toothbrush to get to those hard-to-reach places.

MIRROR

wash mirrors with vinegar and wipe dry with a newspaper or cotton cloth. Smear shaving foam all over your mirror and wipe it off with newspaper to prevent it from fogging up.

SHOWER AND DOORS

this is the rough job, but someone's got to do it. Spray on your homemade general-purpose cleanser, scrub down the walls and doors with a plastic scrubber, and rinse. It's that easy. Make a habit of rinsing your shower doors with vinegar to keep soap scum and green stuff to a minimum. And get a squeegee to wipe your doors down after every shower.

Are your walls to high too reach? Pull out your microfiber mop and use it on the shower walls before you do the floor!

Don't forget the soap dish. Vinegar and baking soda is your buddy.

SHOWERHEAD

if you have hard water, you may get mineral deposits in and on your showerhead. You'll know it's time for a good cleaning when the shower pressure is more like a dribble than a downpour.

1. Carefully remove the showerhead with an adjustable wrench. Lefty loosey, righty tighty.
2. Place it in a small pan with half a cup of vinegar and a quart of water and boil for fifteen minutes.
3. Let it cool, but don't rinse before replacing.

Can't get the showerhead off? Fill a large plastic bag with half a cup of vinegar and a quart of water. Secure the bag around the showerhead with masking tape, rubber bands, or string, and let it soak overnight. Remove bag.

SHOWER DOOR TRACKS

check your shower door tracks once in a while for built-up gunk. They are ripe for growing mold and mildew.

1. With an old toothbrush, loosen up whatever is in there and wipe it out with a sponge. You can even vacuum it out using that long-nosed attachment.
2. Spray tracks with a white vinegar and get to scrubbing with that toothbrush.
3. Use a glass or bowl to rinse the tracks off.

SHOWER CURTAIN

shower curtains are a breeding ground for mold and mildew, but cleaning them can be tricky. Here are three ways to get you started:

1. Throw your shower curtain in the wash with one cup of lemon juice, one cup of vinegar, and a couple of old towels to act as scrubbers. Pull the curtain out of the machine before the rinse cycle and hang it back up to dry.
2. Lay your curtain out flat and scrub it with your homemade general purpose cleaner. Hang to dry.
3. Leave your curtain hanging and spray heavily with your homemade general purpose cleaner. Let it sit for a bit, then rinse being careful not to pull the curtain off the rings.

Help prevent mildew on your shower curtain by soaking it in a salt-water solution and hanging dry.

TUB

if you've got a tub-and-shower combo, clean the tub last. Get it wet and scrub the entire surface with baking soda. Rinse well and wipe clean with a sponge. Pay special attention to the areas around the drain, the fixtures, and where the tub meets the wall. Those are prime areas for soap-scum build up and can usually benefit from a toothbrush and vinegar scrub.

For tough stains in the tub, make a paste from cream of tartar and hydrogen peroxide. Let it dry then rinse the stain away.

Need to get rid of some ugly tub decals? Try prying them up with a hard plastic scraper. Shy away from metal or you may scratch your tub. Lay a vinegar-soaked rag on top of the glue for ten or fifteen minutes and scrub clean with a scrubby sponge. Repeat if necessary, or cover the goop with petroleum jelly and scrub again in ten to fifteen minutes.

CLEAN YOUR TOILET LIKE A HOTEL MAID

who better to emulate than the real porcelain goddesses?

WATER, WATER EVERYWHERE

All that water in the bowl serves no purpose but to dilute your cleanser. Use your toilet brush to push the water out of the bowl in a plunging motion. Eventually you will be able to remove all but about a cup of water. Once the water's gone, leave the brush in the bowl to block the opening into the sewer.

NOW THE CLEANSER

Dump your borax and lemon juice paste into the bowl. About a quarter of a cup will be plenty. Take your little brush, now saturated with cleanser, and swab the inside of the bowl, especially under the rim. You can't see it, but if your bathroom has a smell that won't go away, it may be what's accumulated under there.

NOW WE WAIT

This is the time that a hotel maid uses to change the beds, wipe down the mirrors, sink, tub, etc. She finishes these tasks in ten to fifteen minutes. Find a similar task to amuse yourself for at least ten minutes while the cleanser does its work. When the time is up, swab again. Most of that ring around the water's edge should easily slip off now. If it doesn't, wait for another ten minutes, then swab again. The natural cleanser should start lifting away the grime. You don't even need to scrub.

FLUSH

Hold the brush in the water so it gets rinsed along with the bowl when you flush. Then swab the bowl with the rinse water and swish your brush around to rinse it out. Flush again and tap the puff on the edge of the bowl to shake the water out.

PRETTY ON THE OUTSIDE

After all that work you can't deny the outside of the commode! Use a lemon-juice and vinegar spray to wipe down the bowl, the seat, the lid, and the tank. Don't forget the base. You never know who's been missing the bowl.

WALLS

are you a fan of hairspray? It loves to stick to the walls, trapping hair, dirt, and dust with it. Wipe them down once a month with hot soapy water or with your microfiber mop.

FLOORS

just like the kitchen, dry-mop with the microfiber mop and follow with a wet mop.

MAYDAY, MAYDAY

stuff happens. Whatcha gonna do?

OVERFLOWING TOILET

Act fast! Grab the plunger and pump, making sure the plunger's bell is completely covering the drain inside the toilet. This should suction out whatever's in the way. If that doesn't work, reach behind the toilet and find the tap that controls the water flow into the toilet and turn it off. Then call your landlord to send a plumber out on the double.

NO-FLUSH TOILET

Remove the lid from the water tank and jiggle the flush handle. There should be a chain connecting it to the rubber flapper valve down below. If it's not there, it's lying on the bottom of the tank. Dive on down and reattach to the hole in the handle, leaving a half an inch of slack.

STICKY OR LOOSE-HANDLED TOILET

Check that chain. It's probably a slack issue. Adjust with needle-nose pliers to create half an inch of slack.

MY TOILET'S RUNNING
- Check the chain slack.
- Check the float ball. Is it touching the side of the tank? If it is, bend it back away from the edge. If you lift it above the water level, does the running stop? If yes, gently bend the rod down until the float is resting a half an inch below the opening of the overflow pipe (that open pipe in the tank).
- Your toilet's still on the run? Could be a leaky float ball or a worn-out flapper valve. Call your landlord. He'll be happy to come right away when he realizes his water bill is climbing.

tana's habitat

SLOW DRAINS

Plunge first. Still slow? Try baking soda and vinegar. Let it sit for ten to twenty minutes before flushing with boiling water. If you're still stuck with a dawdler, call your landlord. Those commercial products can cause a lot of damage. Let him decide how to manage.

DRIPPY DRAINS

Most likely you need something simple like a washer or a seal. But because this repair will likely end up in an outing to the hardware store, I'd choose to call the landlord and save myself the trip.

I DROPPED IT DOWN THE SINK

Turn off the water so you don't accidentally flush it further out of reach! Look under the sink for the valves and turn them all the way to the right.

Did you lose a contact lens or something light? Get out your vacuum and the long hose attachment. Cover the tip of the hose with a nylon stocking, pull out the drain stopper, and start sucking. The nylon in combination with the vacuum's suction will trap your contact.

Too heavy for that? It's time for a surgical plumbing procedure.

- Make *sure* the water is off.
- Put a bucket under the P-trap, that U-shaped pipe under the sink.
- If you can't use your hands, use a wrench to unscrew the nuts that attach the trap to the other pipes.
- Yank the trap off and empty it into the bucket to recover your treasure.
- Reassemble the trap and turn the water back on.

SHOWER PRESSURE

Remove the showerhead and clean out the trap. You'll be amazed at how many rocks and deposits end up in there!

it all comes out in the wash

if you can read, you can wash. Everything you ever want to know about how a garment should be cleaned can be found on its label. Follow those instructions and you'll never have a problem.

Here's the key to the symbols you'll find there:

Machine Wash Instructions

| Normal Wash | Permanent Press | Gentle Cycle | DO NOT Machine Wash |

Water Temperature Settings

| Cold (< 85°F) | Warm (< 105°F) | Hot (< 120°F) | Hot (< 140°F) |

Bleaching Instructions

| Bleach as needed | Non-chlorine bleach as needed | DO NOT Bleach |

Special Care

| Hand Wash | DO NOT Wring |

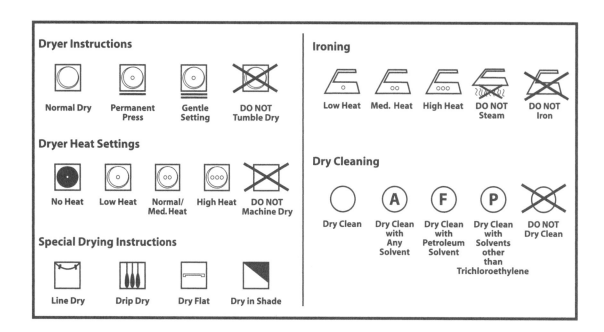

LIFT AND SEPARATE

the road to clean laundry begins with the type of profiling that's only PC in the laundry room.

COLOR AND TYPE

Put same colors together to avoid bleeding dyes, then separate by cycle temperature. If you're unsure, go with cold.

COLORS	MIGHT BE	WASH/RINSE TEMPERATURE
whites	heavy cotton, underwear, t-shirts, handkerchiefs, etc.	**hot/cold**
lights	striped whites, off-whites and pastels, permanent press, synthetics like nylon, polyester, acrylic, and washable woolens	**warm/cold**
darks	blacks, blues, browns, permanent press, denim, cotton, synthetics like nylon, polyester, acrylic, and washable woolens	**warm/cold**
brights	reds, yellows, oranges, fluorescents made from any fabric	**cold/cold**
delicates	fine linens, lingerie, washable silk, some synthetic fabrics	**cold/cold**

PULL IT OUT

Before you proceed:

- Pull super-dirty stuff out to wash together.
- Pull out lint-producing items like terry cloth and chenille to wash together.
- Pull out anything left in the pockets, turn down your cuffs, and turn your jeans inside out if you'd like to keep them from fading quickly.

SEE SPOT RUN. OUT, SPOT! OUT!

take the time to scour your garments before they hit the machine. Pretreat stains with these powerful solutions and let the laundry elves work their magic before they ruin your clothes!

- Baking soda
- Club soda
- Cream of tartar
- Denatured alcohol
- Dishwashing liquid
- Pump hairspray
- 3% Hydrogen peroxide
- Lemon juice—fresh or bottled
- Salt
- Shaving cream, foam not gel
- White vinegar

STAIN BASICS

- Get 'em while they're hot. Treat a stain as soon as possible.
- Walk, don't run. Blot, don't rub. Rubbing will spread the stain.
- Turn the garment inside out and work on the wrong side of the fabric first.
- Use a towel, napkin, or paper towel under the fabric to soak up the stain.
- Keep a stain stick or spray laundry treatment like Ecover by your laundry hamper, aka that mountain of clothes in the corner of your bedroom. Treat the spot before you forget about it and it sinks to the bottom of the pile.
- Never, never, *never* put a stained garment into the dryer unless you are 100 percent sure that the stain or spot is gone. The heat from the dryer will set the stain for life. That's a long time.

COFFEE TALK

Saturate the spot with hairspray—pump, not aerosol. Then work in a bit of bar soap or dishwashing liquid. Rinse with cold water. This will work for a "spot of tea," too.

DEATH BY CHOCOLATE

First, peel or brush off any chocolate left on the fabric and wet the area with club soda. Use a bit of soap and rinse with cold water. If that doesn't do the trick, blot with hydrogen peroxide. Rinse with cold water and follow with regular washing.

PETS AND POOP

If Spot finds a spot to call his own, like your favorite blanket, sweatshirt, or bedsheets, clean up and pick up what you can. Soak up the puddles with paper towels and saturate the area with club soda. Blot with more paper towels.

Still stinky? Use a generous layer of baking soda and let it sit for a day or two to absorb the odor and follow with a regular washing.

STUBBORN SALSA AND PESKY PASTA SAUCE

Spicing up your wardrobe should not involve wearing salsa or tomato sauces. For tomato-based stains try the old shaving-cream trick. Rub it in with a towel and rinse with cool water. Wash as usual. Or try a bit of denatured alcohol (the strong, industrial stuff). It works well when dabbed on the garment and followed with a cool rinse. Then wash as usual.

STOP WINE-ING

Follow these ideas with a cold-water wash.

- Saturate the stain with club soda and blot.
- Use a bit of hand sanitizer like Purell and gently work it into the spot.
- If the stain's still wet, grab the table salt and pour it over the entire spot. The salt will act like a sponge and soak up the wine.
- Make a paste using cream of tartar and water. Let dry and rinse with cold water.
- Squirt unscented shaving foam onto the spot and gently work it into the fabric using a towel or rag. Wet the towel and dab off with cold water. Buy a cheap brand or a store brand (about 99 cents) and stay away from the gels and scented varieties unless you want to smell like your sleazy uncle before a date.

Or try this trick my mom uses for getting wine out of her tablecloths. I swear, the first time I saw it in action, I thought my parents were participating in some voodoo ritual in our very own kitchen!

- Bring a kettle of water (1 quart to 1 gallon) to a rapid boil.
- This part requires two people. Over the kitchen sink, one of you should

stretch the fabric tightly while the other climbs up on a chair/countertop/stepstool with the kettle of boiling water. Slowly pour the boiling water from 4 to 6 feet above onto the stain and be careful not to burn the other person! Watch out for the steam, too.

■ Then, let the laws of physics take over from there and launder as usual. It really works!

BLOOD

For a fresh stain, splash on club soda and rinse with a steady stream of cool water. For dried or fresh spots, hydrogen peroxide (3 percent solution) is amazing. Don't freak out when the solution hits the stain and begins to bubble like crazy. Let the oxygen bubbles work their magic until you see them start to die. Rinse under the tap with a strong stream of cold water.

If a ring remains, try working in a bit of hand soap, rinse, and launder as usual.

SWEAT

If you find your T-shirts turning that pretty corny color under the arms, fill the sink (or a bucket) with warm water and add 1 cup of vinegar. Soak the shirt for at least 1 hour and launder as you always do. If you have a bar of laundry soap or nonchlorine bleach, work it into dampened fabric before you toss it into the washer. This should turn your armpits to charmpits.

INK

Ink is a tough one. Most people go for the hairspray first. But before you do, make sure that alcohol is the primary ingredient. If there is too much oil in the formula, the stain will spread and get worse!

If you don't have hairspray, use regular rubbing alcohol or denatured alcohol. Soak the stain and blot the ink with a rag or paper towel. *Do not rub* or the ink will spread. And, if you use a rag, remember to launder it separately. Throwing it into a regular wash might result in an ink stained load of laundry. Translation: You're scarred for life!

RING AROUND THE RUST STAIN

Try using lemon juice and salt. Put the garment on a hanger and place it outside in the sun to dry. Wash again as usual. Or try making a paste using cream of tartar and water. Let the paste dry a bit, and then soak the garment in a sink full of hot water. Follow it with a regular wash.

LIPSTICK ON YOUR COLLAR

Scrape off as much as possible using a spoon or other flat object, careful not to rub the stain into the garment. Wet the stain and work in some liquid laundry detergent or dishwashing liquid with your thumbs and forefingers and rinse with cold. If the stain remains, soak it in soapy water or a little vinegar. If it still remains, try soaking it in some nonchlorine bleach (Biz is my fave) and wash as usual.

START YOUR ENGINES

now, turn your machine on and choose the proper settings for your load: regular, permanent press, delicate, hot, warm, cold. The choices will vary by machine, so do your best! Add a small amount of detergent into the washer to mix with the water before dumping your clothes in. Be sure not to overload! Your clothes need room to agitate if they're going to get clean.

CHOOSE YOUR POISON

Phosphate detergents lead to algae-clogged lakes and rivers. Look for equally effective detergents with sodium carbonate or sodium citrate instead. Or make your own.

- Grate a third of a cake of pure soap (or buy soap flakes from the supermarket), and mix with one third of a cup of washing soda. Dissolve in hot water and top up with a little more water. The mixture will set to a soft gel. Use 2 to 3 cups per wash load.

BLEACH

Chlorine is found in many cleaning products, including detergents and bleach. Besides creating a mess of hazardous pollutants during the manufacturing process, you may be exposed to dioxins and other compounds as they seep out of your clothes and into your body. Chlorine is listed by the 1990 Clean Air Act as a hazardous air pollutant and federal standards actually regulate workers' exposure to it. Look at the ingredients. If you don't see the word *chlorine*, it may be veiled as *hypochlorite* or *sodium hypochlorite*.[14]

"But what about my whites?" you ask. Try a nonchlorine, color-safe alternative like Biz, or give this a try:

- Use 1 cup of lemon juice in half a bucket of water and soak your garment overnight.
- Too time-consuming? Substitute half a cup of borax per wash load to whiten whites and brighten colors.

FABRIC SOFTENER

I know, it smells yummy and that little bear is so darn snuggly. But guess what? That April freshness comes at a cost.

A few of the petroleum-derived chemicals found in fabric softener and on the EPA's Hazardous Waste list include chloroform, ethyl acetate, and limonene. These neurotoxic, carcinogenic, narcotic substances are passed to us through scent and residue on the clothes we wear and are known to cause cancer, birth defects, central nervous system disorders, and allergic reactions. The residue, which is what makes fabric feel so soft, also inhibits absorbency and may make treated clothes a fire hazard![15]

A cup of white vinegar in the rinse cycle will do the trick just fine. But if you just can't give it up, look for a soy-based softener or, at the very least, use unscented.

If it's the static cling that's got you down, pull your clothes out of the dryer while they're still a bit damp, or line dry—and your problem's solved.

ALL DRIED UP

proper drying can protect garments and minimize wrinkling.

- Check labels carefully for proper drying temperatures.
- Remove clothing from the washer as soon as the cycle ends and shake each piece before throwing it in the dryer.
- Clean the lint trap!
- Overloading will end in wrinkles. Make sure your clothes have room to circulate.

- Take your stuff out as soon as that buzzer goes off and hang or fold everything right away to help reduce wrinkling.
- Overdrying can cause shrinkage or other damage, so check your load for doneness every once in a while.
- Drying a small load reduces the tumbling effect and prolongs the drying period! Add a couple clean and dry towels to help.
- If you don't want it to shrink, don't put it in the dryer. Hang or dry flat on a clean towel or drying rack.

IRON MAIDEN

no matter what you do, some fabrics will beg to be ironed. Check the garment label for special instructions and use this handy reference:

FABRIC	HEAT SETTING
acetate, acrylic	cool heat
cotton, linen, ramie	steam with high or medium heat
nylon	low heat
polyester	low or medium heat
rayon, silk	iron inside-out on low heat
wool, mohair, cashmere, camel, alpaca	steam with medium heat

- Do not iron anything that's dirty or stained or you'll set the stain for life.
- Iron low-temperature garments first, then move on to those needing higher temperatures.
- Iron clothes while they're still damp or sprinkle them with water.
- Make sure fabric is smooth on the ironing board or you'll crease it! Dampen and re-iron if you do.
- Iron with the grain of the fabric.
- Iron rayon, polyester, and silk on the wrong side to eliminate shine.
- Hang newly ironed items immediately.

To starch or not to starch is really a personal question. Some folks like the crispness, that professional look. Spray the entire garment with starch and let it sit a bit before ironing. But make sure to use the proper heat setting or you'll scorch the starch *and* your fabric! Clean your iron with vinegar or nongel toothpaste between uses.

HAND-WASH

for your finest fabrics:

- Separate light from dark.
- Soak garments for five minutes in warm, soapy water. One quarter cup of Woolite works great.
- Dump the water out, pressing the garments against the side of the basin to remove any excess.
- To rinse, fill the basin with clean water, swirl the items around, and press against the side to squeeze out excess while dumping.
- Repeat twice.
- Lay the item flat on a white towel, roll it up, and press down to absorb the water.
- Hang or lay flat to dry.

MAYDAY, MAYDAY

stuff happens. Whatcha gonna do?

BLEEDING

Did your whites turn pink? Don't put them in the dryer! Load them back in the washer with some nonchlorine bleach like Biz and wash on cold.

SHRINKING

It's irreversible! Make sure your dryer is set to the right heat setting for each fabric and don't overdry.

PILLING

What are all those linty little balls on your favorite sweater? They're called pills and they're caused by the rubbing that occurs during normal wear. Minimize them by turning your garments inside out before washing. Remove them by pulling the fabric taut and cutting off the pills with scissors or a safety razor.

PRETTY IS AS PRETTY DOES

although I'd begun making furniture, I was nowhere near making a living at it. Instead, I paid my rent by carting around food for a company who made deliveries for upscale restaurants that didn't offer the service themselves. I made decent enough money doing it. A six-hour shift could sometimes bring in nearly $150 depending on how many people in my area were hungry, but with no mileage, gas, or maintenance allowance, my takings dwindled quickly. Especially on the more common days that only brought in $50.

As a newcomer to this job, my plebe status guaranteed only the worst routes. Mostly that meant that they were far away from our headquarters, which meant more driving. I didn't mind. What were a few more miles in the grand scheme of things? At least I had a job.

One evening, whilst transporting a BBQ Chicken Pizza, two Diet Cokes, and a tiramisu to a ravenous couple in Calabassas, I idled in the left-turn lane, willing the arrow at Topanga Canyon and Ventura Boulevard to turn green. It was a game I often played with myself during my shifts to help the time pass and to test my psychic prowess. But this time my powers had gone awry! I'd made a terrible mistake and, instead, willed the muffler right off my chassis!

Jarred from my hypnotic trance by a terrible clank and a loud roar befitting a NASCAR race on the testosterone patch, I pulled my 1979 convertible Bug to the side of the road and looked back to see my muffler in the middle of one of the busiest intersections in Los Angeles. I navigated my way through the rush-hour muddle. "Excuse me! Excuse me!" I cried, my arms flailing about, running back as if tiptoeing through the tulips to rescue my muffler, abandoned in the middle of the street.

tana's habitat

That thing was hot! I mean I *had* been driving for the last four hours straight. Helloooo! But my pride had been bruised enough by the noise—like Volkswagens aren't loud enough *with* a muffler—and traversing my way through that deadly traffic on foot was not a task I wanted to attempt again. So I bit my lip and hot-potatoed it back to the car, managing to drop it only twice. I found a couple of wire hangers in the trunk and, with the help of some divine inspiration, jury-rigged my muffler back in place so that I could finish my shift with some semblance of self-esteem.

I made it to the muffler shop the next morning, hoping they could do a quick fix, a cheapie. You know, just weld the sucker back on. No such luck. I needed a whole new muffler and it was going to cost me: $89 plus tax and labor. Man. Again, not my day. "Fine," I said. "Get to work. But I'd like to keep my old muffler."

The mechanic looked at me like I was nuts. "Uh, yeah, you can have it." He paused. "But *why?*"

I wasn't sure, really. But I knew that if I was forking out over a hundred hard-earned bucks for a new muffler, I was sure as hell going to get some use out of that old one. Besides, we had a relationship, my muffler and me. I couldn't desert her now; after all we'd been through together!

I took her home and cleaned her up with tender, loving care. As nearly twenty years of grease and grime were (very) slowly stripped away by steel wool and lacquer thinner, a rusty finish emerged. Oh, how I loved rust. Nothing could have been more perfect. And then it hit me. With her beautiful, cylindrical shape and a coat of varnish to bring out her luster, a lamp was just what the doctor ordered.

I'd never made a lamp before, but had once seen Bob Villa rewire one on a television show. It seemed pretty easy, so I dug deep into my memory bank to exhume his directions. I forced holes through her thick steel without breaking my drill and strung the lamp cord all the way through, with maximum effort. I stripped the wire and wrapped and screwed exactly how I remembered seeing him do it. It was a chore, but I did it and she looked gorgeous. There was one major difference, however, between Bob's lamp and mine. His lit up when he turned it on. Mine blew up.

How could she do this to me? After all I'd done for her, she nearly killed me! Twice! Was she getting back at me, traumatized by her new role or my demanding expectations? Maybe she needed a rest? I knew I did, so I put her in the closet. For a year and a half.

When I finally pulled her out from under the bags of art supplies and fabric that somehow found their way into her home, she seemed relieved to have breathing room, happy to see me. I, too, was no longer frightened, excited to reconnect. I brought her a very special gift—instructions, downloaded from the Internet. Together we sat as I found the error of my ways, a negative wire haphazardly connected to a positive post. *If only I'd known*, I thought as I snipped off the old socket and suited her up with a brand-new, shiny gold one. Finally I flipped the switch and she shone brightly, the way she was meant to.

We've been through a lot, my muffler and me, but we're still together, going strong. She still greets me at the door with a dazzling smile when I come home, and I still beam with pride just laying eyes on her.

That's my girl, the light of my life.

tana's habitat

make it, homie

decorating is fun! And it doesn't have to cost you a fortune. Use these concepts to get you started with the big stuff throughout your place.

PICK A COLOR, ANY COLOR

when it comes to painting, choosing a color can be paralyzing! Fear not. Open yourself to inspiration, strategize, and go with your gut. After all, it's only paint. The worst that can happen is a do-over.

MOOD

There's no doubt colors affect our psychology. Think about the kind of mood you want to set in a room, and choose a color that evokes that for you.

COLOR AND EMOTION

red	Love, romance, courage, danger, passion, and rage. Evokes richness, luxury, adventure, and ambition.
orange	Social and exuberant. Evokes warmth and happiness.
yellow	Warm and cheerful. Stimulates activity, communication, circulation, and appetite.
green	Suggests balance. Inspires feelings of restfulness, freshness, and informality.
blue	Peace, tranquility, wisdom, and well-being. Represents serenity, loyalty, and truth.
violet	The color of royalty and noble traits like love, truth, and justice. Dramatic, sophisticated, and sensual. Implies imagination
black	Sophisticated, elegant, dramatic, and formal. Evokes strength and power.
white	Symbolizes light, triumph, innocence, idealism, and joy.

INSPIRATION

- Choose a main color based on something in the room: the background of a rug, a pillow accent color, a painting.
- Use varying tints of the main color to accent spots in the room by mixing white into the paint. Or use a complementary color.
- Don't forget to take the color of your floors into consideration.
- Still confused? Take a look in your closet. That might give you an idea of what colors you're drawn to.

STRATEGY

- Pick up a variety of color chips from the paint store and tape them up on your wall to see how they work. If there are several shades on your sample, mask the others so you don't get confused.
- If you're nervous, do a test. Buy a pint and paint a four foot by four foot patch so you can live with it for a couple days. Experiment with a couple colors at the same time.
- If you can, take your inspiration piece straight to the paint store and have them do a computer color match.
- Because color batches vary, buy all the paint you'll need at the same time.
- Use the same trim color throughout the apartment to pull it all together.

tana's habitat

OIL OR LATEX?

latex paints have come a long way since their commercial beginnings in the 1930s. Thanks to huge technological leaps in acrylic binders and thickeners, latex now easily performs as well as oil. Not to mention, it's easier to clean, it doesn't smell as bad, it dries faster, and doesn't wreak as much havoc on the environment or your lungs. Go latex!

CAN I COVER EXISTING OIL PAINT WITH LATEX?

Yep. But only after you properly prepare the surface to be painted. To ensure proper adhesion, dull the old paint with sandpaper prior to painting. Or prime it.

PRIMER PRIMER

primers can affect the outcome of a topcoat. These undercoats are formulated to create a solid, even base, seal in stains, and ensure that paint goes on smoothly and bonds. Do you need to prime? Try this test: Paint a bit of one wall and let it dry. Put a Band-Aid on the newly painted surface and rip it off. If paint sticks to the bandage, the old paint won't support a new coat. It's prime time.

LOVE THE LUSTER

paint comes in a variety of sheens from dull to super shiny. Choose yours based on personal preference and traffic. Keep in mind, the glossier the appearance, the easier it is to clean.

WHAT YOU'LL NEED

- Paint
- Screwdriver or paint key

- Paint tray and disposable liners
- Roller frame and covers
- Paintbrush for trim
- Drop cloths
- Blue painter's tape
- Razor blade or utility knife
- Fine-grit sandpaper (150–200)
- Spackle and putty knife
- Ladder
- Acrylic varnish and artist's brush (optional)
- Paint stirrers (they're free!)
- Water bucket, sponges, and rags for cleanup

HOW MUCH PAINT DO I NEED?

It depends on how big your room is. Find the area of each wall by multiplying the width by the height. Add them together to find the room's square footage and compare with the specifications on the back of the paint can. Still not sure? Ask for help from the paint guy or visit **www.Glidden.com/products/InteriorCalculator.jsp** for an area calculator.

Looking for a price cut? Ask about returns, discards, or improperly mixed paints taking up space in the back warehouse. You may find a great color for half the price.

ROLL OVER

A roller cover's "nap" refers to the length of its fibers and is associated with wall textures. Choose a smooth, short-napped roller for smooth walls, and a long-napped roller for textured walls. Most important, make sure the roller cover you choose fits your frame. Don't walk out of that store with a nine-inch cover for your twelve-inch frame or you'll face spending another two hours in line at Home Depot.

HOW TACKY

I know what you're thinking. You're standing there in the tape aisle, staring at all the pretty colors, wondering just what the big deal is. How can one possibly warrant twice or even three times the price? Tape is tape, right? Just grab the cheap stuff.

Don't kid yourself. The right tape can make or break your effort.

When it comes to painting, tape's stickiness, or tack, is very important. If the tack's too high, you'll pull off whatever it's stuck to. If it's too low, all your taping will be for naught when the paint bleeds under the seams. Bite the bullet and shell out the extra cash for the blue stuff. It's made exclusively for this job and is superior to any other choice.

PREP TIME

take the time to carefully prepare. It will make a big difference in the end.

- Give yourself some space! Remove all the furniture from the area. At least pile it in the center of the room and cover it with a drop cloth.
- Take everything off the walls including pictures, nails, electrical switch plates, and receptacle plates. Don't forget cable TV outlets and phone jack covers. Store it all in a Ziploc bag for safekeeping.
- If you're painting the ceiling, remove any fixtures or cover them with plastic.
- Cover everything that can't be moved. Use plastic and painters' tape to cover receptacles, switches, radiators, and floors.
- Wipe down the walls with soapy water to remove dirt, cobwebs, and anything else that may stop your paint from sticking.
- Check the surfaces of your walls for cracks and holes. Fill them with spackle paste and sand lightly when dry.
- Use silicone calking to fill in gaps between wooden trim and walls. Squirt it into the cracks, then smooth with a finger.
- If your walls have extensive flaking, cracking, blistering, peeling, mildew, watermarks, tell your landlord and ask him to fix the problem.
- Rough up any glossy surfaces with sandpaper and wipe clean.
- Mask trim last, including baseboards, doors, windows, and ceilings with blue tape. Run a clean putty knife along the seams to ensure adhesion. Take an extra step for super-straight edges and use a small artist's brush to paint a thin layer of varnish where the tape meets the wall.

Caution: If your apartment was built before 1978 you may have lead paint. Sanding can be hazardous to your health. If you are worried, contact the **National Lead Information Center** at **1-800-424-LEAD**.

TAKE IT FROM THE TOP

start off with good lighting and ventilation. Open a couple windows and make sure you can see what you're painting to avoid streaks and missed spots. Always work from top to bottom beginning with the ceiling, then the walls, and finally the woodwork.

- Stir a spoonful of vanilla extract into the paint to reduce fumes.
- For the ceiling, use a brush to paint out 2 to 3 inches onto the ceiling from the wall to provide an overlap for the roller. Then, with a handle extension, work your way across the room from one corner, working in four-foot-wide strips until you're finished.
- When the ceiling is dry, start on the walls. Use a brush to paint corners, ceiling lines, and around woodwork.
- Dip your roller in the paint tray and roll it back and forth on the ridged part of the tray to squeeze out excess paint, avoid blobs and drips, and evenly spread the paint around the roller.
- Paint with diagonal, zigzag strokes like an N, and then go back over the area with longer up and down strokes to even it all out. Work in four-foot blocks and try to get to adjacent blocks before the previous ones dry to avoid lap lines.
- Keep a couple rags on hand for quick cleanups. Get 'em while they're wet.
- Wait four hours and apply a second coat. Wrap your rollers and brushes in a plastic bag and stick them in the fridge to avoid cleaning between coats.
- When the second coat is dry, carefully remove the tape. Try scoring the edge with a razor blade and ruler to avoid peeling.
- Trim time. Paint the woodwork, moldings, baseboards, and doors with a brush. Slow and steady wins the race.

THE CLEANUP

- Clean brushes and rollers right away with soap and water. A wire brush works wonders, too. Once the paint hardens, that's it.
- Save leftover paint to use for touch-ups later. Keep it fresh by placing plastic wrap over the mouth of the can before hammering down the lid.

tana's habitat

■ Label the paint can to remind you which room you used it in. Example: bedroom trim and the date used.

PROTECT YOUR HARD WORK

It takes at least two weeks for paint to cure and bond to your walls, so use caution when hanging your artwork and moving furniture around.

HOW ABOUT THE EMPTIES?

Hold on to empty paint cans, used trays, and drop clothes until your community has a hazardous material collection day. Call your city hall to find out when and where the next one is.

MORE FUN WITH PAINT

- ■ Use different colors for each wall.
- ■ Paint stripes, shapes, and patterns.
- ■ Visit **www.Zinsser.com** for tips on faux finishes.
- ■ Use chalkboard paint on one wall so you can change your décor daily.
- ■ Copy a picture onto a transparency and cast it onto a wall with an over-head projector. Trace the outlines with paint, pens, markers, or crayons. Or tap in small nails and connect the dots with string, embroidery thread, or fine wire.

MORE BIG IDEAS FOR YOUR WALLS

- ■ Wallpaper a room with fabric. Use liquid starch as glue and trim the edges after it's dry.
- ■ Use a billowy curtain to cover walls or divide rooms. Hammer grommets into the top end of a flat sheet and string on a wire.

THE GREAT COVERUP

next to choosing colors, coming up with creative window treatments may be the most difficult task you face when fixing up your place. The choices are great: sheers and shades, tiebacks and tea stains, velvet valances and satin swags. The list goes on and yet you still end up with the same old dreary drapes that cost you an arm and a leg.

Boring be gone! From paper to Plexi, use what you've got to add wow to your windows and you'll see why less is more when it comes to curtains and cash.

NO-SEW CURTAINS

Use sheets, tablecloths, or vintage towels to create a variety of great-looking windows.

WHAT YOU'LL NEED

- Flat sheets, tablecloth, or vintage towels
- Curtain rod or curtain wire
- Curtain clips
- Eyelet kit and hammer
- Hooks
- Decorative thumbtacks
- Stitch Witchery bondable webbing
- Iron, ironing board, and wet rag
- Ribbon

DIRECTIONS

1. Install your rod or curtain wire per manufacturer's instructions.
2. Use an eyelet kit to hammer grommets into the fabric every five inches and string on curtain wire.[16]
3. If the fabric's too long for the window, fold it over to make a valance. Attach a curtain clip every three inches and slide onto the rod.[17]
4. Forget the rod and wire and attach hooks to the moldings instead.
5. Skip the hooks and grommets and use thumbtacks. Decorate them with hot glue and seashells or silk flowers.[18]
6. Trim plain sheets with ribbon by using a hot iron and Stitch Witchery.
7. For a fuller look, use Stitch Witchery sheets together to extend the width of your fabric.

BRIGHT IDEA: Look for curtain wire and clips at Ikea or Home Depot. Don't forget to check near the shower curtains! And find Stitch Witchery, eyelet kits, and ribbon at Michaels, Jo-Ann Fabrics, or your favorite fabric store.

BOX YOURSELF IN

Since you've just moved into your new home, chances are you'll spend more time pawning off all those boxes than you did rounding them up. Put them to good use instead!

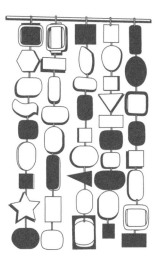

WHAT YOU'LL NEED

- Cardboard
- Utility knife
- Paint and brush
- Twine or string
- Tape
- Curtain rod
- Screws and screwdriver

DIRECTIONS

1. Using a utility knife, cut a variety of shapes from the boxes: circles, squares, rectangles, whatever you like.
2. Paint the shapes. Use one color or an assortment and be sure to get both sides.
3. While the paint's drying, hang the curtain rod above the window.
4. Tie several pieces of twine or string to the curtain rod and trim to the desired length.
5. Use clear packing tape to attach the cardboard shapes to the strings.

 BRIGHT IDEA: Get creative with your curtain rod. Use a pipe, a broomstick, rebar, or a bamboo pole.

BAMBOO AS THE ROMANS DO

With the big yoga craze, bamboo mats are as common as downward-facing dogs. Look for them at the dollar store or other discount import markets and make yourself a Roman shade with Asian flare.

WHAT YOU'LL NEED

- Bamboo mats
- Yarn or string
- Scissors
- Embroidery needle or crochet hook
- Curtain rod
- Self-adhesive Velcro dots

DIRECTIONS

1. Cut five 10" pieces of string or yarn per mat.
2. Use an embroidery needle or crochet hook to attach and knot the strings along the top edge of the mats, equally spaced.
3. Tie the strings (and, hence, the mats) to the curtain rod and hang above the window.
4. Place two sets of self-adhesive Velcro dots on the back of each mat. Put the soft sides on the bottom corners, ½" up from the bottom and ½" in from the sides. Position the hard sides halfway up the mat, ½" from the edge.
5. Want some light? Fold the mats backward and let the Velcro do all the work!

BRIGHT IDEAS
- Since the mats are so cheap, buy a bunch and tie them on top of each other for a layered look.
- Experiment with the placement of the Velcro to allow each layer to fold at a different length.

CATCH SOME RAYS

One part sun catcher, all parts eye-catcher, this colorful Plexiglas covering will cast its hue on you.

WHAT YOU'LL NEED

- Plexiglas or Lucite
- Jigsaw
- Goggles and work gloves
- Wax pencil
- Drill or Dremel
- 1" split rings or wire
- Needle-nosed pliers
- Fingernail polish remover and rag
- Curtain rod

DIRECTIONS

1. Draw shapes onto Plexiglas with a wax pencil. Make a template from cardboard and trace it to make your shapes all the same.

2. Cut out each shape using a jigsaw. Without question, wear goggles and work gloves, as the friction from the saw can cause the Plexi to melt and hurl itself into your eyes and onto your skin. Ouch.

3. Use fingernail polish remover on a rag to clean off the saw blade as necessary and remove any spikes or rough edges from the cutouts.

4. Drill holes at each end of the cutouts, not too close to the edge. The high speed of a Dremel works great for this project, but a drill will work, too, if you let it do the work. Don't push too hard or you'll end up with a bunch of broken pieces. Again, recall the melting plastic? Goggles and gloves are a must.

5. Insert split rings into each hole and link the pieces together with extra split rings until you reach the preferred length. If you've never used a split ring before, it's simple. Just open it up with needle-nosed pliers, run it through the hole, and close the rings back up. You can just as easily use wire or string.

6. Hang chained Plexi lengths by sliding the curtain rod through the rings. If your rod is too thick, pick up some shower curtain rings at the discount store. They always do the trick.

DESIGNER RUG OR DESIGN-A-RUG?

are you stuck with ugly linoleum or boring beige carpeting? Do you have gorgeous wood floors but want to warm up a room? Make your own ultra-hip, one-of-a-kind rug and save a bundle.

SAMPLE RUG

All carpet stores have samples. Some stores will even *give* you their old ones! Piece them together to make a great patchwork pattern of various colors and textures.

WHAT YOU'LL NEED

- Carpet samples
- 6–8 rolls of carpet tape
- Scissors
- Some imagination

Standard sample size is thirteen inches by eighteen inches. You'll need about thirty-five to make a nine-foot by six-foot rug.

DIRECTIONS

1. Go to carpet stores and beg for their old samples. You may have to visit more than one, but you'll find most stores to be pretty generous.
2. Clear the room and lay out the samples.
3. When you have your rug laid out like you want it, flip over each sample and connect each adjoining section with carpet tape.
4. Once complete, have a friend help you carefully flip it and move your furniture back into place.

MYPOD RUG

Try a variation with circular doormats or bathmats.

WHAT YOU'LL NEED

- Circular rugs
- Nylon cable ties
- Knife
- Scissors

DIRECTIONS

1. Lay out the rugs in a random pattern to fit the room.
2. Carpet tape won't work with circular rugs so you'll have to attach them together with nylon cable ties. Poke a hole inside the edge binding with a small knife or scissors where the two rugs meet.
3. Run the cable tie through the holes so they meet in the back. Pull the tie through the lock and cut off any excess.
4. Tie all rugs together until they are securely connected.

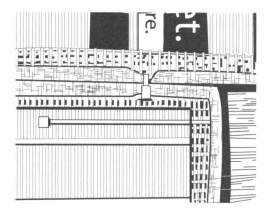

REMNANT RUG

Remnants are leftover pieces from rolls of wall-to-wall carpeting too small to use for a full-size room. Most carpet stores will have loads of them which can usually be purchased for a fraction of the price just so they can free up some space.

WHAT YOU'LL NEED

- Carpet remnants
- Carpet tape
- Carpet knife, utility knife or Xacto blade
- Paper and pencil to design your rug
- Measuring device

DIRECTIONS

1. Design your rug.
2. Shop for remnants
3. Lay out your pieces and cut to size with a sharp blade. Cut from the back. It's easier.
4. Attach remnants together with tape. Be sure to run the entire length of the seam.

IN A BIND

Give your rug a finished look and keep it from fraying by having it bound. It isn't necessary, but it sure does look pretty. They can do it for you at the carpet store. It'll cost you about a buck a foot (and up) depending on the type of binding you want.

SHE LOVES ME PILLOW

make this pretty little daisy sham or personalize it to your own taste.

WHAT YOU'LL NEED

- Fabric (white for petals, contrasting for pillow)
- Pillow form
- Ribbon
- Thread
- Straight pins
- Sewing machine
- Glue
- Iron
- Ironing board
- Scissors

DIRECTIONS

1. Cut a piece of fabric large enough to cover your pillow, envelope style.
2. The face and back will be equal with a smaller flap folding over the top.
3. Leave a two-inch seam allowance on the edges.
4. Check out this diagram.

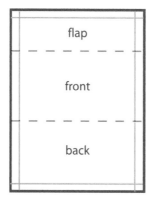

– – – – – – fold here
——————— sew here

5. Fold over ribbon to form loops using a straight pin to secure them.

6. Stitch the loops closed with a sewing machine and you've got leaves.

7. Just wind and wind three or four colors of thread into a mish-mash clump.

8. If you're having a tough time making it stay in a ball, use a little glue and a straight pin.

9. Cut a handful of petals from your white fabric.

10. Arrange the stem, petals, and leaves on the good side of your fabric. Pin everything in place.

11. Tack down the ribbon with your machine.

12. Use a dab of glue to put your petals in place. Once it's dry, just sew a little stitch down the center of each one for the vein.

13. Put a head on it! Use glue and a lot of it.

14. Clean the edges by sewing a small hem on the short ends of the fabric.

15. With the good sides facing, fold the fabric in three with the shorter flap on the inside.

16. Sew up the sides and trim the edges.

17. Turn it outside in and stuff it with your pillow.

18. Put the finishing touch on by handwriting "she loves me" on a prominent petal.

HANG IT UP

when you're staring at a bunch of blank walls, hanging artwork can seem a little menacing. Don't let it get you down. Just follow a few guidelines to help you plot your course.

- Use small pictures for narrow walls and larger pieces for big spaces.
- When hanging art over a piece of furniture, it shouldn't be longer than 75% of the width of the furniture.
- Make a grouping of art or photographs on a wall to create an interesting focal point.
- Choose groupings based on a theme to create a story.
- Use frames and mats that are different sizes and shapes but complement one another.
- Consider lighting to emphasize your arrangement.
- Always hang pictures at eye level: 58" from the ground is a good benchmark.
- Tight spacing between prints should be two inches or less. Normal spacing should be between four and six inches.

GROUPINGS

group similar pieces   symmetrical arrangement

asymmetrical arrangement

museum arrangement

gallery arrangement

spacing

even number arrangements

HOW'S IT HANGIN'?

would you trust a tiny little nail to save you from seven years of bad luck? That's exactly what you're doing if you don't take the proper precautions to choose the right hardware for your mirrors and masterpieces. Choose your fastener by considering wall surface, size, and weight.[19]

DRYWALL

The safest way to hang a picture on drywall is to locate a wooden beam behind the wall (the stud) and drive a screw into it. But how do you find the stud?

- Stud finder to the rescue! These electronic devices sense the density changes in the wall and signal where the stud is. You can get one for as little as $10 at the hardware store.
- Tap, tap, tap the wall until the sound goes from hollow to dull. There's the stud!
- Find two, you've found them all. Generally, studs are equidistant from each other, 16", 20", or 24" apart. Mark them all the way around the room by measuring the distance between two adjacent studs!

Stud's in the wrong spot? Choose your hanger carefully.

- Picture hooks are rated by how much weight they can bear. For light frames and mirrors, regular picture hooks, elite picture hooks, or EZ hangers work great. Just hammer the nail in at an angle to provide the support required.
- For medium or larger pictures, use a toggle bolt or molly bolt for additional support. These have expanding wings once inserted into a wall.

PLASTER

Plaster is a lot harder than drywall, so attempting to hammer a nail through it is likely to cause cracking and chipping. Use a masonry bit to drill a hole and insert a wall anchor (or sleeve) that expands in the wall when you drive in a screw to provide more grip.

- Drill a hole just large enough to insert the anchor and tap the anchor until it's flush with the wall.
- Drive a screw into the sleeve, leaving a small amount protruding to hang your picture on or attach a fastener.
- Anchors and screws usually come packaged together with instructions on which size drill bit to use.

MASONRY OR BRICK

Use the same technique as plaster hanging. Or:

- Drill a hole with a masonry bit into the wall and fill it with epoxy.
- Place a fastener rated to hold the proper weight into the wet epoxy and let it harden completely.
- Use a chisel to remove the epoxy when you take your piece down.

FAUX SHUI

feng shui (pronounced "fung shway") is a Chinese system of living in harmony with the natural elements and forces of earth. Its goal is to achieve harmony, comfort, and balance, first in your environment, then in your life. Feng shui is an art that can take Chinese masters thirty years to perfect! So rather than trying to decode this evolved and involved science in a thousand words or less, here are some **faux shui** basics you can apply to your habitat in minutes.

THE FIVE ELEMENTS

The five elements are one of the basic building blocks of feng shui. According to Chinese belief, each of these elements depicts a different aspect of ch'i, or vital energy flow. Fire stimulates, earth stabilizes, water softens and blends, wood expands, and metal strengthens and concentrates. Feng shui says that if you apply these elements to your environment in a harmonious way, you can bring balance into your life.

YIN AND YANG

According to feng shui philosophy, these fundamental energies yin (feminine) and yang (masculine) are everywhere and in everything. The goal is to create balance so that neither force dominates.

FENG FACTS

Numbers and shapes have significance in feng shui. Incorporate them into your space to bring prosperity into your life.

NUMBERS AND THEIR MEANINGS	
0	completeness, harmony
1	beginnings, independence
2	polarity, complementary forces
3	creativity, growth
4	strength, permanence
5	change, action
6	collaboration
7	withdrawal, introspection
8	money, good fortune, material power
9	satisfaction, completion

SHAPES AND THEIR MEANINGS	
circle	completeness, harmony, continuity
square	solidity, permanence, strength
triangle	change, movement toward a goal
rectangle	growth, expansion
curved or wavy lines	flexibility, adaptability
straight lines	rapid movement

THE WAY TO THE BANK IS THROUGH YOUR KITCHEN

The Chinese believe wealth is generated in the kitchen, so keep your kitchen clean and well organized.

GET LUCKY

- Fill a red envelope with rice and leave it in your kitchen. Rice is a symbol of prosperity and red is for luck. It also works as your "in case of emergency" meal.
- Display a gold star in your work area. It's a good reminder to do your best.
- Display the number 8 in your house; the Chinese consider it very lucky.
- The symbol of good fortune and success is a circle with an X through it. Make a bunch and display them everywhere you spend a lot of time to remind yourself that you're lucky. Your room, your office, your car. You can't have too much good luck or happiness.
- Place an item from each element (earth, metal, wood, and water) in a red container and place it in your living room. (I know, I know, fire's an element, too, but the red container takes care of that). This harmonious combo is said to encourage good luck and a well balanced home. Chinese brides typically wear red because it's considered lucky. Of course, that symbolizes a whole different kind of lucky in America!
- Put a live plant in your living room. Plants symbolize growth, life, and emotional well-being and add a nice decorative touch. Bamboo is a good choice. The Chinese consider it lucky because of its ability to grow quickly.

MAKE CHANGE

- Put a live plant in your kitchen. Plants symbolize growth. If you're a cook, plant an herb garden in your kitchen. For an added bonus, tape three coins to the bottom of the plant to encourage financial growth.
- If money is burning a hole in your pocket, place a large stone near your back door to block the ch'i from leaving your house.
- Burn some incense in a bamboo holder to stimulate prosperity. The Chinese believe incense will carry requests to the heavens and bamboo is considered lucky. Make a wish for added measure.

GOOD ENERGY

- Use your stove every day—it helps stir up the ch'i in your kitchen.
- Place a circular glass bowl near your front door. Symbolically, circles represent harmony and glass improves communication. And it's a great place to keep your keys, sunglasses, and all the other items you take with you every time you leave the house!
- Get rid of stuff you no longer need. It reduces clutter thereby freeing up space for ch'i to move about freely.
- Ringing a bell in your living room helps stir up the ch'i that may get stuck in the corners. You'll probably want to make sure no one is home or your roommates may think you're crazy.
- Hang a wind chime between you and a noisy neighbor or a loud street. It will help break up the negative energy before it gets to your house. It's definitely more effective than yelling, "Shut up!"

live it up

have you seen something outrageously cool in someone's apartment lately? Chances are they didn't buy it. And if they did buy it, they probably got ripped-off! The newest wave in second-generation retail has boutique and antique storeowners finding flea market bargains and side-of-the-road giveaways, slapping on a coat of paint or whitewash, and calling it vintage. Oh yeah, and marking it up 1000 percent. (Not an exaggeration.)

Skip the racket and save by beating them at their own game. Hit the road and find your own treasures. And remember, if it's in the free zone, it's yours.

DUMPSTER DIVING IS A EUPHEMISM

a recent study of emergency room visits strongly suggests that one should not actually dive into a Dumpster. And for good reason! Dumpsters are filled with broken glass, needles, rotten food, and dirty diapers. Look before you leap.

ZEN AND THE ART OF DIVING

There is no such thing as a bad neighborhood for Dumpster diving. But there is a bad time. Get out there early! Most *wanna-be* divers head into trendy neighborhoods after a leisurely Saturday brunch. Guess what? The early bird already got the worm. True divers have their eyes open all the time, through every alley diversion and roundabout course.

FOR RICHER

Exclusive neighborhoods have the best stuff, and people throw that good stuff away. However, residents can afford to have their junk hauled away, or zoning laws prohibit untidy trash heaps, or the servant who was asked to toss it in the trash throws it in his trunk instead.

FOR POORER

The theory is that poor folks are out of touch with what's hip and trendy. They don't know the chic value of what they're tossing, making low income neighborhoods lucky for some divers. I don't buy it. More likely, residents of these areas don't have much to begin with. Besides, these neighborhoods are densely populated. When a priceless item appears, it's claimed in less than 3.5 seconds. Only a well-trained, seasoned professional can compete under such rigorous conditions.

FOR PERFECT

Forget about the extremes—the fat middle is a diverse, fascinating place. Find the right old working-class neighborhood and you just might stumble upon a cool 1950s red linoleum kitchen table. Or a street of aging upscale professionals may give up a groovy deco lamp. And don't forget about businesses. Some of the best finds are behind shops and retail outlets.

START CRUISING

Drive down alleys. Turn down the street you'd never take in a million years. Keep your eyes peeled for rehabs, and don't forget, cool stuff often follows crappy stuff. Spring-cleaning may start with piles of old magazines and threadbare socks. But day three may end with the decision to finally get rid of the chair and magazine rack that have just been sitting in the basement all these years.

MIND YOUR MANNERS

Of course, you want to stay out of jail, not get beatup, and make it through the day without getting yelled at by someone's grandfather.

STAY OFF PORCHES

You could get shot, dragged into a strange living room, bleed to death on shag carpeting, and be immortalized in a Charlton Heston speech.

OBEY THE "RULE OF THE GRASS"

Don't be confused between *house grass* and *median grass*. Median grass is the grass between the street and the sidewalk. Unattended items in the median grass are fair game. Items on the other side of the sidewalk are sitting in house grass. Taking from house grass is called stealing.

STAY OUT OF ABANDONED BUILDINGS

First of all, it's trespassing. Second, just because a place is abandoned doesn't mean no one lives there. And it's probably somebody you don't want to meet in a dark stairwell.

TWO COLLECTORS CANNOT DIVE TOGETHER

They just butt heads. Your companion should be a curious assistant, not a serious collector.

WORDS OF WISDOM

Get on out there and start cruising! But before you hit the road, keep these final words in mind:

- Wear gloves
- Give anything upholstered the sniff test
- Drive someone else's vehicle whenever possible. Pee-eew.

DO YOU DO WINDOWS?

the day I moved into my new apartment building, I went on a little treasure hunt. Searching through hallway closets and laundry room cupboards, I lucked into a stack of French windows that had been removed from someone's apartment years ago. "These are too cool to sit in the laundry room," I thought to myself. "They'd look much better under my bed!"

And there they sat for what seemed like an eternity, calling my name, begging to be shaped into something wonderful and something useful.

And so they were. The coolest, best conversation piece of all time. My coffee table.

WHAT YOU'LL NEED

- A window
- 4 legs
- 4 pieces of 1" × 2" pine for apron
- Wood screws: 2" and 1" (nails will do in a pinch)
- Drill and bits (or hammer if you're pinching)
- 8 corner brackets (L brackets)
- Tape measure
- Pencil
- Liquid Nails or wood glue

LEG ROOM

Home Depot and most lumberyards or big hardware stores sell premade legs. They come in lots of styles and sizes so you can customize the height of your table to suit your cousin in the WNBA or the sawed-off couch you found in the alley.

STANDARD ISSUE

- Kitchen tables and desks are usually around 29" high.
- Coffee tables are usually around 16" high.

table height = window thickness + leg height

APRON STRINGS

The apron is a piece that runs along the bottom outer edge of the table top, forming a lip. Not every table's style calls for one, but in this case, it is important because it will hold the legs in place. I use 1" × 2" pine because it's cheap. The quality isn't always great, but I paint it in the end anyway, so it doesn't really matter.

In theory, each leg will sit on one corner of the window and the space between the legs, along the perimeter, will be filled with the apron. So how long should each piece of the apron be?

**size of apron = length (or width) of window
– combined width of two legs**

> **BRIGHT IDEA:** Not all legs are square at the top, so make sure you're measuring the side of the leg that corresponds with the side of the table you are measuring.

MEASURE TWICE, CUT ONCE

The lumberyard should be able to cut your apron pieces to size for you. Double-check your measurements before they cut and make sure their cuts match your specs. There's nothing more frustrating than getting home to find your pieces are all wrong.

ENOUGH MATH, LET'S BUILD

Lay your window flat on the floor, topside down. Set up the legs and apron pieces to make sure everything fits together as you wish. If something is not right, this is the time to fix it. Act now or live with it!

1. Glue the apron pieces in place with wood glue or Liquid Nails and let that dry. Make sure they're exactly where you want them because once dry, they're on there!
2. Predrill small holes straight through the apron and into the window every 4" to 6". Predrilling holes that are too big will inhibit the screws' ability to grip, so use a smaller bit.
3. Drive screws into the holes, being careful not to push them in past their limit until all the apron pieces are secured.

BRIGHT IDEA: Make sure your screws are long enough to go through the apron and part of the window without poking through the other side.

A LEG TO STAND ON

1. Nestle the legs into place.
2. Snuggle your L bracket so that it sits flush against the leg and the apron.
3. Mark the holes with a pencil.
4. Predrill the holes, being careful not to cut all the way through.
5. Replace the bracket and screw into place.
6. Continue until all of your legs are firmly attached.

KICK YOUR FEET UP!

- Turn over your window and you'll find you've got yourself a table! Kick up your feet and relax a bit while you decide how best to decorate your new conversation piece.
- Paint works wonders!
- Take off the original hardware and place a sheet of glass over the panes.
- Leave the hardware on and the panes uncovered for a sense of authenticity.

STACKED LAZY SUSAN STORAGE

this lazy Susan is simple, Simon. Use it to display knick-knacks, hold books, or store stuff. Spin the boxes and everything's out of sight.

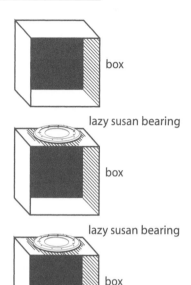

box

lazy susan bearing

box

lazy susan bearing

box

feet

WHAT YOU'LL NEED

- 3 wooden storage boxes
- 4 plastic furniture feet
- 2 lazy Susan bearings
- Drill

1. Decorate boxes with paint, stain, stickers, etc.
2. Attach feet to the bottom four corners of one box according to the manufacturer's instructions.
3. Place the lazy Susan bearings and mark. Predrill holes and attach per manufacturer's instructions.

OTTOMAN

rest your weary feet on this easy ottoman. Build a bunch and, poof, it's a couch!

WHAT YOU'LL NEED

- Plywood cut to size
- Sandpaper
- 4 furniture feet
- Contact cement
- High-density foam cut to size and thickness
- Fabric
- Staple gun and staples
- Scissors

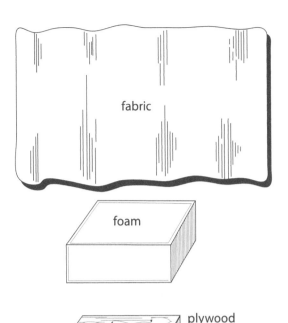

1. Sand the edges of your plywood smooth and attach the feet per manufacturer's instructions. Inset them one inch from the edge.
2. Coat the top of the plywood and the bottom of the foam liberally with contact cement. Once dry, connect the glued surfaces carefully.
3. Lay fabric flat, wrong side up, and place ottoman form in the center.
4. Staple fabric to underside of plywood on one side. Moving to the opposite side of the ottoman, pull the fabric tight as you staple it to the underside. Start stapling in the center and work your way out to the edges, smoothing out any wrinkles as you go.
5. Repeat with other two sides and trim the excess.
6. The corners are the hard part. Pretend you're wrapping a birthday present. Tuck, fold, and smooth.

BRIGHT IDEAS
- Get high-density foam at an upholstery supply shop or fabric store. Try Jo-Ann or Michaels.
- How much fabric you need will depend on the size of your ottoman. Add 6" to both height and width of combined plywood and foam measurements.
- Decorate with buttons, bric-a-brac, or dingle balls.
- Play with shapes. Try round, paisley, or rectangular.

MEDIA CABINET

make this stylish media cabinet to hold all your components, CDs, and DVDs to boot.

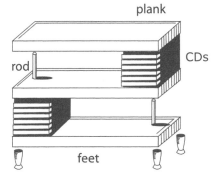

WHAT YOU'LL NEED

- 3 2" × 12" pine planks cut to desired length
- 4 furniture feet
- 2 wooden or metal CD cases
- Measuring tape
- Saw
- Curtain rod
- 2 sets of rod flanges
- Drill

1. Paint or finish wood as desired.
2. Attach furniture feet to bottom plank per manufacturer's instructions.
3. Measure height of CD cases and cut two pieces of curtain rod to match.
4. Attach flanges as shown in diagram per manufacturer's directions and insert rods.
5. Slide CD cases into place.

sample CD case

WHAT THE HECK'S A FLANGE?

Flanges are the end pieces that hold a closet rod in place!

ORGANIZE ME

- Label media cables with tape and a Sharpie so you know what's what.
- Use old dressers, lingerie drawers, or apothecary cabinets to store CDs and DVDs.
- Scrap your jewel cases and get flip books for your music and movie collection.
- Stack hardbound coffee table books and top with a sheet of sturdy glass to use as a side table.
- Fill this media stand with baskets instead of your electronic equipment to store magazines, pamphlets, maps, or travel books.

tana's habitat

peking ducks in a row

o pantry, great Food Stash, Giver of Life, Supplier of Infinite Snacks, why do you have to be such a total disaster area? I will try to love you despite your dented, aging cans; skunky, gummy shelves; and weevils out the wazoo. Yet more often than not, I fear you will frustrate, even repulse me as I turn my back on you to order take-out from that excellent Thai place up the street.

PARTY IN THE PANTRY

map out your new food-storage system before you even begin stocking up on snacks. As you plan, remember the three ideal conditions of a perfect pantry:

DRY

Humidity fosters the growth of mold and causes crackers and cereals to go undesirably soggy. Keep all bulk products in moisture-proof containers with reliably airtight lids. If you live in a moist climate, keep an open box of baking soda on the shelves and change it regularly.

DARK

Light causes accelerated deterioration of nutrients. Therefore, when using clear jars for storage, hang a door curtain to shield exposed goods from the light. Or choose opaque containers.

COOL

The ideal temperature for food storage is 50° F. Air temperatures lower than 40° or higher than 80° will cause food to spoil quickly. Avoid storing food near heating ducts, ovens, or refrigerator motors.

HAVE IT ON HAND

experts may have a tried-and-true pantry checklist to foist upon you. But I say what you keep in your pantry is entirely dependent upon the eating habits of your bad self. This isn't an outline of what you *should* keep in stock, but rather what you *could*. Base the contents of your pantry on the items you are most likely to use and remember to check labels of each and every item just in case special ingredients mandate cold storage.

THE RUNDOWN

- Canned meats (with the exception of some hams)
- Sweeteners like honey, molasses, and sugar
- Cooking oils such as canola, sesame, olive, and grape seed
- Pasta and noodles of every ilk: rice, egg, soba, wheat, udon
- Nuts
- Prepared cereals
- Coffee, tea
- Dried beans, peas, and lentils
- Snacks galore: chips, crackers, and cookies
- White rice

- White flour
- Spices (see exceptions below)

These goods belong in your refrigerator or freezer, as room temperature is simply unsuitable:

- Whole-grain flours made from wheat, barley, or rice
- Ground meals including those made from corn, flax, almonds, and oats
- Paprika, red pepper, and chili powder

As you load your shelves, date each and every item with the month and year. Keep a Sharpie handy to date your goods every time you bring home a new bag of groceries. Group common items together and keep older items near the front, rotating the new from behind as you use the old.

When all is neatly arranged, breathe a sigh of relief. You're one step closer to a functional, user-friendly kitchen.

USE ME

efficiency is excellent

- Keep equipment near the place it will normally be used, e.g., pots and pans close to the stove, knives by the work surface.
- Hang a towel rack over the stove and use S hooks to hold pots, pans, and lids
- Nail a trellis or some chicken wire onto a wall to hang utensils on.
- Put a shelf above the stove for commonly used things like wooden spoons, spatulas, timers.
- Organize your cupboards with heavy stuff underneath the counters, lighter things above.
- Keep like items together.
- Store appliances and pots and pans that are rarely used in an out-of-the-way place.
- Use a three-ring binder to keep take-out menus and loose recipes together.
- Use an acrylic cookbook holder instead of a can of soup to keep your recipe book open and stain-free.

- Use a wall-mounted magnetic rack for keeping knives handy and in great condition. Look for one meant to hold screwdrivers and wrenches at the hardware store and save a bundle.
- Hang a stemware rack under a cabinet to save valuable cupboard space.
- Display your serving platters or fancy dishes on a wall with the use of plate fasteners. Gourmet art!

OOH, SPICY

do you love to cook? Are you lost without curry? Find an accessible and space-saving place for your spice rack.

- Look for wall-mounted or pyramid racks.
- Stack your spices on a lazy Susan to make use of an out-of-the-way corner of countertop.
- Line an empty drawer with a spice jar liner.
- Use an undercounter spice rack below kitchen cabinets or under the sink.
- Try door-mounted racks for the back of your pantry door.
- Use magnetized spice jars and arrange them on the fridge.

RUSTED CABINET INLAY

if you've got inset cabinet doors, try this little trick to gussy them up. They're great to hang magnetized clothespins on to keep your recipes at eye level.

WHAT YOU'LL NEED

- Sheet metal cut to fit your inlay
- Instant Iron Kit (*Available at stores like Home Depot, Michaels, and Jo-Ann Fabrics*)
- Sponge brush
- Sandpaper
- Sponges
- Disposable brush
- Velcro dots

1. Start by brushing Instant Iron onto the sheet metal with a sponge brush.
2. Sand when dry and repeat until covered.
3. Lightly sand.
4. Brush Instant Rust solution onto dried stainless steel in a random pattern and let it dry.
5. Continue rusting until you've got the desired effect.
6. Lightly sand between coats if desired.
7. Attach to door panels with sticky-backed Velcro.

BRIGHT IDEAS
- Buy sheet metal at a roofing supply store. Bring your measurements and let them cut it for you.
- Watch the edges—they're sharp.
- Vary your rust-applying technique. Use a sponge, pour, or speckle to get an authentic, textured outcome.

REFRIGERATOR POETRY

homemade refrigerator magnets are sure to entertain you as you cook or just pop into the kitchen for a refreshment. Want to leave a message for your sweetie? Got a message for one of your roomies? Leave it on your fridge.

WHAT YOU'LL NEED

- Magnetic printer paper
- Printer
- Scissors
- Words of wisdom

DIRECTIONS

1. Simply print up your favorite words and icons and print them out onto magnetic paper. Cut them out and start getting creative. It's fun and a whole lot cheaper than buying the store-bought versions.

2. Magnetic paper can be found at any office supply store.

sleepy time

outfit your bedroom with the right gear and make it a retreat, a comfort, a place you like to be.

PUT IT TO REST

a mattress is the high-ticket item you'll be spending a third of your life on! Arm yourself with some knowledge and buy the best you can afford. To soften the blow, remind yourself that it will probably last you ten years.

THE FOUNDATION

A box spring is made to work with a mattress to provide maximum support and should be considered in your buying process. Look for steel-reinforced box springs and significantly increase the life of your mattress.

TO THE CORE

The most important part of the mattress, made up of metal coils, is the core. The number of coils in a mattress corresponds to how much support it provides. The more coils, the more support.

High coil count = firm mattress
Low coil count = soft mattress

A coil's gauge refers to the thickness of its wire. Heavy gauge coils offer more support than light gauge coils. Steer clear of mattresses with low count, heavy gauge coils or you're bound to go lumpy at lightening speed.

High number = low gauge = thinner coil wire
Low number = high gauge = thicker coil wire

Coils are kept in place by other wires called interconnecting wires. The more of these, the less likely your coils will spring a leak.

FIRM FACTOR

Soft or firm is a matter of preference. The only way you'll know your mattress style is to try a bunch out. But beware the fluff! Fancy features like pillow tops and foamy fillers will increase the price without adding any value. In fact, these extra elements will likely wear out well before your mattress does. If you're down with down, buy a removable feather bed, pillow topper, or egg-crate mat. They're much more affordable to replace.

LOOKING FOR THE PEA

- Test-drive lots of mattresses before you buy.
- Check the warranty. Most premium mattresses come with at least a ten-year warranty, though they may be voided if the mattress has been stained.
- Get comfortable. Take off your shoes and take a nap! Ask for a pillow or bring your own. Don't pick your mattress until you've lain on it for at least fifteen minutes straight.
- Roll around from the center to the edges to make sure the support is even. And check for extra support around the edges for sitting.
- Will you be sharing your mattress? Bring your partner and figure out how much space you need before choosing a size.

- Check the ticking (the fabric cover). Quality fabric will be cotton blend or damask, though it may also be a synthetic.
- There's always room for negotiation. Don't be afraid to haggle.

MATTRESS SIZES	
king or eastern king	76" wide by 80" long
california king	72" wide by 84" long
queen	60" wide by 80" long
full or double	54" wide by 75" long
twin or single	39" wide by 75" long
twin extra-long	39" wide by 80" long

BRIGHT IDEA: Buy a mattress at least six inches longer than the tallest person sleeping on it.

ON GUARD

Watch for sneaky salesmen. They like to push for the extras. What's more, manufacturers make the same bed with different names and price points to sell at different stores making comparison-shopping virtually impossible! Feel it out.

CARE FOR ME

Keep your mattress clean by covering it with a cotton mattress pad. It will absorb perspiration and can be removed and washed. Also:

- Rotate your mattress per manufacturer's instructions.
- Only use the handles for positioning. Lifting may cause damage.
- Don't sit on the same spot or you may cause sagging.
- The "do not remove" tag? They mean it. You'll need it if you have to file a claim against the warranty.

TRANSFORMER

not ready to take the leap? If you're starting out with a less-than-stellar mattress, find support to transform your lumpy, bumpy bed into a nest fit for Goldilocks.

FEATHER BEDS

BAFFLE BOX

Square boxes stitched through the feather bed to allow for an even distribution of feathers. Usually the most expensive construction, prices for a twin start at around $99, king-size around $199. Department stores like **Bloomingdale's** or **Macy's** are a good place to go to check out top quality options, but for buying on a budget try a bedding specialty shop like **Bed Bath & Beyond** or a retailer like **Target**.

BAFFLE CHANNELS

These divide the feather bed lengthwise but do not have the crosshatches for box construction. Prices for baffle channels start at about $99 for twin size as well, with king-size retailing for around $150.

MATTRESS TOPPERS OR EUROBEDS

A thinner version of the traditional feather bed, these are usually made with a baffle channel stitch. **Target** offers down mattress toppers in all sizes with prices ranging from $89 to $110.

THE FILLER FACTOR

A combination of down and feathers is standard, but some manufacturers use synthetic fillers, which will not give the same insulation as natural down. That's the soft and fuzzy first growth of ducklings (which stays on the soft under-bellies of mature ducks) and is a much better insulator than feathers. Be sure to check the tags.

EGG CRATES

A foam mat is a great way to comfy up a questionable mattress and leave little worry about allergy issues if the very thought of feathers brings tears to your eyes.

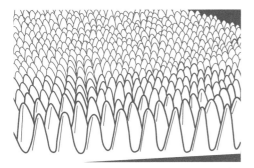

BRIGHT IDEA: **Pacific Coast Feather Company** has an Allergy-Free Warranty. The feathers are washed up to eight times to remove dust, dirt, and allergens. They claim that this process leaves the down and feathers at a neutral pH and back up the warranty with a 100 percent refund if returned within thirty days. **Pacific Coast Feather Company** products are available at retailers like **Bed Bath & Beyond, Linens 'n Things,** or online at **www.PacificCoast.com.**

PILLOW TALK

a walk down the pillow aisle at your favorite department store is bound to leave you with your fill of choices. Take some basics into consideration before you buy to get the pillow of your dreams.[21]

SIZE

The two common pillow sizes are standard and king, with a queen or a European thrown in here and there for good measure. Beyond the obvious match to the size of your bed, take your personal preferences into consideration. If you're a Munchkin and like being in control of your pillow, the colossal king may not be your best choice.

SLEEP STYLE

The main function of a pillow is to support your neck and spine, keeping it all aligned. Back sleepers will probably prefer flat pillows while side sleepers may go for something more sizeable to support their head.

FILLING

Do you like squishy or solid? Firm or flexible? Choose from a variety of fillings like down, synthetic, foam, and fusions to get the density you desire. Keep in mind, foam's life span is two years or less while good quality down can go up to ten years!

- **Natural** pillows are generally more expensive than synthetic pillows and contain down feathers and 100 percent cotton covers.
- **Synthetic** pillows are more reasonably priced. Filled with manmade materials such as polyester or foam latex, they're often preferred by allergy sufferers. In fact, they even make synthetic down, though it will cost you the same as the real stuff.

FIRMNESS

Firmness is determined by the amount of filling in the pillowcase.

- **Extra-firm** pillows are best for side sleepers. They fill in the space between your bed and shoulders to keep your neck and spine aligned.
- A **firm** pillow cradles the head and neck making it a good choice for back sleepers.
- **Medium** pillows are best for stomach sleepers. A softer pillow means your head won't be as tilted upward and won't create as much stress on the neck and spine.

COVERS

Pillow protectors are a great way to lengthen the life of your pillow. You just zip them over the pillow, and they protect it from perspiration or other stains. They come in several materials including 100-percent cotton, allergen-free, and waterproof. Satin protectors are made to lessen friction between hair and the pillow. A cure for bed head?

CARE

- Fluff your pillows regularly to help them maintain their shape and get some fresh air. Throw them in the dryer for fifteen minutes with a couple tennis balls for a professional plump-up.
- Most synthetic pillows can be thrown in the machine. Even some down pillows are labeled machine washable, but for best results, they should be dry-cleaned. Read the manufacturer's care tag and follow their instructions.
- Is your pillow pooped? Fold it in half and press down. If it springs back into shape when you let go, it's still supporting. If not, happy hunting!

SPLITTING THE SHEETS

in the modern bedding industry, there are no standards or laws to regulate sheet quality, making it hard to compare. Generally speaking, you get what you pay for. Factor in the following:

THREAD COUNT

Thread count refers to the number of horizontal (weft) and vertical (warp) threads in one square inch of fabric.[22] Bed sheets range in thread count from 80 to 1200, though you're more likely to see 180 to 500. But because many factors like ply and yarn size influence the measurement, a high thread count doesn't always imply high quality. For instance, a manufacturer can increase a thread count by twisting two thin threads together. By using two-ply thread, a 300 thread count sheet can instantaneously become 600 thread count!

The soft, luxurious feel that most people desire in their bedsheets is created with a thread count between 180 and 420 using 1-ply thread with a yarn size between 40 and 100. Check out the labels.

FABRIC

Bedding comes in fabrics from polyester to pima cotton, linen to silk. Read the labels to know if you're getting a blend.[23]

COTTON

Quality cotton is defined by the length, fineness, and strength of the fiber. The highest-quality cottons come from "long staple" fibers like Pima and Egyptian. These natural fibers offer breathability, softness, and durability making cotton the most popular sheet fabric in America.

TYPES OF COTTON	
pima cotton	grown primarily in the southwestern United States, Australia, and Peru.
supima cotton	a licensed trademark owned by Supima, a grower's organization promoting 100% American-grown Pima cotton.
egyptian cotton	cultivated in Egypt, offers superior softness and durability.

COTTON WEAVES	
cotton sateen	a soft, smooth feel and subtle sheen, you'll see no visible patterns of weaving.
cambric cotton	a soft, tightly woven fabric with one slightly glossy side, used with many down products.
percale cotton	a medium, plain weave found in low to medium count fabrics.

OTHER COMMON BEDDING FABRICS	
linen	made from flax, this crisp fabric is twice as durable as cotton and available in light and heavy weights.
polyester	a synthetic fabric offering greater softness than in previous years. extremely durable and wrinkle resistant.
microfiber	made from nylon, rayon, acrylic, or polyester. luxurious feeling, washable, and extremely durable.
modal/cellulose	made from the fiber of Beech trees, this fabric starts off soft and continues to soften with each wash. brilliant colors and sheen.
silk	luxurious, lustrous, and lightweight, this natural fiber reduces static cling, but has limited durability.

You'll even find sheets made from wool, merino wool, and cashmere!

TRUE FIT

Last but not least, make sure your linens will fit! Confirm the size of the sheet set matches your mattress; i.e. king, queen, full, single. And if you've got an extra thick mattress, make sure the pocket depth of the fitted sheet is deep enough. To find out, measure the edge of your mattress from highest point to bottom edge including mattress pads, feather beds, or any other extras.

ORGANIZE ME

get the most out of your bedroom with some of these space-saving tips:

- Maximize closet space with double-hung clothing bars, shoe racks, and stackable wire drawers.
- Maximize door space by hanging full-length mirrors and storage caddies on the backs.
- Display collections on your walls: belts, hats, scarves. Use decorative drawer pulls as hangers.
- Clutter under the bed is considered bad feng shui, but if you want to risk it, find boxes made specifically for that purpose. It's a great place to store out of season clothes.
- Enlist nightstands to hold your reading materials and other necessities.
- Eliminate the clothes pile by making a hamper handy. Make it pretty so it can be part of your décor rather than taking up your limited closet space.

PLATFORM

this simple, adaptable platform bed sets the stage for REM state.

WHAT YOU'LL NEED

- Particleboard or plywood for platform
- 1" × 4" pine boards for trim
- 1" × 12" pine boards for base
- Straight metal straps
- Wood glue
- 8 L-brackets
- Wood screws
- Wood putty
- Drill and bits
- Putty knife
- Sandpaper

tana's habitat

1. Cut all your wood to size or have the lumberyard do it for you. The measurements of the platform are based upon your mattress size. So if your mattress is larger than a twin, you'll need to join a couple pieces of particleboard to achieve a big enough piece.

Platform length = Mattress length + 2"	**depends**
Platform width = Mattress width + 2"	
1 x 3 Side trim = Platform length	**2 pieces**
1 x 3 Head/Foot trim = Platform width + 3.5"	**2 pieces**
1 x 12 Side base = Platform length – 2'	**2 pieces**
1 x 12 Head/foot base = Platform width – 2'	**2 pieces**

2. Sand everything smooth!
3. Attach platform pieces together by sealing the entire seam with metal straps.
4. Metal strap side up, center the four base pieces on the platform. Glue them together in a box, and, when dry, drive three screws into each end to hold the box together.

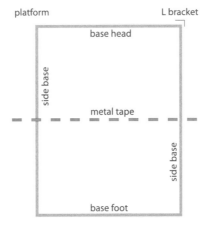

5. Attach an L bracket to each corner, too, for added support.
6. Use L brackets to attach the base to the platform and flip it over. It'll be heavy, so get some help.
7. Mark the trim boards so they rise above the platform by one inch to create a lip to hold the mattress in place. Predrill pilot holes, then use wood screws to mount the trim onto the platform. Putty any holes when done.
8. Sand the wood puttied areas, and paint, stain, or varnish the bed.

EASY HEADBOARDS

use this headboard idea with your new platform or any bed.

- Cut a piece of sheet metal to size and mount it on the wall behind your bed with bolts. Leave it as is, paint it with high-gloss enamel, etch a pattern into it, or create a design with a hand sander.
- Cover a piece of plywood with foam and staple fabric onto it for an upholstered look. Experiment with shapes and textures.
- Hang a tapestry or sheer behind your bed. Use a towel rod or hang it from the ceiling. Change the tapestry with the seasons.
- Weave plywood and dowels like this:

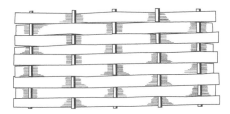

WHAT YOU'LL NEED

- A piece of plywood (4" wider than your mattress)
- Five 36" wooden poles (dowels)
- Stain
- Paintbrush
- Staple gun
- Picture brackets
- Drill
- Measuring tape
- Pencil
- Hammer

CUTTING AND STAINING

1. Have the lumberyard cut an ⅛"-thick piece of plywood down to 4" wider than your mattress, then cut into 4"-wide strips.

2. Lay out all the strips onto newspaper and stain the topsides of every piece. Let dry, then stain the backsides.
3. Stain the poles, too, but make sure you stand them on end; otherwise, you'll ruin the stain with newsprint.

STARTING OUT

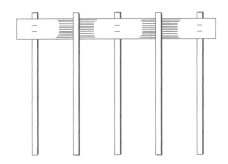

1. Mark all the poles one inch from the tops and the bottoms.
2. Center one plank over a pole on the one-inch mark. Staple the plank in place. Use a hammer if it doesn't go all the way in.
3. Staple a pole on each end of the plank at the one-inch mark, six inches in.
4. Place the remaining poles on top of the plank, so they're equidistant, fifteen to sixteen inches apart.

MOVING ON

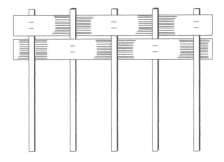

1. Weave the next plank around the poles opposite the first. Slide it up, snug against the other.
2. Staple it to the second and fourth poles.
3. Continue weaving and stapling until all the planks are stapled securely in place.
4. The even-numbered planks will get stapled only to the second and fourth poles. Odd numbered planks will get stapled to the first, third, and fifth poles.

IN THE END

1. With a measuring tape and pencil, mark spots for your picture brackets on the end poles behind the second plank.
2. Drill pilot holes and screw in the brackets. . . and you're done.
3. Turn it over and hang it up behind your bed. Notice all the staples are in the back? Nice work.

IT'S A THEME

with a little creativity, design is just a matter of subject.

BEACH ON THE BRAIN

Try an island motif on for size and it may just feel like vacation all year round.

BEDTIME

- Cut up a grass skirt or two and attach them to your bed frame with hot glue to make a bed skirt.
- Sew two colorful sheets together on three sides to make a duvet cover. Decorate the top by sewing different color fabrics to make a palm tree or hibiscus flowers.
- Make pillowcases with wave fabric or cut out surfboards or hula dancers from different materials and sew them on. Use a grass skirt as fringe around the edges!

TIME MANAGEMENT

- Make a clock from a vintage Beach Boys or Don Ho album cover.

LIGHTEN UP

- Glue bamboo rods around a lampshade and trim the top and bottom with plastic flowers. Pile seashells and starfish around the base of the lamp and hot glue them together.
- Hang your summer sarong or pareo over your window or above your bed like a canopy.
- String up palm tree lights around the perimeter of the room for mood lighting.

ACCESSORIZE

- Frame an old mirror with seashells.
- Use coconut shells for candleholders.
- Use shells, surfboards, seaweed, dancing hula girls, etc., as accent pieces around the room.
- Get a plant. Or even two! Orchids or palms. Don't forget to water!

Customize your own chic tie-dyed sheets on the cheap!

WHAT YOU'LL NEED

- 100% cotton sheets (white or light in color)
- Big plastic bucket
- Rit dye
- Wooden spoon
- Rubber gloves
- Garbage bag
- Rubber bands
- Squeeze bottle
- Scissors
- Sink or shower
- Washing machine
- Detergent

DIRECTIONS

1. Prewash your sheets, but don't dry them. They need to be wet.
2. Mix the Rit with water according to the manufacturer's directions and pour the solution into the squeeze bottles. Each color gets its own container.
3. Grab one wet sheet and start tying. The more wrinkles you tie into the fabric, the crazier the design will be. Wrap rubber bands or pinches of fabric in any way that strikes your fancy. There's no wrong way to do it as long as it's tight.
4. Place the tied sheet inside the garbage bag, and then start dyein'.
5. Rotate the fabric several times while evenly "injecting" the dye. Keep the nozzle directly on the fabric while you squeeze, and be sure to get the dye into the middle of every bundle. Be careful that the rest of the sheet's not sitting in a puddle of dye at the other end!
6. When you're convinced every millimeter you want covered with dye is covered with dye, wrap it up in the garbage bag to make sure it stays moist. Repeat with the rest of the sheet set.
7. Now let it sit. One to four hours is good. Read the manufacturer's directions on the bottle of dye for specifics.
8. Done? Snip off the rubber bands and rinse out the excess dye in warm (then gradually cooler) water till the water runs clear.

9. Wash with detergent and dry.
10. Have a luau!

IT'S A MOD, MOD WORLD

Give your bedroom a modern mood with clean lines, simple funky patterns, cool colors, and a healthy dose of whimsy.

YOU ARE GETTING SLEEPY, VERY SLEEPY

Most of your discount department stores have tons of choices for **mid-century inspired duvets** and **bedding** for you to choose from. If you don't find a duvet you like, make your own from two sheets that fit your bed.

- Sew up the edges leaving one short side open.
- Sew some Velcro onto the remaining side so you can insert or remove the duvet.

Add some pillows in cool hues, fancy designs, or fake fur.

Make a bed skirt from coordinating fabric, cut to size. Hot glue it to the inside of the bed frame. And yes, you only have to do the sides that show.

MOD MOODS

Set the mood by giving your ordinary lamp a makeover.

- Cover the shade with leftover fabric from your bed skirt. Cut the fabric to fit the shade, spray the shade with adhesive, and apply the fabric. Be sure to leave the fabric a bit long on the top and bottom to wrap to the inside to hide the edges.
- Why not leave the original shade and paint a lightbulb? Most any large craft store will have **lightbulb paint**. Any painted design will work to create a gobo effect on your walls. While you're at it, paint a bunch. Bulbs won't last forever.

A mobile is a great modern touch. Make one from bamboo skewers, string\, and old CDs. What about cocktail umbrellas? Or paper clips? Hang them from the ceiling with a self-adhesive hook.

Does your mirror need an update? Try gluing cheesy plastic flowers or other fun objects around the edges.

HOT MOROCCAN NIGHTS

If you're looking for a unique and fun space, take a trip to Africa. Rich in textures, patterns, and colors, **Moroccan style** is exotic and, above all, comfortable.

SUMPTUOUS BEDDING

- Make a duvet cover out of rich, colorful embroidered or intricately patterned fabrics. Feel free to mix and match fabrics for your duvet. Moroccan is all about layering textures, colors, and patterns.
- Use the same types of fabrics to make your bed skirt. Measure the distance from the top of your bed frame to the floor and add 2". Wrap the extra 2" around the bed frame and hot glue around the perimeter of your bed.
- For pillows, the more colorful and elaborate the geometric patterns, the better. For floor pillows you'll want to use heavier woolen fabrics stuffed with cotton. For the bed go with silks and velvets. Soft and smooth.

LAYERS

- Start with a **Kilim** rug. It'll warm up the room and create a space for lounging. Use one large rug or several smaller ones. If you use smaller rugs let them overlap. Layer, layer, layer!
- To dress up your window, make several strings of glass beads to hang in front of your curtains. You don't need a lot of beads; a few will go a long way. Attach the string to the top of the curtain with a needle and thread and let them dangle.

AMBIENCE

- Add a henna lamp or **Moroccan lantern** for mood lighting.
- Make your own **mosaic table**; it's easy to do. Cover a tabletop with small tiles arranged in a geometric pattern and glue them in place. Let the glue dry. Grout between the tiles, wipe away the excess with a sponge, and you're done.
- Make a **canopy**! Drape fabric from the ceiling above your bed or your whole room with tacks, Velcro, or even double-sided tape.
- Turn up the Afropop! Check out some hot **Rai** and **Shaabi** musicians at **www.AfroPop.org** for a mix of tradition and rebellion. Or search out African rapper Pitch Black Afro at **www.OneWorld.co.za**.

SHANGHAIED

Take a cue from Ancient China and add an Eastern edge to your room.

SLEEP TIGHT

- Make a duvet cover by sewing two twin sheets together on three sides. Decorate the top sheet by fabric painting a giant Lucky Buddha or pagoda on it. Trim the corners with big red tassels.
- Cut out colored-paper koi fish and tape them together to form a bed skirt.
- Make felt pillows with your favorite anime or Superflat illustrations on them.

IN THE MOOD

- Hang paper lanterns for mood lighting.
- Get a big Oriental umbrella and hang twinkle lights from the spokes underneath. Ooh, romantic.
- Get a bonsai plant or a lucky bamboo stalk.

OTHER FUN STUFF

- Make a message board! Get a piece of sheet metal from the hardware or roofing supply shop. Decorate the border with Chinese candies or toys. Glue the same (candy or toys) onto magnets and use them to post pictures or dream suggestions. Hang your board on the wall with self-adhesive Velcro.
- Use indoor/outdoor carpeting to create a lily pad rug.

private time

don't get bogged down in the bathroom. Make space for all the things you use regularly and keep everything else elsewhere.

ORGANIZE ME

- Mount shelves on the walls to hold wicker storage baskets.
- Use a wall-mounted soap dish, toothbrush, and cup holder to save counter space.
- Hooks are great space savers for towels or accessories like blow-dryers, brushes, etc.
- Hang a hotel caddy for towels over the toilet to store extra towels or rolls of toilet paper.
- Section off drawers with dividers and the space under the vanity with wire drawers.

JEWELRY AND MAKEUP

- Toss anything half used or over a year old.
- Attach magnets to the inside of the medicine cabinet to hold tweezers, clippers, and other metal bathroom tools.
- Keep a nice-looking basket or bowl handy on the countertop with all the items you use every day so you can grab them as you run out the door.
- Hang a shoe organizer on the back of the door to hold jewelry, makeup, shaving supplies, etc.
- Use an old spice rack and tins with clear tops to hold jewelry.

LINEN CLOSET

- Divide linens into categories and arrange by size.
- Keep sheet sets together by storing them in a coordinating pillowcase.
- Stack towels with folded sides out to make it easy to remove them from the shelf.
- Rotate fresh linens when putting them away so that one set does not get more worn than another. Newly washed stuff goes on the bottom.
- Store tablecloths and other little-used linens inside out so as not to collect dust on the creases.
- Hang tablecloths on towel racks or hooks mounted to the back of the door to save space.

PORCELAIN CONTEMPLATION

admit it. you read in the bathroom. Magazines, catalogs, newspapers, photo albums. You've probably even resorted to Band-Aid boxes and shampoo bottles. We are a nation of bathroom bibliophiles! Toss technology aside and let the bathroom door delineate one of the few sacred spaces available.

PERIODICALS IN THE PRIVY

Magazines are the most popular bathroom fare. Whether you just like the pictures or actually read the articles, try going beyond the usual ***People***, ***Vanity Fair***, and

Newsweek. Experiment with some wackier titles like ***Barbie Collector***, ***Varmint Hunter***, and ***Pasta Connoisseur***. If you're short on space, check out yard sales for old magazine racks or make your own by stringing a piece of twine or wire between two nails mounted on the wall next to your toilet. Hang your mags there!

> ## BRIGHT IDEAS
> - Decorate the nail heads by gluing on dice, marbles, or bottle caps.
> - If your wall is tile, use heavy-duty suction cups instead of nails.
> - Make sure your new rack is strong enough to carry the weight of the Travel and Tanning issue of *Wallpaper*!

I SEE LONDON, I SEE FRANCE

Is your old View-Master in storage somewhere? Pull it out and hang it near the toilet and watch your friends line up for a turn to use your W/C.

WHAT YOU'LL NEED

- View-Master
- Hook with screw tip
- Long, coiled phone cord
- Hot glue gun

DIRECTIONS

1. Drive the hook into the ceiling above and just to one side of the toilet so that when the View-Master is hanging from it, you won't get bonked in the head.
2. Find the middle of the phone cord and hang it on the hook so you've got two equal lengths of cord hanging down.
3. Sit on the pot. Find the height at which the average Joe or Josephine will easily access your 3-D view and snip the ends accordingly. Then snip about six more inches as the weight of the View-Master will pull on the cord, placing it at the right level. Some phone cord is more stiffly coiled than others, so you might need to experiment to get this just right.

4. Use a hot glue gun to attach the ends of phone cord to each side of the View-Master.
5. Fan the 3-D reels in an elegant container and place it on the tank.
6. Don't be late for work.

OTHER TIPS FOR YOUR TOITY

■ **Guinness World Records** was written to be read on the throne. Other reference books like small atlases make excellent quick-trip reading as well. Dorling Kindersley, a British publisher, makes a colorful, informative series of little books about things like the weather, wild animals, the solar system, which fit nicely into a small container left on a counter or the back of the toilet.

■ Collect autographs? Leave your book in the bathroom (with a pen, of course!) and wait for your friends to get famous!

■ How about a box of Trivial Pursuit cards nicely displayed on the back of the commode? There are also informational cards put out by the Discovery Channel, Bill Nye, and other educational publishers. Leave them in a little basket, box, or dish on the back of the toilet.

■ Are you a poet but ya don't know it? Mount a piece of sheet metal on the wall to display your set of magnetic poetry. This is the perfect setting for musings and deep insights.

■ Cover your walls with brown paper or butcher paper. Then invite your friends over to graffiti your walls! Here I sit, broken-hearted . . .

Bathroom readers of America, stand up and be counted!

On second thought, stay seated.

STEP INTO THE LIGHT

stop bumping into the walls, tripping over the cat, and waking up your neighbors every time you come home after dark with this funky night-light made with your Chinese Zodiac animal.

- Liquid resin and dye
- Resin hardener
- Soap mold (Michaels)
- Latex gloves
- Disposable mixing cup and stirrer
- Night-light fixture

DIRECTIONS

1. Mix the resin and hardener according to the directions on the back of the can and add a few drops of resin tint. Start small, a little goes a long way.
2. Fill the mold with resin one color at a time and let set.
3. After each layer hardens, mix and color more resin and fill to desired thickness.
4. Place the night-light attachment arm into the bottom center of the mold and let it sit until hardened. Overnight is good.
5. After the resin has completely hardened, peel back the mold. You may need to use scissors
6. Attach the night-light base, plug into the wall socket, and voilà! Let there be life—I mean light!

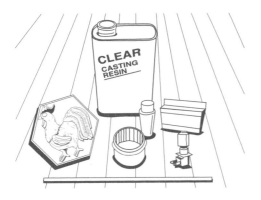

nothing, nothing on my walls

is yours the most boring apartment of all? Personalize your place with some simple, stylish accessories.

ALL BOTTLED UP

hang on to those clear glass bottles. You know the ones from sodas, store-bought Frappuccinos, olive oil, salad dressing, and the like? They make perfect frames for those photos of friends, family members, and vacations of long ago that sit in a box deep in your closet.

- Empty clear glass bottles
- Dish soap, water, and a sink
- Chopstick or pencil
- Scissors
- Photos

DIRECTIONS

1. Wash thoroughly inside and out.
2. To remove paper and glue rub the bottles with dish soap and let them soak in a sink of water until the glue easily separates from bottle. I like to let them sit overnight for total ease of cleaning. But an hour could work. If the glue is really sticky, try using a hair dryer and rubbing alcohol.
3. Let the bottles dry completely on the inside or the condensation will ruin your pictures.
4. Gently roll up photo and slide it into the bottle. You may need to use a chopstick to help unroll and push the photo in place. If the photo is too large for a bottle you might need to trim it a bit to make it fit. Or get a bigger bottle.

Prominently display your new collection of bottled photos. Your friends will think you're an artistic genius—as long as you've included them in the pack.

 BRIGHT IDEA: If you're short on shelf space, try hanging your bottles from the ceiling or on your wall with string or wire.

CAN IT, SISTER

don't throw out your soup cans, vegetable cans, or any other tin can. Clean them up and use them for unusual picture frames. They can be displayed anywhere you like.

- Empty tin cans in various sizes
- Tape
- Dish soap, water, and a sink

DIRECTIONS

1. Peel off the paper, then wash and dry the cans thoroughly.
2. Choose photos and trim if necessary.
3. Turn the can upside down and wrap the photo around it. Just run a piece of tape down each side.

STRING 'EM UP, BROTHER

run to Target and grab some clothespins, then hang your pictures out to dry.

WHAT YOU'LL NEED

- Mini clothespins
- 1 ¼" finishing nails
- Steel wire or string
- Hammer
- Measuring tape

DIRECTIONS

1. String some clothespins on a wire and hang between finishing nails! Super simple.

nothing, nothing on my walls 235

FRAME AND FORTUNE

what's in your wallet? If it's a collection of fortunes from years of fabulous Chinese dinner dates, you've got what it takes to create your destiny. Or at least a pretty picture frame . . .

WHAT YOU'LL NEED

- Picture frame
- Fortunes
- ModPodge
- Foam brush
- A picture

DIRECTIONS

1. Coat the frame with a light coat of ModPodge.
2. Place your fortunes randomly. Be sure to smooth out any bubbles.
3. Let it dry, then paint on another layer of ModPodge to seal the deal.

IT'S HIP TO BE SQUARE

Rubik's Cube meets alphabet soup! This whimsical, interactive wall hanging is made from sliding wooden blocks so you can change it as often as your mood.

WHAT YOU'LL NEED

- ⅞" casing bead
- Tin snips
- 2 10' × 6" × ¾" wood planks

- 1 4' × 1" × 1" piece of wood
- Paint and paintbrush
- Level
- Tape measure
- Phillips head screwdriver or drill
- 50–60 drywall screws
- Pencil
- Rollerball pen

Casing bead: L-shaped piece of metal used for hanging drywall. It comes in 8' or 10' lengths and will cost you around $2 per length.

DIRECTIONS

1. Paint both sides of each square.
2. Once the paint has dried, paint letters on every block, a different one on each side. Leave a few blank to use as spaces between words.

   - Remember to make more vowels than consonants and more Ls, Ms, Ns, Ss, and Ts than Xs, Ys, and Zs.
   - Mix up the fonts, upper and lower case, and colors of the letters. The more diversity you have the better.
   - If you have trouble with free-handing, print out letters from your computer and trace!

3. Cut casing bead to 4' lengths with tin snips.

BRIGHT IDEAS
- Try different painting techniques such as wiping off the paint to let the grain come through.
- Paint a couple with chalkboard paint or try staining a few.
- Glue on a mirror.
- Paint a design.
- Attach a photo.

THAT'S WHAT FRIENDS ARE FOR

The next few steps may require a second pair of hands.

4. With a level, mark the wall where you want the bottom of the first row. Make sure it's level.

5. Hang the casing bead here, one screw every few inches.

6. Measure 6" up and mark.

7. Install a second casing with screws to form a sliding track here.

8. Make sure it works! Slide a letter from one end to the other. It should slide easily, but not fall out.

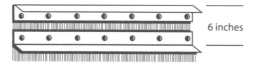

MOVING ON

9. Measure up 1" from the top track, mark, and level. Place the bottom of the second casing bead along this line and screw it in.

10. Measure up 6" to finish installing the next track.

11. Continue until all tracks are up.

12. Slide letters on tracks to form words or sentences and voice your opinion.

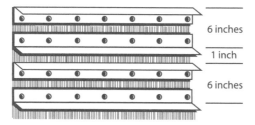

PHOTO GRIDLOCK

are your bookshelves filled with long-forgotten coffee table books? Get to rippin'! This cheap and unique piece of wall art is a great way to display those gorgeous pictures.

WHAT YOU'LL NEED

- Plywood or particleboard
- Pencil
- Box of 1" finishing nails
- Photos from coffee table books
- 120' of 28-gauge steel wire
- Measuring tape
- Masking tape
- Hammer
- Pin or needle
- Level
- Scissors or wire cutters
- X-Acto knife

HOW'S IT HANGIN'?

Do this project on a board you can hang or nail the grid directly onto the wall.

1. Measure the size of your wall space and decide how large you want to make your grid.
2. Add 2" to the length and 2" to the width. Cut your particleboard or plywood to this size or tape out the space on your wall.
3. From the edges, measure in 1" and mark lightly with a pencil to define a 1" border around the board.
4. From the left corner of this line, measure in 1" and mark, measure down 1" and mark. Repeat for each corner of the frame. You'll end up with eight marks.
5. Divide the space between the marks on each edge of the border into equal parts and mark.
6. On each mark, hammer in a nail leaving ½" above the board.

nothing, nothing on my walls 239

7. Choose your photos and gently tear or cut them out of the book with an X-Acto knife.

8. Arrange the photos on your board in the pattern you like.

9. Wind the wire around the nails creating a grid pattern over the photos. (Leaving the pictures in place will help you remember where each photo goes when you start attaching them to the wire.) Make sure to leave plenty of extra wire on the ends to make it easier to wrap and rewrap as you weave in the pics. You can always trim later or leave them long for an extra industrial feel.

10. Starting with the one in the center, determine how you wish to weave the wire through each photo, then make your holes with a pin. There is no right or wrong way to wire the photos, so do what pleases you. Go crazy. It's fun! Work your way out until you're all wired up!

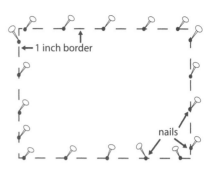

LET THERE BE LIGHT

are you an avid reader? Make this awesome book lamp from a copy of your favorite book. Rigged with a groovy push-button switch, you just squeeze the book and it's on—squeeze it again and it's off. The Clapper has finally met its match.

WHAT YOU'LL NEED

- Hardback book
- X-Acto knife and blades
- Push-button switch (we used UPC #17903)
- Electrical (power) cord with plug attached (at least 6' in length)
- Light socket (this should be a two-piece socket without an on/off switch)
- Hollow threaded rod (approximately 6"—the light socket attaches to the rod and must extend from the center of the book to approximately 2–3" above the book.)
- Lightbulb
- Lampshade
- Needle-nose pliers
- Screwdriver
- Pencil or pen
- Ruler
- Electrical tape

PREPARE THE BOOK

1. Open the book to the first page.
2. About halfway down the page, lay the push-button switch down with the cords running toward the binding and draw around the entire thing, cords and all.
3. Use an X-Acto knife to hollow out this area large enough for the push-button switch to sit in snuggly. Don't cut too deep. The button needs to stick out ¼" above the level of the first page in order to work.

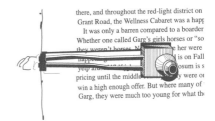

4. Where the push-button switch cords meet the binding, cut a hole large enough to pull an electrical cord through.

ELECTRICAL

5. Run an electrical cord through the spine of the book, bottom to top.

6. Next, run the cord through the hollow threaded rod and the base of the light socket, in that order.

7. Attach the wire to the socket. To do this, loosen the screws on both sides of the socket and wrap the exposed wires around each of the screws.

8. Tighten the screws.

9. Attach the base of the socket.

STRIP IT

10. Most cords will come stripped, but just in case . . . Split the cord with the X-Acto knife giving yourself some room to work (about 1½" should be sufficient). Next, cut around the protective plastic about ½" from the end—careful not to cut into the wire. Carefully pull off the end of the plastic revealing a bare wire.

ATTACHING THE SWITCH

11. With your needle-nose pliers reach through the hole in the binding and pull the electrical cord through about 4".

12. Split this section of the cord in two with the X-Acto knife. Be careful not to cut into the wiring.

13. Cut one of these newly separated sides in half and strip the ends about ½".

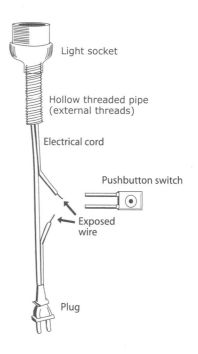

Light socket

Hollow threaded pipe
(external threads)

Electrical cord

Pushbutton switch

Exposed
wire

Plug

Screw in a lightbulb and add a shade and you're done. Plug it in and give it a squeeze. Repeat. Repeat. Repeat. Now isn't that fun?

BRIGHT IDEA: To really make it your own, try writing out your favorite passage from the book onto the shade with a magic marker.

AND NOW IT'S A LAMP

from decanters to bottles, you've got lighting options all around you.

WHAT YOU'LL NEED

- Decanter
- Lamp wire
- Plug and on/off switch
- Copper plumbing fittings
- Mini light socket
- 25-watt or less bulb
- Screwdriver
- X-Acto knife
- Wire strippers

BRIGHT IDEAS
- **Find a cool vase, bottle, or decanter.**
- **Find a socket and lightbulb that will fit inside the decanter.**
- **Find copper plumbing fittings that fit snuggly inside the opening of the decanter like a stopper. This little decorative touch will also hide the socket.**

DIRECTIONS

1. Slip one end of the lamp wire through the copper fitting.
2. Split the end of the wire down the center seam with your X-Acto knife approximately 1½–2". **See diagram.**
3. With the wire strippers, remove ½" of the plastic from each end, twisting the newly exposed wire around itself to prevent any stray filaments.
4. To attach the socket, loosen the screws with a screwdriver. Wrap the exposed wire from one end around one screw, the other end on the other screw and tighten. If your socket has a cardboard cover, slide it on.
5. Attach the plug and on/off switch. Be sure to place the switch where it'll still be easy to get to but also out of sight.
6. Screw in the lightbulb, slide the copper fitting over the socket, and fit the mechanism into the opening of the decanter.

Now turn it on and marvel at your beautiful new creation.

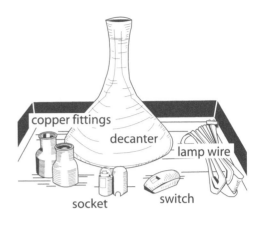

copper fittings
decanter
lamp wire
socket
switch

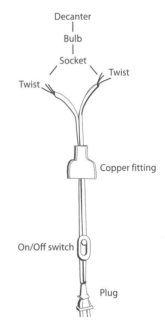

Decanter
Bulb
Socket
Twist
Twist
Copper fitting
On/Off switch
Plug

WALL OF SOUND

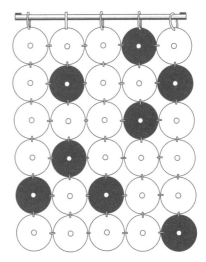

every apartment has a sore thumb that stands out against the rose garden of your style. In my case, it's an exposed water heater welcoming guests into my bedroom where a maze of space-age tubes and rusty old pipes makes its way up the twelve foot ceiling, open for all to see. Pretty.

I've tried it all. Curtains, shades, bamboo, beads. But nothing I concocted could hide this monstrous flaw without calling more attention to it until now. Constructed from old data, audio, and AOL trial-offer CDs, this modern masterpiece is the perfect piece to disguise your defects, separate your sectionals, or beautify your bedroom.

WHAT YOU'LL NEED

- A whole bunch of CDs
- Spray paint
- Dremel and bit
- Wire and wire cutters
- Rod and hangers
- Shower curtain rings
- Measuring device

DIRECTIONS

1. Measure the space that you wish to cover, height and width.
2. Divide the height by 4.75 (the height of a CD) and the width by 4.75 (the width of a CD).
3. Multiply those numbers to figure out how many CDs you'll need.

   h x 4.75 = a
   w x 4.75 = b   **a x b = CDs**

4. Dust off the CDs, then give them a couple coats of spray paint in a well-ventilated area.

5. Be sure they're completely dry before you handle them or they'll all stick together.
6. Lay them out on the floor in the pattern you like and then get drilling. Put holes at 12 and 6, 9 and 3, as if on a clock. Let the Dremel do the work. If you push too hard, you'll crack the discs.
7. Try doing a few at a time. But three seems the limit.
8. Two at a time, connect the CDs by threading short pieces of thin-gauge wire through the front of the CDs and twisting them closed behind until your panel is complete.
9. Attach the shower curtain rings to the top row of CDs and slide onto rod.
10. Hang rod.

BRIGHT IDEA: The high speed of the Dremel works wonders for this project. But if you don't have one, a drill will work fine with some patience. CDs are synthetic. The friction of the drill essentially melts it to get to the other side, sending hot molten shards of material across the room, onto your bare wrists, and potentially into your peepers. Wear your goggles and some gloves.

THE ABCs OF CDs

don't know what to do with all those empty CD cases? Use them for storage on your wall. With double-sided tape or self-adhesive Velcro, create a fun pattern on your wall. Better yet—cover the wall. Use them as picture frames or even to store your CDs. But if you're keeping CDs in them, be sure to use plenty of tape or there's bound to be a disaster.

it's alive!

plants and pets are great ways to add more life to your home and your health.

NOT JUST ANOTHER PRETTY FACE

we all know that plants release oxygen into the air, but did you know they might offer other real health benefits? Through research, surveys, and studies, scientists have built a bank of information that proves how beneficial plants are beyond their beauty.[24] For instance:

- Plants emit oxygen we need to breath and absorb the carbon dioxide we exhale.
- Plants absorb Volatile Organic Chemicals (VOCs) caused by man-made building materials like adhesives, some paints, carpets, etc.
- They reduce headaches, sore or dry throats, dry or itchy skin, and fatigue.

- Plants keep us calm.
- They help us to recover from surgery more quickly.
- They can absorb noise.

Put some potted pretties in your place and reap the benefits of what you sow!

PICK 'EM

don't have much time to spare? Steer clear of plants that require daily care. If you're a city dweller, some plants are better than others in terms of cleaning pollutants. Do you want a burst of seasonal flowers or long-lasting foliage? Choose plants based on your lifestyle, where you're going to put them, and what your growing conditions are.

LIGHT

Low light (L): North-facing windows and interior spots are good places for these plants that thrive on minimum light.

Medium/Indirect Light (M): These plants love bright light but not direct. Place these plants a foot or two away from west- or south-facing windows.

Bright/Direct (B): These babies love the sun! Put them right on a south- or west-facing windowsill.

WATER

Moist (M): Keep soil uniformly moist to the touch, but don't saturate with water.

Intermediate (B): Allow soil to dry to the touch between watering.

Dry (D): Allow soil to dry completely between watering.

TEMPERATURE

Plants have critical temperature minimums and maximums, specifics of which can be found on the instructional stake. Generally, daytime temperatures between 65° F and 75° F are best, cooling ten degrees at night. Heat and A/C can really damage houseplants so watch for vents and drafts.

PLANT NAME	LOW MAINTENANCE	AIR CLEANERS	FLOWERS	PET FRIENDLY	LIGHT	WATER
spider plant	x	x		x	m	m
devil's ivy	x	x			m	m
mother-in-law's tongue	x				b/m	b
jade plant	x				b	b
christmas cactus	x		x		b	d
rubber tree	x				l,m,b	b
parlor palm	x	x			m	m
african violet	x		x	x	m	m/d
aloe	x				b	b
dragon tree	x	x			m	m
ficus		x			b	m
ferns		x			m/l	m
chrysanthemum		x	x		m	m
philodendrons		x	x		m/l	b
peace lilly		x	x		b/m	m

PUTTING DOWN ROOTS

your plant will have to get used to its new home, so give it some time to adjust. It may even lose a few leaves. Remember, too, that plants grow toward the sun. So if it only has one light source, turn it regularly to prevent growing in only one direction.

FEED ME

- Put your plant pots on saucers or plates to avoid staining furniture or carpet.
- Water when the compost surface is no longer moist. Test it by sticking your finger in half an inch.
- Most plants can be watered from the top. But if the pot is small, fill the saucer with water and let the compost soak it up.
- Don't let plants stand in water; dump the excess from the saucer.
- Don't overwater.
- If your plant dries out and flops, submerge the entire pot (but not the plant) in water and hold it there until the air bubbles stop.
- Don't go overboard on fertilizer. A little goes a long way.

A NEW HOME

Are roots coming through the hole on the bottom of the pot? It's time to repot.

1. Buy a pot that's one size bigger, and some fresh houseplant compost.
2. Pour a little compost into the base of the pot.
3. Ease your plant out of its original pot and place it so that the rootball is about an inch below the top of its new pot, adding more compost to the bottom if necessary.
4. Fill with compost, and tamp it down with your hand.

BROWN LEAVES, YELLOW LEAVES. WHAT DOES IT MEAN?

use this handy troubleshooter to save your plants if they're looking less than stellar.

SYMPTOM	CAUSE	SOLUTION
Tiny white or brown shells on leaves, stems, or both	Scale insects	Remove the insects, using a strong water spray, tweezers, a toothpick, or a cotton swab dipped in alcohol.
Sticky honeydew on leaves; waxy white insects on the undersides	Mealy bugs	Wash the plant with a solution of 2 tsp. dishwashing soap to 1 gallon water.
Loss of vigor; roots and soil particles covered with white, waxy powder (most often on cacti and other succulents, African violets, ferns, and fuchsias)	Root mealy bugs	Wash the roots thoroughly and repot the plant in fresh soil and a clean pot. In severe cases, discard the plant; sterilize the pot before you use it again.
Barely visible dots moving slowly on the undersides of leaves; fine webbing sometimes visible when you hold the plant up to light.	Spider mites	Spray the plant with water to dislodge the mites. Wash the plant with soapy water (see "Scale insects," above).
Clouds of tiny white flies around the plant; sometimes sticky honey-dew on upper leaf surfaces	Whiteflies	Spray the plant with water to dislodge mites. Wash the plant thoroughly with soapy water and a soft brush.
Reduced growth; leaves small and yellow	Nitrogen deficiency	Apply a high-nitrogen fertilizer; consult a houseplant book for specific guidelines.

SYMPTOM	CAUSE	SOLUTION
Wilting foliage and sometimes stems; leaves yellow and falling; roots peeling or disintegrating	Overwatering or poor drainage	Cut back on water. Replant in a better-draining potting mix, and make sure the pot has drainage holes.
Poor growth; wilting leaves	Too little water	Water more frequently; consult a houseplant book for your plant's specific requirements. Improve the moisture retention of the soil by adding compost or commercial water-retention granules.

Still need some help? Visit **www.suite101.com/course.cfm/17497/lessons** for everything you need to know about houseplants.

MAN'S BEST FRIEND

having a pet can be a wonderful, rewarding experience. Just ask the nearly 100 million dog and cat owners in America! Besides making loyal, lovable friends, they're actually good for your health. It's said that people with pets live longer, happier lives.

However, owning a pet is also a huge responsibility and a life-altering commitment.

TILL DEATH DO US PART

You are responsible for your pet for its *entire* life, not just the first few weeks until the novelty wears off. Rodents, frogs, and fish have a life span of less than five years while dogs and cats usually live fifteen to twenty. Turtles can live up to fifty years! Can you commit to that many years of love and care?

TIMING IS EVERYTHING

How much time do you have every day to devote to the care of your pet? Dogs need to be exercised regularly, fed twice a day, groomed, and given plenty of attention. They may also need to be trained or taken to obedience classes. Cats require less time, but still need to be fed, groomed, and given plenty of affection. Gerbils, fish, and turtles require even less time, but you still need to schedule feeding and cleaning cages or tanks. Can you fit that into your schedule?

BUDGET BUSTER

Pets can be expensive. The price you pay at the pet store or shelter is only the beginning.

Your pet will need:

- Food
- Supplies including some kind of habitat (tank, cage, bed), a litter box, toys
- Health care including regular check-ups, shots, and flea medicine
- Licensing
- Boarding care if you can't get your neighbor to babysit when you go home for the holidays
- Grooming
- Training or obedience lessons
- Unexpected expenses including extreme health care like chemotherapy, operations, or accident-related care

TOTALLY HIGH MAINTENANCE

Getting the right pet is really important. Ask yourself some questions:

- Why do I want a pet?
- Am I really ready to take care of an animal's needs? Will I resent having to get up early or come home right after work to feed Fido?
- Am I allergic to any animals? How about my roommate?
- How much space do I have for a pet? Is there a backyard? Is it fenced? Are pets allowed?

MAINTENANCE LEVEL	TYPE OF ANIMAL	TIME COMMITMENT	FRIEND-O-METER
lowest	fish, snakes, lizards, turtles	15 minutes daily for feeding, 1 hour per week habitat cleaning	**low**
low	cats, small birds, rabbits, rodents	15–30 minutes daily for feeding, 1 hour per week habitat cleaning	**medium/high**
medium	dogs	2 hours daily for feeding, walking, grooming, poop scooping	**high**

WHERE TO LOOK

pet stores have a variety of animals from puppies and kittens to rabbits, fish, lizards, rats, mice, birds, and more. For low maintenance pets, this is probably a good place to start your search. But if you're planning on adopting a cat or dog, consider a shelter, humane society, or pet adoption fair instead, especially if you want a puppy.

Why? Many pet stores buy their puppies from puppy farms, inhumane breeders who make a lot of money by producing as many dogs as they can, as fast as they can. Bitches often live in horrible conditions, three to a cage, and are abandoned or killed once they pass their reproductive years. Ask your pet store where they get their puppies and look up the breeder to make sure they're reputable. Don't buy from any pet store that encourages the practice by selling puppy farm dogs. In fact, report them to your local humane society.

Find a shelter, adoption agency, or foster care near you by visiting **www.PetFinder.com** or **www.1-800-Save-a-Pet.com**. Gotta have a pure-bred? Find a rescue that specializes in your breed of choice.

PICK ME, PICK ME

don't pick your pet on impulse. No matter how cute that kitten is, make sure you've done all your homework before you pull out the plastic.

- Research the species or breed you're considering to find out what kind of pets they make and how much care they require.
- Get to know animals. Visit a shelter and interact with some animals. Many places will let you take a dog for a walk so you can get to know each other's personality.
- Find out about leash, licensing, and vaccination laws in your area before you bring a pet home. Visit your city government website or give them a call.

PET PROOFING

before you bring your new pet home, make sure your house is pet-ready.

- Fix anything your pet could get hurt on, stuck on, hang itself on, or escape through.
- Cover electrical cords that could be chewed through.
- Pick up anything that can be choked on.
- Put away whatever you don't want in your pet's mouth or in his paws.

CAUTION

- Never leave a pet alone in a car on a hot day. Just like babies, they overheat.
- Never feed your pet chocolate. Ever. No matter how much they beg. Dogs can't digest chocolate and can die from eating too much.
- Never give pets human medicine.
- If you're unsure about how to care for your pet, ask your veterinarian.

SNIP, SNIP

every day in the United States, animal shelters are forced to destroy 30,000 dogs and cats. These numbers could be greatly reduced if every pet owner just got their animal friend spayed or neutered. The surgical removal of a pet's reproductive organs, spaying and neutering reduces the population of unwanted animals by keeping down the number of homeless animals. It also prevents reproductive cancer and aggressive behavior.

Most veterinarians recommend that female cats and dogs be spayed before they're six months old, males between six months and a year.

DANGER, WILL ROBINSON

and there, as if suddenly transported into the climax of an after-school special where the good girl takes a wrong turn to find herself facing adversity on the other side of the tracks, I found myself, trapped in a dead end alley in South Central Los Angeles, alone but for the loitering gangsters, jive talking and smoking a jay behind their apartment. "Hmmm," I thought as I watched a tricked-out minivan pull in behind me, blocking my only exit. "Maybe this wasn't such a good idea."

Indeed, this was a place I'd only heard about, a few blocks from the infamous intersection of Florence and Normandie, the site of the Rodney King beating that had incited days of rioting in Los Angeles just a few years earlier. Magnified by this incident and nightly reports of drive-by shootings, South Central's reputation was bound to scare anyone unfamiliar with its turf, not just me.

"Hey, is Anthony around?" I asked the pavement, trying to keep my cool as I got out of my car. Never let 'em see you sweat, right?

"I'm Anthony," I heard. "What can I do for you?"

A sea of groupies parted ways as a handsome man emerged from a garage packed with Volkswagens. Covered head to toe in Pennzoil and tattoos, his hair beautifully and intricately braided in zigzags, he looked exactly like the stereotype character I expected, blue jumpsuit, red oil rag, gold tooth, and all. "I'm Tana," I said as we air-shook hands so as not to dirty my dainty little manicure. "We spoke this morning."

I'd discovered Anthony's number buried deep in the classifieds of the *LA Weekly*, a free "alternative" newspaper known mostly for its extensive calendar

tana's habitat

section and escort service listings, after my unfortunate incident with the back end of a Suburban. The front end of my Bug was totaled, as if the Incredible Hulk had wrapped the hood of my trunk around and around the entire car like a woman wraps her wet hair in a towel after a long, luxurious bath. Duct tape and twine could barely hold it in place to make it drivable. The body shops all said the same thing. "You're gonna need a new front end. And let me tell you, that ain't cheap." I knew I was going to need to get creative if my car was going to get fixed. After all, I had no car insurance and was also responsible for the $500 cost of replacing the bumper of the stopped truck I'd slammed into. . . at 30 mph.

My friend Eduardo day-lighted at a body shop and, eager for a challenge, offered to do the job for a nominal fee, after work, at his convenience. Not only would he cut off the front end, weld on a new apron, and replace the fenders, he would also install the Suburban's new bumper, which I'd already purchased from an after-parts dealer in the Valley. All I had to do was find the parts.

VW body parts. Used. Cheap.
Anthony: 213.555.6972

"Let me show you what I've got," Anthony said, opening the door to his pickup truck. "Get in."

"Gee," I thought, twirling my momentarily blond locks around my finger, ignoring my inner child screaming at the top of her lungs to step away from the car, step away from the car! "Can he really fit the front end of a Volkswagen in the cab of a truck?"

Anthony at the wheel, his assistant Duane next to me on the passenger side, we pulled out of the alley and into the street. The minivan moved dutifully out of the way to let us pass, then resumed his spot, blocking the entrance. My heart was pounding. We drove less than a mile, through a residential neighborhood filled with children playing in the streets and running through sprinklers, past a rundown church and several liquor stores. The homes were well kept, the lawns maintained. It looked like any other regular neighborhood I'd seen, but with a resounding air of oppression punctuated by the bars on every window.

As we silently approached a vacant lot, fenced in by chain link and tarp, Anthony honked the horn twice. What did that mean? Was it a signal? Duane slipped out the door to open the padlock as two German Shepards lunged through the gate, growling and snarling, foaming at the mouth with a rage like Sasquatch defending his litter from a vicious pack of *National Enquirer* photographers. "Good boys," Anthony said with a laugh as he grabbed some doggie treats from the glove compartment and tossed them out the window. "These are my babies," he said to me with a soft smile, his gold tooth gleaming in the light as the dogs fervently devoured their treats and licked their chops.

Anthony drove through the gate into a veritable VW boneyard, junked Bug after junked Bug after junked Bug, every model, every year, every color imaginable. Duane closed and locked the gate behind us as we parked and jumped out of the truck, the dogs sniffing me, uncomfortably close. "J.T., Echo. Get over here." They were the first words I'd heard from Duane, and the last. The dogs obeyed and played catch with him while Anthony took me on a tour of the place.

tana's habitat

"Oh my God," I thought, following Anthony around the lot as he carefully and quietly examined each and every heap of jettisoned German engineering. "What am I doing? I've got to get out of here. This is not how I want to end up on the eleven o'clock news!"

"This is it," Anthony said, turning to me sharply, as if reading my mind, interrupting my scan of the layout for an escape route.

"What?" I asked nervously, scared, suddenly not sure why I was even there. *Is he really going to kill me?* I wondered.

"This is it," Anthony repeated. "This is your new apron."

"Great," I answered without even looking at it, anxious, relieved. "I'll take it. Now let's get out of here."

We made our way back to the alley the same way we came, Anthony, me, and Duane, leaving a little pile of doggie treats for J.T. and Echo. We passed the same kids, the same church, the same liquor stores, and the same guarded windows. As we approached the alley, now inhabited by many more Anthony devotees, the minivan blocking the entrance moved automatically to let us in and returned to its guard post.

I paid the man his cash and agreed to come back in two days to pick up the part he would have to slice off the orange Beetle we'd seen in the yard. While I waited for Anthony to scrawl a receipt on the back of a flyer, the only white guy in the group approached me to converse. I quickly learned that Mike had just been released from prison and was living in a halfway house up the street. Anthony had been kind enough to give him a job to help him with his transition into society. I secretly hoped this was not his way of picking up chicks, thinking he desperately needed help on his spiel, though I knew I would not be the one to give it to him.

Anthony delivered the receipt. "Thanks," I said. "See you soon." We shook hands, dirty or not.

I leaped into my mangled car and started her up. "Open sesame," I said to myself as the minivan pulled over to let me out, driver still anonymous. "Thanks," I mouthed and waved with a faint smile, thinking it would be safe to return to pick up my apron, knowing I would not come alone.

Like every good parable, the events of my after-school special revealed no shortage of lessons when I replayed the scenes in my head on the long drive home to West Hollywood, my heart still beating wildly.

- Safety first
- Self over savings
- Look before you leap

These were the biggies, the obvious, the head-bangers. It was perfectly clear that I put myself into a potentially dangerous situation and that my day could have ended quite differently.

But there was something more to my cautionary tale, an embarrassing discovery that my fear begat unwarranted stereotyping and that my snap judgments needed some real attention.

Lucky for me, my daytime drama went deeper than its theme song.

tana's habitat

you were robbed

with over 10.4 million robberies in the United States in 2003, property protection is something to consider. Take some simple precautions to limit the likelihood of becoming a victim.

APARTMENT SAFETY

- Rekey your locks and get a deadbolt and peephole.
- Place a wooden rod in the track so your sliding-glass door can't be opened.
- Leave a light on.
- Even if you are just going out for a few moments, lock your door and take the key with you.
- If someone comes to your door asking to use the telephone, make the call yourself or send them on their way. Don't invite them in.
- Let your building manager or neighbors know when you're going out of town.[26]

- Make sure the walkways, entrances, parking areas, elevators, hallways, stairways, laundry rooms, and storage areas are well lit night and day.
- Make sure the fire exit stays locked from the outside so you can exit, but no one can enter.
- The mailbox area should be well lit and well traveled.
- Get someone to pick up your mail and newspaper subscription every day while you're away.
- Make sure the landlord or building manager stays on top of maintenance like burned-out lights, trash, landscaping, and snow removal.

THE NEIGHBORS

- Meet your neighbors. Attend apartment-wide social events if you have to.
- If your building has a tenant patrol, use it.
- Suggest security improvements to your landlord.

THE ART OF BEING MUGGED

think you're down for a good conversation with a stranger? What about this one?

Stranger: "Give me your wallet."
You: "No."
Stranger: (pulls out gun) "Give me your wallet."
You: "OK."

WHAT'S SO SECURE ABOUT SOCIAL SECURITY ANYWAY?

Nothing. Leave your Social Security card out of your wallet.

CANCEL YOUR CARDS AS SOON AS POSSIBLE

If you lose a credit card or have one stolen, call immediately and cancel it. They can send you a new one in a matter of days, so just do it as soon as possible. Keep the numbers to your credit card companies somewhere handy, at work maybe, just in case. Just don't keep them in your wallet. Because that would be ironic, wouldn't it?

ZEN AND THE ART OF NOT GETTING SHOT FULL OF HOLES

Muggings happen really quickly. Muggers just want your cash. They're not interested in long, dramatic confrontations. They get what they want, and then they split. So, if you're smart, you won't give them any reason to stick around. It's not worth getting shot for a small amount of money.

YOU'RE NOT CARRYING A LOT OF MONEY, ARE YOU?

You are? Well, that's planning ahead, isn't it? Just about anywhere you go you can use a credit or a debit card. Yes, having some cash is always handy, but there's no need to carry too much of it. Don't make yourself a target. Minimize your risks.

DARKEST BEFORE THE DAWN

If you have to walk around late at night, stay in well-lit areas. And most important, be aware of your surroundings. Could I have avoided being mugged if I had been more aware of my surroundings? Absolutely. I just might have noticed the guy following me from the subway.

HEADS UP

Muggers want an easy target and they want to surprise you. If you look like you are aware of what's going on, if you look like you might be prepared to deal with a mugger, they'll most likely leave you alone. Interviews with criminals show that street crime is not so random. They carefully select their targets using visual clues, so make sure you don't look like a victim. For example, no headphones late at night. Put the iPod away, 'cause they'll want that, too.

Stay alert. If you see something that makes you nervous, go back inside. Try to go where there are people around.

INSURANCE

if you find you have been robbed, mugged, or have witnessed a crime, call 911 as soon as possible. Write down everything: the date, time of day, list of goods stolen or damaged. Then contact your renter's insurance company or agent (if you have one) to report the loss and get the appropriate claims form.

IF I FILE A CLAIM, WILL MY POLICY BE CANCELED?

Your policy probably won't be canceled, but your rates may increase depending on the specifics of your case.

WHAT IF MY INSURANCE COMPANY DOES NOT RESPOND TO A CLAIM?

File a complaint with your state insurance department or local consumer protection office.

JEEPERS PEEPERS

peeping toms, stalkers, and abusive neighbors can be serious threats to your personal safety. Treat them as such. If you *ever* feel uncomfortable or threatened, *do not* hesitate to call 911. The police *will* come and they *will* take you seriously. It's their job.

MAY I SEE YOUR ID?

everyone is a target for identity theft. Find out how you can decrease your risk by visiting **www.IDTheftCenter.org/idthefttestc.shtml**.[27]

How do thieves get my information?

- They go through your trashcan, looking for straight cut or unshredded papers.
- They steal your mail or your wallet.
- They listen in on conversations you have in public.
- They trick you into giving them the information over the telephone or by e-mail.
- They buy information on the Internet or from someone who might have stolen it.
- They steal it from a loan or credit application form you filled out or from files at a hospital, bank, school, or business that you deal with. They may have obtained it from Dumpsters outside of such companies.
- They get it from your computer, especially those without firewalls.
- They may be a friend or relative or someone who works for you who has access to your information.

PREVENTION

While no one can totally prevent this crime from occurring, here are some positive steps to take to decrease your risk.

- Check your credit reports once a year from all three of the credit reporting agencies to confirm all the activity is yours.
- Guard your Social Security number. Don't carry it around with you.
- Don't put your SSN or driver's license number on your checks.
- Guard your personal information. You should never give your Social Security number to anyone unless they have a good reason for needing it.
- Watch for people who may try to eavesdrop and overhear the information you give out orally.
- Carefully destroy papers you throw out, especially those with sensitive or identifying information. A crosscut paper shredder works best.
- Be suspicious of telephone solicitors. Never provide information unless you have initiated the call.
- Delete without replying to any suspicious e-mail requests.
- Use a locked mailbox to send and receive all mail.
- Reduce the number of preapproved credit card offers you receive by calling **1-888-5OPT-OUT** (they will ask for your SSN).

I'VE BEEN STOLEN

If you think your identity has been stolen, contact the fraud department of any of the three major credit bureaus to place an alert on your account asking any creditors to contact you before opening any new accounts or making changes to existing accounts. Alert the Federal Trade Commission at **www.Consumer.gov/idtheft** or **1-877-IDTHEFT** and the police. They'll walk you through the rest.

For more information on identity theft, visit **www.idtheftcenter.org/index.shtml.**

Above all, always choose safe over sorry.

CHAPTER 17

landlords and you

you've done everything right. Before you signed on the dotted line, you understood the conditions of your tenancy, you got everything in writing including rent and security deposit payment and refund terms, you photographed existing property damage, understood repair procedures, and hashed out your privacy rights. And yet, your landlord still doesn't seem to be living up to his end of the bargain.

KNOW YOUR RIGHTS

according to the U.S. Department of Housing and Urban Development (HUD), these renters' rights are inalienable, provided you comply with the rules and guidelines that govern your lease[28]:

- The right to live in decent, safe, and sanitary housing that is free from environmental hazards such as lead-based paint hazards.

- The right to have repairs performed in a timely manner, upon request, and to have a quality maintenance program run by management.
- The right to be given reasonable notice, in writing, of any nonemergency inspection or other entry into your apartment.
- The right to equal and fair treatment and use of your building's services and facilities, without regard to race, color, religion, gender, disability, familial status (children under 18), national origin (ethnicity or language), or in some circumstances, age.

HOME IMPROVEMENT

sure your landlord is required to keep your apartment in livable shape. But what does that mean? Habitable is partly a matter of personal standards!

As long as you didn't cause the damage yourself, your landlord is responsible for the big stuff, like maintaining a structurally sound building including floors and roofs. He must keep electrical, heating, and plumbing systems in safe operation, provide you with a reasonable amount of hot and cold water, and keep your place free of bug infestations.

However, he is not necessarily responsible for fixing minor things like cosmetic repairs, even from normal wear and tear. Peeling paint, leaky faucets, stained carpets, or mildewed grout may only require your landlord's attention if they serve a clear and present danger, making your home inhabitable.

IT'S THE LITTLE THINGS

Even if your landlord is required by law to fix some minor damages, getting him to do it is another story. Most states allow tenants to make repairs and deduct them from the rent, though this approach is not necessarily the best for maintaining an amicable relationship. In the end, you really just want your place to look nice and be comfortable.

After an oral inquiry, try writing a letter. A written request is a great tactic because, not only does it give you an open medium to describe your problem in detail, it also gives your landlord a chance to mull it over in his own time, without feeling the pressure of having to give a yes or no answer on the spot as the dollar signs mount in his mind. Be sure to explain why fixing it would benefit him. If the problem may potentially cause more damage, it will cost him more money down the road. If there is a safety or security issue, he may be held liable down the road. Get him thinking.

tana's habitat

If you are ignored, contact a mediation service to help you and your landlord come to an acceptable solution. Check out **www.Mediate.com** for information on finding a mediator. Beyond that, your options are reporting him to your local building or housing agency, which enforces code violations, or good old small claims court. If you get to this point, you may also want to look for a new place to live.

GIVE IT TO ME, GIVE IT TO ME

landlords can take deductions from your security deposit, but they have to be reasonable. In fact, lots of states require landlords to provide you with an itemized list of repairs beyond normal wear and tear with the deposit balance.

What is this normal wear and tear? Unfortunately, it's subjective. That's why it's smart to have documentation and pictures of your pre-move-in condition. Some examples:

WEAR AND TEAR	
ORDINARY WEAR AND TEAR: LANDLORD'S RESPONSIBILITY	DAMAGE OR EXCESSIVE FILTH: TENANT'S RESPONSIBILITY
curtains faded by the sun	cigarette burns in curtains or carpets
water-stained linoleum by shower	broken tiles in bathroom
minor marks on or nicks in wall	large marks on or holes in wall
dents in the wall where a door handle bumped it	door off its hinges
moderate dirt or spotting on carpet	rips in carpet or urine stains from pets
a few small tack or nail holes in wall	lots of picture holes or gouges in walls that require patching as well as repainting
a rug worn thin by normal use	stains in rug caused by a leaking fish tank
worn gaskets on refrigerator doors	broken refrigerator shelf

WEAR AND TEAR	
ORDINARY WEAR AND TEAR: LANDLORD'S RESPONSIBILITY	DAMAGE OR EXCESSIVE FILTH: TENANT'S RESPONSIBILITY
faded paint on bedroom wall	water damage on wall from hanging plants
dark patches of ingrained soil on hardwood floors that have lost their finish and have been worn down to bare wood	water stains on wood floors and windowsills caused by windows being left open during rainstorms
warped cabinet doors that won't close	sticky cabinets and interiors
stains on old porcelain fixtures that have lost their protective coating	grime-coated bathtub and toilet
moderately dirty mini-blinds	missing mini-blinds
bathroom mirror beginning to "de-silver" (black spots)	mirrors caked with lipstick and makeup
clothes dryer that delivers cold air because the thermostat has given out	dryer that won't turn at all because it's been overloaded
toilet flushes inadequately because mineral deposits have clogged the jets	toilet won't flush properly because it's stopped up with a diaper[29]

GIVE IT TO ME NOW

how long can your landlord keep your deposit? It varies by state, but usually between fourteen and thirty days after your departure.

STATE	DEADLINE FOR RETURNING SECURITY DEPOSIT
No statutory deadline	Alabama
Alaska	14 days if the tenant gives proper notice to terminate tenancy; 30 days if the tenant does not give proper notice
Arizona	14 days
Arkansas	30 days
California	Three weeks
Colorado	One month, unless lease agreement specifies longer period of time (which may be no more than 60 days); 72 hours if a hazardous condition involving gas equipment requires tenant to vacate
Connecticut	30 days, or within 15 days of receiving tenant's forwarding address, whichever is later
Delaware	20 days
District of Columbia	45 days
Florida	15–60 days depending on whether tenant disputes deductions
Georgia	One month
Hawaii	14 days
Idaho	21 days, or up to 30 days if landlord and tenant agree
Illinois	30–45 days, depending on whether tenant disputes deductions
Indiana	45 days
Iowa	30 days

STATE	DEADLINE FOR RETURNING SECURITY DEPOSIT
Kansas	30 days
Kentucky	30–60 days, depending on whether tenant disputes deductions
Louisiana	One month
Maine	21 days (tenancy at will) or 30 days (written rental agreement)
Maryland	30–45 days, depending on whether tenant has been evicted or has abandoned the premises
Massachusetts	30 days
Michigan	30 days
Minnesota	Three weeks after tenant leaves, and landlord receives mailing address; five days if tenant must leave due to building condemnation
Mississippi	45 days
Missouri	30 days
Montana	30 days (10 days if no deduction)
Nebraska	14 days
Nevada	30 days
New Hampshire	30 days
New Jersey	30 days; five days in case of fire, flood, condemnation, or evacuation
New Mexico	30 days
New York	Reasonable time
North Carolina	30 days
North Dakota	30 days
Ohio	30 days
Oklahoma	30 days
Oregon	31 days

tana's habitat

STATE	DEADLINE FOR RETURNING SECURITY DEPOSIT
Pennsylvania	30 days
Rhode Island	20 days
South Carolina	30 days
South Dakota	Two weeks to return entire deposit or a portion of it, and to provide reasons for withholding; 45 days for a written, itemized accounting if tenant requests it
Tennessee	No statutory deadline
Texas	30 days
Utah	30 days, or within 15 days of receiving tenant's forwarding address, whichever is later
Vermont	14 days
Virginia	45 days
Washington	14 days
West Virginia	No statutory deadline
Wisconsin	21 days
Wyoming	30 days, or within 15 days of receiving tenant's forwarding address, whichever is later; 60 days if there is damage[30]

YOU'RE OUT OF HERE

we've all heard horror stories about families getting evicted, kicked to the curb to live in their cars. But guess what? Landlords can't just kick you out; they need to get a court ordered judgment first.[31]

Laws on terminating tenancies vary from state to state, but generally speaking, it's a long process. A landlord must first give you sufficient written notice in the proper form, giving you the chance to remedy the situation. If you don't, he can file a lawsuit to get a court-ordered judgment to have your bum banned.

Termination notices include:

Pay or quit: Late rent? This notice gives you three to five days to pay the rent or move out.

Cure or quit: If you are in violation of your rental agreement, this notice will give you a set amount of time to fix it (cure) or move on.

Unconditional quit: This notice requires you move out on the spot, no chance to pay, no chance to cure. In most states, unconditional quit notices are allowed only if you have:

+ repeatedly violated a significant lease or rental agreement clause
+ been late with the rent on more than one occasion
+ seriously damaged the premises
+ engaged in serious illegal activity, such as drug dealing on the premises

I GOT A NOTICE. WHAT HAPPENS NOW?

If you got the slip and are unwilling or unable to remedy the situation, your landlord must serve you with a summons and complaint for eviction. It's your invitation to see the judge.

If you can validate your existence in the building by proving that your apartment is uninhabitable, that your landlord served you with incomplete or illegal papers, or that your landlord is trying to get back at you for insisting on repairs, you may have a shot at staying in your home. However, even if the landlord wins, he must turn the judgment over to a local law enforcement officer who, in turn, will give you notice that he will be back to escort you off the property. Kicking and screaming, no doubt.

MY LEASE IS UP

If the term of your lease is up or you're on a month-to-month, your landlord may have the right to give you a thirty-day or sixty-day notice, even if you haven't violated anything! If you live in a rent-control area, however, they may have to prove a just cause. Check with your local housing authority for answers.

for your health

whether it's an earthquake, a tsunami, or a terrorist attack, no one wants to think about disaster striking. Unfortunately, it does. Prepare yourself for the worst and minimize the stress if it ever happens to you.

EMERGENCY SUPPLIES

water, food, and clean air are essentials for survival. Customize an emergency preparedness kit to meet your personal needs. Make two, one for home and one for the car.

The Department of Homeland Security recommends the following:

- Water. One gallon of water per person per day, for drinking and sanitation
- Food. At least a three-day supply of nonperishable food, paper plates, cups, towels, and plastic utensils

- Can opener
- Battery-powered radio and extra batteries
- Flashlight and extra batteries
- First-aid kit and manual
- Whistle to signal for help
- Dust mask or cotton T-shirt, to help filter the air
- Moist towelettes for sanitation
- Wrench or pliers to turn off utilities
- Plastic sheeting and duct tape to shelter-in-place
- Prescription medications you take every day such as insulin, heart medicine, and asthma inhalers and medical supplies like glucose and blood pressure monitoring equipment
- Garbage bags and plastic ties for personal sanitation
- One complete change of warm clothing and shoes per person, including a jacket, long pants, long-sleeved shirt, closed-toe shoes, hat, and gloves
- A sleeping bag or warm blanket
- Rain gear
- Cash or traveler's checks, change
- Fire extinguisher
- Tent
- Compass
- Matches in a waterproof container
- Signal flare
- Paper, pencil, scissors
- Feminine supplies and personal hygiene items
- Disinfectant
- Household chlorine bleach
- Copies of important family records such as insurance policies, identification, and bank account records in a waterproof, portable container.

Download a checklist of financial documents you may want to keep in your kit at **www.ready.gov/pdf_eefak.html**.

FIRST-AID KIT

We all need a Band-Aid every once in a while. Put together a first aid kit in a portable box and keep it well stocked. Better yet, learn how to use it! Find a basic first-aid pamphlet by contacting your local Red Cross. They can even help you get certified in CPR.

First-aid kit contents:

- Activated charcoal (use only if instructed by Poison Control Center)
- Adhesive tape
- Antiseptic ointment
- Band-Aids (assorted sizes)
- Blanket
- Cold pack
- Disposable gloves
- Gauze pads and roller gauze (assorted sizes)
- Hand cleaner
- Plastic bags
- Scissors and tweezers
- Small flashlight and extra batteries
- Syrup of Ipecac (use only if instructed by Poison Control Center)
- Triangular bandage
- Pain and fever reducers, such as acetaminophen and ibuprofen
- Anti-itch medications, like hydrocortisone cream
- An antihistamine, like Benadryl, for allergic reactions
- Laxative

CUTS AND SCRAPES

if your cut or scrape doesn't stop bleeding on its own, apply gentle, continuous pressure with a clean cloth or gauze for twenty to thirty minutes. Resist excessive peeking or you'll rip the fresh clot right off and make it bleed again!

- Rinse it with clean water and tweeze out any particles that may be stuck inside. If you can't get them all, get to the doctor to avoid infection.
- Once you're cleaned up, apply a thin layer of antibiotic cream like Neosporin or Polysporin. It won't help you heal faster, but it will inhibit infection.
- Exposure to air speeds healing, but bandages can help keep your wound clean and bacteria-free. It's your choice, but if you choose to cover, change your dressing daily.

- See your doctor if the wound isn't healing or you notice any redness, drainage, warmth, or swelling.

WHEN DO I NEED STITCHES?

If your cut is deep and you cannot easily tape the mouth of the wound shut, you need stitches.

DO I NEED A TETANUS SHOT?

Doctors recommend you get one every ten years anyway. If your wound is deep and dirty, or if you haven't received one in five years, go for a booster.

BRUISES

Bruises aren't pretty, but there's not much you can do about blood trapped beneath your skin.

For some relief, try elevating your injury or applying ice or a cold pack for 30 to 60 minutes at a time for a day or two after the injury.

SPRAINS

A sprain is an injury to a ligament caused by excessive stretching. They occur most often in your ankles, knees, and the arches of your feet, and swell quickly. Generally speaking, the bigger the pain, the bigger the injury

TREAT YOURSELF WITH P.R.I.C.E.

- **P**rotect yourself from further injury by using splints or crutches instead of your joint.
- **R**est your injury, but don't avoid activity all together. Even with a sprained ankle, you can usually exercise other muscles with stationery cycling and free weights.
- **I**ce it. Apply ice, a cold pack, or cold compression pack as soon as possible after the injury. Use ten to twenty minutes three times a day. Don't go over twenty, though, or you'll cause damage to the nerve tissue.
- **C**ompress the area with an elastic wrap or bandage. Elastic and neoprene are the best.

■ **E**levate to help prevent or limit swelling.

If your sprain isn't improving after the first two or three days, you have a fever, or the area around the injury is red and hot, you may have an infection. Call the doctor.

WRAP IT

Using an Ace bandage can be confusing, especially if you're in pain! Try these instructions to wrap an ankle and alter to wrap a hand, wrist, elbow, or knee. Don't wrap too tight, though. You may cut off the circulation. You'll know it's too tight if you feel numbness or tingling, or if your appendages turn blue.

■ Hold the rolled bandage in one hand and put the loose end on top of the foot with the other.
■ While holding the loose end tight to the foot, wrap the bandage around twice between the arch and the ball. Be sure to overlap the Ace wrap and smooth out any wrinkles.
■ Continue wrapping toward and around the ankle like a figure 8, leaving the heel uncovered.
■ Repeat several times and fasten the end with tape or metal clips.[32]

ANIMAL BITES

domestic pets cause most animal bites. And though dogs are more likely to bite, cat bites are more likely to cause infection.

Worried about rabies? It's pretty uncommon in domestic pets because they're usually immunized. Wild animals like raccoons, skunks, bats, and foxes are more likely to carry rabies than the usual suspects like rabbits, squirrels, and rodents!

■ If the bite barely breaks the skin, treat it like a minor cut.
■ If the bite causes a deep puncture, skin tear, or severe bleeding, apply pressure and see the doc.
■ If you notice signs of infection like swelling, redness, pus, or pain or have any reason to suspect rabies, it's time to call the doctor.

INSECT BITES AND STINGS

most reactions to insect bites are mild, causing little more than a bit of itching, stinging, and mild swelling. Delayed reaction may cause fever, painful joints, hives, and swollen glands. Only a small percentage of people develop severe reactions to insect venom, but if you're one of them, look for facial swelling, difficulty breathing, and shock. Bee, wasp, hornet, and yellow jacket bites are the most troublesome, though mosquitoes, ticks, and biting flies can also cause mild reactions.

MILD REACTIONS

- Scrape or brush off the stinger with a straight-edged object like a credit card or the back of a knife and swab the site with a disinfectant like rubbing alcohol or hydrogen peroxide. Don't try to pull out the stinger with tweezers *or* with your fingers; doing so may release more venom.
- Apply ice or a cold pack to reduce pain and apply 0.5 percent or 1 percent hydrocortisone cream, calamine lotion, or a baking soda paste several times a day until the symptoms subside.
- Take an antihistamine containing diphenhydramine (Benadryl, Tylenol Severe Allergy) or chlorpheniramine maleate (Chlor-Trimeton, Teldrin).

SEVERE REACTIONS

Severe reactions progress rapidly. Call 911 immediately if you experience difficulty breathing, swelling of your lips or throat, faintness, confusion, rapid heartbeat, hives, nausea, cramps, or vomiting.

VENOM ER

you got your black widow. You got your brown recluse. You got your rattlesnake. Although these bites are uncommon *and* the most inaccurately self-diagnosed, if you think you've been bitten by one, get yourself to the emergency room immediately. Better safe than sorry.

CHOKING

choking strikes fear! But don't panic. If the victim can speak, then the windpipe is not completely blocked and oxygen is reaching the lungs. If choking really is occurring, it's time for the Heimlich maneuver.

PERFORMING THE HEIMLICH

- Stand behind the choking person and wrap your arms around his or her waist, bending them slightly forward.
- Make a fist with one hand and place it slightly above the person's navel.
- Grasp your fist with the other hand and press hard into the abdomen with a quick, upward thrust. Repeat this procedure until the object is expelled from the airway.

AUTO HEIMLICH

- Position your own fist slightly above your navel.
- Grasp your fist with your other hand and bend over a hard surface like a countertop or chair.
- Shove your fist inward and upward.

PREGNANCY/OBESITY HEIMLICH

- Position your hands a little bit higher than with a normal Heimlich maneuver, at the base of the breastbone, just above the joining of the lowest ribs.
- Proceed as with the Heimlich maneuver, pressing hard into the chest, with a quick thrust.
- Repeat until the food or other blockage is dislodged or the person becomes unconscious.[33]

I DON'T FEEL SO GOOD

feed a fever? Starve a cold? Who can remember? Especially when you're struck down by runny nose, watery eyes, sneezing, and congestion! If you're like most adults, you're likely to get a cold two to four times a year. The good news is, you should be feeling better within a week. If you're not, get to the doctor to rule out a bacterial infection.

Also seek medical attention if you have:

- Fever greater than 102° F
- High fever accompanied by achiness and fatigue
- Fever accompanied by sweating, chills, and a cough with colored phlegm
- Symptoms that get worse instead of better

WHAT IF I DON'T HAVE A DOCTOR?

You're not alone. More than 45 million Americans are stuck without health insurance![34] But lack of insurance is no reason to disregard your health. There are lots of resources out there to help you find low and no-cost care including prescription drugs, wellness tests, and annual checkups.

- Visit **www.GovBenefits.gov/govbenefits/index.jhtml** to search state and federal health programs you may be eligible for.
- Check the Yellow Pages for free or low cost clinics.
- Call Planned Parenthood at **1-800-230-PLAN** or visit **www.PlannedParenthood.org** to find a clinic near you.
- Go to the emergency room. It's illegal for them to turn you away for inability to pay.

FIX ME

There's no cure for the common cold. Antibiotics are of no use against cold viruses, and over-the-counter cold preparations won't cure a common cold or make it go away any sooner. However, over-the-counter medications can relieve some symptoms.

For fever, sore throat, and headache, try acetaminophen (Tylenol, others) or other mild pain relievers. For runny nose and nasal congestion, you can take an antihistamine or decongestant. Don't use decongestant drops and sprays for more than a few days, though, because prolonged use can cause chronic inflammation of your mucous membranes.

MAKE YOURSELF COMFORTABLE

Drink lots of fluids. Avoid alcohol, caffeine, and cigarette smoke, which can cause dehydration and aggravate your symptoms.

- Get some rest. Take a sick day if you have a cough or fever and rebuild your strength.
- Adjust your room's temperature and humidity. Keep your room warm, but not overheated. If the air is dry, a cool-mist humidifier or vaporizer can moisten the air and help ease congestion and coughing. Be sure to keep the humidifier clean to prevent the growth of bacteria and molds.
- Soothe your throat. Gargle with warm salt water several times a day or drink warm lemon water with honey to soothe a sore throat and relieve a cough.

DO I HAVE THE FLU?

some signs and symptoms, such as a runny nose, sneezing, and sore throat, may initially seem like a cold. But if you are an adult and have a fever of 101° F or more, you may have influenza. Your fever may last from one day to as long as a week and, in rare cases, may reach as high as 106° F.

You're likely to feel much worse with the flu than with a cold and may experience other symptoms like chills and sweats, headache, dry cough, muscular aches and pains, fatigue and weakness, nasal congestion, and loss of appetite. In most cases, you should feel better in about a week to ten days unless you develop a serious post-flu lung infection like pneumonia bronchitis. Beware: You're probably contagious for up to a week after your symptoms first occur. Even if you feel better!

FIX ME

Sad but true, unless you're at risk of complications from the flu, your doctor may suggest nothing more than bed rest, plenty of fluids to prevent dehydration, and over-the-counter medicines such as acetaminophen. But in some cases, he may also prescribe an antiviral medication.

Help yourself:

- Drink plenty of liquids. This will help you to avoid dehydration.
- Rest up. Get more sleep.
- Try chicken soup. It's not just good for your soul. It really can help relieve flu symptoms by breaking up congestion.
- Take pain relievers. Use an over-the-counter pain reliever such as acetaminophen (Tylenol, others) or ibuprofen (Advil, Motrin, others) cautiously, as needed. Remember, pain relievers may make you more comfortable, but they won't make your symptoms go away any faster and may have serious side effects.

SHOULD I GET A FLU SHOT?

The injected vaccine is made from an inactivated form of the flu virus, so you can't get the flu from a flu shot. You may, however, have a slight reaction to the shot, such as soreness at the injection site, mild muscle aches, or fever beginning six to twelve hours after you've been immunized. These viruses are grown in chicken eggs, so if you're allergic to eggs or have any other immunity issues, you may want to refrain.

DIARRHEA

eeeewww. what does it mean? A simple case could be caused by anything from stress to food poisoning. But chronic diarrhea can be a sign of a serious disorder. If yours persists or you become dehydrated, see your doctor.

FIX ME

Diarrhea caused by viral infections typically ends on its own without antibiotics. Over-the-counter (OTC) medications may slow diarrhea, but they won't speed your recovery. Certain infections may be made worse by OTC medications because they prevent your body from getting rid of what's causing the diarrhea!

Take these measures to prevent dehydration and reduce symptoms while you recover:

- Drink plenty of clear liquids including water, clear sodas, and broths, plus gelatin and juices every day.
- Add semisolid and low-fiber foods gradually as your bowel movements return to normal. Try soda crackers, toast, eggs, rice, or chicken.
- Avoid dairy products, fatty foods, high-fiber foods, or highly seasoned foods for a few days.
- Avoid caffeine and alcohol.[35]

HANGOVER? GET OVER IT

since inventing alcohol several centuries ago, humans have sought to avoid the agony that often follows the ecstasy. Ancient Egyptians ate boiled cabbage for prevention, sailors of old claimed that saltwater could save them, and to this day we continue to seek a cure for the common hangover. There is only one surefire prevention. Abstinence. But odds are pretty good that anyone seeking hangover cures is not likely to "just say no." So, when you wake up with the Mojave Desert in your mouth and a vice tightening around your skull, get some relief.

WHAT CAUSES A HANGOVER?

Experts seem to agree that the big culprits are congeners, toxic impurities created during the fermentation process. The presence of these organic chemicals causes at least some of the discomfort we feel when we drink too much.[36]

Since not all alcoholic-beverages are created equally, your choice in libation tonight can greatly impact the effects you feel tomorrow. "Cleaner" liquors like vodka contain fewer congeners and may therefore do less damage than darker, more congener-heavy choices like bourbon.

VODKA	GIN, SCOTCH	BRANDY, RUM, SINGLE MALTS	BOURBON
x	xx	xxxx	xxxxxx

x = congener

Wines and champagnes follow the same color guidelines: white has fewer congeners than red. Wines can also contain a great deal of sulfites, a preservative known to trigger asthma, migraines, and other adverse reactions in some. Generally speaking, the higher the quality, and consequently, the more expensive the product, the less of these additives you'll find. Pay now, or pay later.

WHAT IS A HANGOVER?

Medical sources agree on a few physiological effects of drinking that cause a general malaise:

1. Alcohol evaporates body fluids, causing dehydration.
2. Alcohol is toxic to your liver and to your nervous system, resulting in a kind of nervous shock.
3. Alcohol irritates your urinary system and upper digestive tract, creating an "upset stomach."
4. Alcohol can deplete your bodily reserves of many nutrients such as:
   - Vitamins—A, B, B_6, and C
   - Minerals—calcium, magnesium, niacin, and potassium

CAN ANYTHING RELIEVE A HANGOVER?

Given that there are no real cures, the best we can hope for is some relief. And knowing what a hangover is helps us define a plan of attack. So when you wake up to the pain of life after a binge, the task at hand is two-fold: first, rehydrate and nourish your body to replace what the alcohol took away and second, metabolize the remnants of your toxic alcohol overdose.

REHYDRATE

Drink water, and lots of it! Knowing that the last thing you'll want to do when you wake up is actually get up, consider setting out a tall glass or pitcher of water as you stumble into bed after a night of excess. This way you can begin to repair the damage you've done without leaving the relative comfort of your covers.

When you finally do get up, continue drinking clear fluids all day. Water and real fruit juice are the best choices. Not only does fruit juice contain a good deal of water, but the fructose found in it is reputed to aid in metabolizing the toxins still at work in your system. Stay away from coffee. That hot cup of Joe may be a tempting "wake-me-up," but it will actually dehydrate you further and may prolong your agony.

Eating may not feel like a priority but, unless you turn green at the thought, try to eat at least a little something to help replenish what the alcohol has taken away. Keep it simple. Given that eggs and dairy products (other than yogurt) can be tough to digest, you may want to avoid them for now. Some toast and fruit are good choices.

But food alone may not replace all the vitamins and minerals that your cocktails "washed away." Taking a few supplements the day after overdoing it is a good idea. Get yourself a good B-complex vitamin as well as 500 to 1,000 mg of vitamin C. Also get a supplement with calcium, magnesium, niacin, and potassium—you may be able to find a single multivitamin that contains all of the vitamins and minerals you'll need. Groovy Dr. Weil (of TV, book, and Internet fame) suggests adding 100 mg of thiamin to your hangover-recovery plan.

METABOLIZE

Now that you've rehydrated and refueled it's up to your body to purge the alcohol's remaining toxins. Unfortunately, the only sure remedy for metabolizing those impurities and completely relieving your agony is time. But a little exercise can increase your intake of oxygen and help to speed up the metabolizing process. It has also been said that the fructose in honey and fruit juice can offer a similar effect.

HOW CAN I AVOID A HANGOVER?

If you're looking to party without punishing your body, here are a few things to keep in mind:

1. Eat before you drink. Fatty foods like dairy products can be a good preventative measure. Things like cheese and milk will not only line your stomach and inhibit alcohol irritation; they can also slow your body's absorption of alcohol and its toxins. That can mean less pain in the a.m.
2. Pick your poison wisely. When choosing your beverage, remember those nasty congeners and what they can do to you tomorrow. Selecting a "cleaner" alcohol like vodka, gin, or a quality white wine may reduce your regret. And heed the warning: you get what you pay for. Paying a little more for premium drinks tonight may save you in the morning!
3. Pace yourself. Taking your time with each drink can help to keep your total intake down.

4. Drink water. Not only will drinking plenty of water throughout the evening help to keep your body hydrated, but also by increasing your water intake, you may effectively reduce the amount of alcohol you consume.

OTHER POINTS OF INTEREST

Because prevention is not always 100 percent effective and patience may be hard to come by when in pain, many of us will try to medicate a hangover. Read on. . .

RESIST PAIN RELIEVERS

New research indicates that acetaminophen, aspirin, and ibuprofen should never be taken with alcohol, unless directed by a physician. Apparently, acetaminophen (an active ingredient in pain relievers such as Tylenol) is metabolized in the liver and can cause highly dangerous reactions in those who have consumed alcohol. There is currently not enough known about the possible adverse effects of other liver-metabolizing pain relievers such as ibuprofen. But researchers do know that ibuprofen products like Advil, as well as aspirin, are stomach irritants and combining them with alcohol is a bad idea.

BEWARE OF THE DOG THAT BIT YA

Some swear by "the hair of the dog" approach to relieving a hangover. But experts caution against this remedy for two reasons. First, while a little nip the next day may provide the sedative effects of alcohol and mask some of your hangover symptoms, it only pollutes your body further and prolongs the much needed recovery process. Second, drinking the day after a binge is a good way to cultivate a rather unhealthy behavior that may put you on the fast track to a drinking problem.

SWEAR OFF THE SWEET STUFF

Sugary drinks can dramatically increase hangover symptoms for some. And the sweet taste masks the alcohol content and may tempt you to drink more than you should.

CUT THE CARBONATION

Those tickly little bubbles in tonic and soda may look harmless, but carbonation speeds your body's absorption of alcohol and may defeat some of your preventative measures.

ET, PHONE HOME

moving out on your own can be one of the most exciting and fulfilling experiences of your life. It may, at times, feel overwhelming, but don't be scared! You are prepared!

- Feel confidence in knowing that millions of people have done it before you and millions will follow. How hard can it be?
- Remember that everyone's got their own way, so don't feel obligated to follow the herd.
- Know that you're not alone when you have questions! Put Mom on speed dial, reread this book, or shoot me an e-mail (**tana@tanashabitat.com**). There's an answer somewhere.
- Create the life you want to live by following your instincts. You can do it!

American author John Burroughs said it best when he wrote: "Leap and the net will appear."

Take it from me, it will.

sources

CHAPTER 2

1. http://news.zdnet.com/2100-1035_22-5445712.html
2. http://www.vonage-forum.com/printout227.html
3. http://www.vonage-forum.com/printout1150.html

CHAPTER 4

4. http://interiordec.about.com/od/moving/a/org_movetips.htm
5. http://www.upack.com/moving-resources/site-map.asp

CHAPTER 5

6. http://www.arc.govt.nz/arc/library/w30650_2.pdf
7. http://www.zerowasteamerica.org/index.html
8. http://www.campaignearth.org/intro.asp
9. http://www.epa.gov/epaoswer/non-hw/muncpl/compost.htm

CHAPTER 6

10. http://www.trivia-library.com/guide-to-kitchen-utensils/index.htm
11. http://www.chefdepot.net/sanitation.htm
12. http://www.ciwmb.ca.gov/wpie/healthcare/epamicromop.pdf
13. http://www.mercola.com/2003/dec/6/household_items.htm

CHAPTER 8

14. http://www.organicstyle.com/feature/0,8028,s1-41-30-46-428,00.html
15. http://www.immuneweb.org/articles/perfume.html

CHAPTER 9

16. http://www.bhg.com/bhg/story.jhtml;jsessionid=5R3X4URQPAHBFQFIBQPR5VQ?
    storyid=/templatedata/bhg/story/data/12598.xml&categoryid=/templatedata/bhg/
    category/data/WindowIdeaCenter_Decoration.xml&page=2
17. http://www.bhg.com/bhg/story.jhtml?storyid=/templatedata/bhg/story/data/12598
    .xml&categoryid=/templatedata/bhg/category/data/WindowIdeaCenter_Decoration
    .xml&page=1
18. http://www.bhg.com/bhg/story.jhtml?storyid=/templatedata/bhg/story/data/12598
    .xml&categoryid=/templatedata/bhg/category/data/WindowIdeaCenter_Decoration
    .xml&page=3

19. http://www.cbsnews.com/stories/2003/09/30/earlyshow/contributors/dannylipford/main 575960.shtml

CHAPTER 11

20. http://www.realsimple.com/realsimple/gallery/0,21863,1037805,00.html

CHAPTER 12

21. http://interiordec.about.com/cs/bedlinenindex/bb/aabyb1001bpillo.htm
22. http://www.selectcomfort.com/research/researcharticledisplay.cfm?site Location=001~003~300~011~002-1657
23. http://www.selectcomfort.com/research/researcharticledisplay.cfm?site Location=001~003~300~011~002-1659

CHAPTER 15

24. http://www.flowercouncil.org/uk/Pressroom/plantsforpeople/default.asp

CHAPTER 16

25. http://www.fbi.gov/pressrel/pressrel04/crimestat102504.htm
26. http://www.securityworld.com/library/home/apartmentsafety.html
27. http://www.idtheftcenter.org/index.shtml

CHAPTER 17

28. http://www.hud.gov/offices/fheo/FHLaws/FairHousingJan2002.pdf
29. http://www.nolo.com/article.cfm/objectID/1FA7B262-72D8-4388-ADBEF5E4AE2407B0/213/178/117/ART/
30. http://www.nolo.com/article.cfm/objectID/491C49DA-D208-4876-BEA5092CCB39FE1D/catID/F952FED3-0C94-4431-862E21322CCD72B6/104/138/305/ART/
31. http://www.nolo.com/article.cfm/objectID/6D164165-C439-45B9-9FED82FC4701FD40/catID/F952FED3-0C94-4431-862E21322CCD72B6/104/138/305/ART/

CHAPTER 18

32. http://www.drugs.com/CG/HOW_TO_USE_AN_ACE_WRAP.html
33. http://www.mayoclinic.com/invoke.cfm?objectid=58F86124-269C-49E1-834BBE72273246D6
34. http://www.census.gov/hhes/www/hlthins/hlthins03/hlth03asc.html
35. http://www.mayoclinic.com/invoke.cfm?id=DS00292
36. http://health.howstuffworks.com/hangover3.htm

about tana

tana march is currently editor-in-chief of **tanashabitat.com**, webmaster for the College of Letters, Arts, and Sciences at USC, and a regular contributor to *Teen* magazine, *Teen Beat* magazine, **TEENMag.com**, and HGTV. Her designs and philosophy have been featured in publications ranging from the *Washington Post*, *Entrepreneur*, *U.S. News & World Report*, and the Nikkei Business Associé, and her advice and opinions are featured frequently in periodicals throughout North America, Japan, and Europe.

In her spare time, Tana likes to play golf, cook for friends, road trip, and eat cheese.

about scott

the year was 1998. Los Angeles–based artist and designer **Scott Acord** was looking for a creative challenge in a galaxy far, far away from Hollywood, so he took a multiyear sabbatical from a successful career in corporate television publicity and marketing.

After twelve years of working at such innovative companies such as **MTV Networks** and **Dreamworks**, Scott began pursuing the design career he'd always dreamed of, but never thought possible. Enrolling at the world renowned **Art Center College of Design** in Pasadena, California, Scott immediately put his "I can do that" attitude into play. He emphasizes, "To me, success is doing what you love. Once I began to pursue my passion of design, I knew I was already successful."

While honing his penchant for creating stunning custom designs for his house, Scott met designer Tana March through a mutual friend in the summer of 2002. Immediately recognizing their similar design philosophies, Scott and Tana began meeting regularly for "arts and crafts days." Experimenting with a variety of materials and projects, the duo created design lighting with found objects, utilized Polaroid transfers, and designed rugs, among a myriad of other creative endeavors. It wasn't long before they decided to team up and Scott became a partner in **tana's habitat.**

Up next for Scott is a series of DIY books for kids to create and customize their bedrooms and living spaces for little to no money. "I believe your living (and working) environment should be reflective of your personality and I want to teach people of all ages how to be resourceful and achieve this on their own."

When Scott isn't playing in his art studio or working on a new series of DIY books, he spends an exorbitant amount of time watching sports, hiking, snowboarding, playing golf, or reading.

about ian

ian rogers is an illustrator and designer by day but masquerades as a fine artist and animator by night. He makes mysteriously eccentric, whimsical images with pencils and mice. He hibernates in his Brooklyn studio where his creations are currently holding him hostage. Visit **www.ianrogers.info** for more information on the situation.

index

Page numbers in *italic* indicate illustrations; those in **bold** indicate tables.

Interactive Wooden Block Wall Hanging
project, 236–38, *236*, *238*
ironing, 161–62, **161**

i

junior (JR), 68

k

kitchen:
appliances, 128
bakeware, 128
cleaning equipment/surfaces, 132–39
daily cleaning, 139–40
efficiency in, 205
germs and bacteria, 139–40
Homemade Refrigerator Magnets project, 208, *208*
knives, 128–31
other tools for, 131
pantry, 203–5
pots and pans, 127–28
Rusted Cabinet Inlay project, 207–8, *207*
spice rack ideas, 206
troubleshooting, 140–43
knives, 128–31

l

Lamp From Favorite Book project, 241–43, *241–42*
landlord:
questionnaire, 78–79
renters' rights, 269–70
requirements of habitability, 270–71
security deposit deadlines, **273–75**
terminating tenancies, 275–86
wear and tear, **271–72**
landlord questionnaire, 78–79
latex paints, 171
laundry:
drying, 160–61
garment cleaning symbols, 153–54, *153–54*
hand-washing, 162
ironing, 161–62
separating clothes, 154–55, **155**
stains, 155–59
troubleshooting, 162–63
washing machine use, 159–60
lease, 11, 83–84
lightbulb, broken, 126
lipstick stains, 159
loan consolidation, 64
location, 8–9
loft, 68

m

masonry walls, 189
mattresses, 209–11, **211**
mattress toppers, 212–13, *212, 213*
Media Cabinet project, 201, *201*
medical attention, 284
medical insurance, lack of, 284
mega complex, 69
microfiber mop, 138–39, 149
microwave, 137
mid-rise, 69
mirrors, 146
money:
banking, 38–42
costs of settling in, 43–55
cutting expenses, 35–38
debt-to-income ratio, 29–30, **30**
incoming, 30
outgoing, 30–34
money market account, 42
money market fund, 42
month-to-month lease, 11
moving:
boxes for, **91**
cross-country, 100
day of, 102–4
expenses for, 53–54, **54**
packing, 90–94
purging unwanted items, 89–90
truck for, 98–99, **98**
u-pack, we drive companies, 99–100

muggings, 264–65
Mypod Rug project, 182, *182*

n

neighbors, 264
noise, 10
nonstick coating, 133
No-Sew Curtains project, 176–77, *177*
numbers, **190**

o

one bedroom (1 BD; BDR; BDRM), 68
online bill payment, 41
organization:
    bathroom, 227–28
    ideas for, 202
Ottoman project, 199–200, *200*
oven, 135
oven fire, 142
over-the-counter medications, 284–86

p

packing, 90–94
painting, 101–2
    amount of paint, 172
    choosing color, 169–70
    cleanup, 174–75
    fun ideas, *101–2*, 175
    luster, 171–72
    oil vs. latex, 171
    pointers for, 174
    prep time, 173
    primers, 171
    rollers, 172
    tape, 172–73
    tools for, 171–72
pantry, 203–5
paring knife, 129
parking, 9–10
peeping Toms, 266
penthouse (PH), 69
pet deposit, 43

pets, 11–12
    expenses of, 253
    house and pet-proofing, 255
    life span, 252
    plants and, **249**
    questions to ask, 253
    researching, 254–55
    sources of, 254
    spaying and neutering, 256
    time requirements, 253, **254**
pet stains, 157
pilling, fabric, 163
pillows, 184–85, 214–15
plants:
    benefits from, 247–48
    light requirements, 258, **249**
    pet friendly, **249**
    repotting, 250
    temperature requirements, 249, **249**
    troubleshooting, **251–52**
    water requirements, 248, **249**, 250
plaster walls, 188–89
plastic, 134
Platform (bed) project, 218–19, *219*
Plexiglas Window Treatment project, 180, *180*
porcelain, 132–33
pots and pans, 127–28
prewar, 69
P.R.I.C.E., 280–81
primers, 171
public transportation, 12

r

recycling, 122–24
refrigerator, 135–36
refrigerator, used, 48
Remnant Rug project, 183, *183*
rent, 29–30, **34**
rent control (RNTCTL), 69
rental characteristics, 70–73
rental types, 68–70
renters' insurance, 97–98
renters' rights, 269–70